Praise for *The New Odyssey*

'A fine piece of work.'

Jonathan Ross, BBC Radio 2

'An absorbing read that shakes up compassion fatigue with gripping witness accounts, vivid historical context and serious analysis that goes way beyond the momentary spotlight of news grabs.'

Australian Books of the Year

'Explores the human stories behind Europe's refugee crisis. One of the most important books you will read this year . . . Kingsley's experience reporting from the front lines of the crisis gives an unrivalled perspective . . . powerful.'

Suzanne Lynch, *Irish Times*

'A fascinating study . . . *The New Odyssey* starts to do for the refugees what British abolitionists did for the slave trade . . . mobilises eyewitness testimony to promote empathy, and through empathy, better policy.'

Guardian

'Analytical, consistently trying to make sense of information and pin down the facts. Kingsley has gone further than the others in trying to explore the economics of the smugglers and their accomplices. He writes at fascinating length about the "second sea", the Sahara, which most people from the Horn of Africa have to cross and where many die even before they reach the Mediterranean.'

Caroline Moorehead, *New Statesman*

'Vivid and moving.'

Joshua Hammer, *New York Review of Books*

'Attempts to make the return journey back to reality: to a place where the humanity of the immigrant can not only be understood but deeply felt.'

Niki Seth-Smith, *New Humanist* Books of the Year

'A remarkable book.'

Frankfurter Allgemeine

'A brilliant, humane, sweeping account of the European refugee crisis. Kingsley has produced the great piece of reporting this issue so badly needs.'

Alan Rusbridger

'Kingsley tells the story of the greatest exodus of modern times in richly recognisably human terms, investigating and illuminating so much that gets routinely misreported and misrepresented . . . Compelling.'

Maurice Wren, Chief Executive of the Refugee Council

'The pile of half-read books by my bedside is a guilty embarrassment but this was so engaging and well written that it was, almost uniquely for me, consumed in full over a few days . . . A gripping and frequently emotional read.'

Crispin Blunt, MP, Chairman of the Foreign Affairs Select Committee, House of Commons

The New Odyssey

The Story of Europe's Refugee Crisis

PATRICK KINGSLEY

First published in 2016
by Guardian Books, Kings Place,
90 York Way, London N1 9GU

and Faber & Faber Limited
Bloomsbury House
74–77 Great Russell Street
London WC1B 3DA

This paperback edition published in 2017

Typeset by Agnesi Text
Printed and bound by CPI Group (UK) Ltd, Croydon, CRO 4YY

The right of Patrick Kingsley to be identified as author of this work
has been asserted in accordance with Section 77 of the Copyright,
Designs and Patents Act 1988

Maps by Bill Donohoe

A CIP record for this book
is available from the British Library

ISBN 978–1–783–35106–0

2 3 4 8 10 9 7 5 3 1

To my mother and father

Contents

List of Illustrations

List of Maps

. . . no one puts their children in a boat
unless the water is safer than the land.
from 'Home' by Warsan Shire

If any god has marked me out again
for shipwreck, my tough heart can undergo it.
What hardship have I not long since endured
at sea, in battle! Let the trial come.
from Homer's *Odyssey*

Prologue

Wednesday, 15 April 2015, 11 p.m.

Routes into Europe

In the darkness far out to sea, Hashem al-Souki can't see his neighbours but he can hear them scream. It's partly his fault. They are two African women – perhaps from Somalia, but now is not the time to ask – and Hashem is spreadeagled on top of them. His limbs dig into theirs. They want him to move, fast, and so would he. But he can't – several people are sprawled on top of him, and there's possibly another layer above them. Dozens are crammed into this wooden dinghy. If anyone tries to shift, a smuggler kicks them back into place. They don't want the crammed boat to overbalance, and then sink.

It is perhaps eleven at night, but Hashem can't be certain. He's losing track of time, and of place. Earlier in the evening, on a beach at the northernmost tip of Egypt, he and his companions were herded into this little boat. Now that boat is who-knows-where, bobbing along in the pitch darkness, lurching in the waves, somewhere in the south-eastern Mediterranean. And its passengers are screaming.

Some of the screams are in Arabic, some not. There are people from across Africa here, others from across the Middle East. There are Palestinians, Sudanese and Somalians. And Syrians, like Hashem. They want to get to northern Europe: Sweden, Germany, or anywhere that offers them a better future than their collapsed homelands. For that distant hope they are risking this boat trip to the Italian coast. All being well, they should reach Italy in five or six days. But, for now, Hashem doesn't know if he'll survive the night. Or if anyone will.

An hour passes. They reach a second boat, a bigger one, and then a third, bigger still. At each new vessel, the smugglers toss them over the side like bags of potatoes. Now they have a bit more space, but they're soaked. They had to wade through the waves to get to the dinghy, and the second boat was full of water. Their clothes drenched, they shiver. And they retch. The person squeezed to his left pukes all over Hashem. Then Hashem pays the favour forward, spewing all over the person to his right. He looks up, and realises everyone's at it; everyone's clothes are caked in other people's vomit. Each has paid more than $2000 to spew over fellow refugees. 'It's a vomiting party,' Hashem thinks to himself.

Perhaps the most extraordinary part of this scene is just how ordinary it has become. The world is currently witnessing the biggest wave of mass migration since the Second World War – and the most dramatic example of this phenomenon is occurring in the Mediterranean sea. Since 2014, over 1.5 million people crossed the Mediterranean in leaking boats like this one,[1] as civil wars in Syria, Afghanistan and Iraq – and repression and poverty in Africa – push an unprecedented number of people towards Europe. For years, the burden of the global refugee crisis has largely been borne by the developing world, which the UN says is home to 86 per cent of refugees. Now Europe is also waking up to the crisis.

Migration to Europe is by no means new. African migrants have long tried to reach Spain from Morocco, or the Canary Islands from Senegal. For years, Libya, Turkey and Egypt have been springboards for people hoping to get to Italy, Greece and Bulgaria. But never before have migrants come in such extraordinarily high numbers.

To begin with, in 2014, the spike was driven mainly by Syrians, Eritreans, and sub-Saharan Africans. Back then, they sailed mainly to Italy from Libya (as law and order there broke down in the aftermath of the Arab Spring), and to a lesser extent from Egypt. Some 170,000 reached Italy in 2014, nearly triple the previous record.[2] In 2015, sub-Saharan refugees continued to leave from Libya and Egypt at almost the same record rate as during the previous summer. But the game-changer in that year was Greece, which overtook Italy as the most popular gateway to Europe. Changing visa restrictions for Syrian refugees meant they could no longer easily reach north Africa, and the war in Libya meant they no longer wanted to. So they began departing en masse from Turkey to the Greek islands, along with émigrés from an increasingly unstable Afghanistan and Iraq. Tiny islands that had previously been sleepy holiday hideaways on the fringes of the Aegean sea were turned overnight into the ground zero of the Middle Eastern refugee crisis. Already struggling with an economic meltdown, the Greeks were utterly unprepared.

Suddenly, a problem that was once just a western European one became a challenge for eastern Europe too. In 2015, more than 850,000 refugees left Turkish shores[3] – and the vast majority marched northwards through the Balkans, all in the hope of reaching the safety and stability of northern

Europe. Among other things, this book records what happened in that extraordinary year of 2015, why it happened, and how it changed Europe.

In 2015 Hungary, which only five years earlier had seen just 2,400 migrants cross its southern borders,[4] suddenly had to deal with a hundred times that number. Its government eventually erected a fence along its southern flank. When people simply re-routed into Croatia, the Hungarians built a second barrier along their Croatian border too.

For the rest of the European Union the crisis created divisions of a more metaphorical kind. Italy and Greece saw no reason why they should cope with such a huge wave of immigrants by themselves and tried various ways of getting the rest of Europe to share the burden. First the Italians and Greeks simply waved many refugees on with a nudge and a wink, instead of encouraging every boat arrival to settle on Italian or Greek soil, as required by current EU rules known as the Dublin treaties. Then they tried the negotiating table, attempting to persuade their neighbours to take in the migrants voluntarily. But throughout months of endless and fruitless conferences and summits, most other EU countries refused to relieve the Greeks and Italians of more than a token few migrants. In the autumn, most governments finally agreed to a deal that would see 120,000 migrants taken off the hands of the frontline states, and shared among the rest of the continent. For the wonks in Brussels, it was seen as a small victory, and the creation of an important precedent. But in reality it was a pitiful response. The 120,000 amounted to around a ninth of the total that reached Italy and Greece in 2015,[5] making the so-called deal almost meaningless. One of the EU's key founding principles – solidarity among member states – seemed to have vanished.

As the year went on, more and more countries erected fences along their borders to direct the flow of refugees, and a few threatened to seal their borders entirely. In the process, they endangered another value central to the EU's soul – the concept of free movement between mainland European countries, a principle that had first been enshrined with great fanfare by the Schengen agreement of 1985 and which is still considered one of the greatest achievements of the European project. Later, the crisis helped stoke some of the fears that led to Britain's Brexit vote, and gave Viktor Orban, Hungary's far-right leader, a platform on which to call for the end of liberal Europe, and the start of what he termed a counter-cultural revolution within the EU. In short, the migration crisis had become one of the biggest threats to the cohesion of the European Union in the organisation's history.

It was also one of the most unnecessary. In a way, the refugee crisis is something of a misnomer. There is a crisis, but it's one caused largely by our response to the refugees, rather than by the refugees themselves. The figure 850,000 sounds like a lot – and in terms of historic migration to Europe it is. But this is only about 0.2 per cent of the EU's total population of roughly 500 million, an influx that the world's richest continent can feasibly absorb, if – and only if – it's handled properly. There are countries whose social infra-structure is at breaking point because of the refugee crisis – but they mostly aren't in Europe. The most obvious example is Lebanon, which houses well over one million Syrian refugees within a total population of roughly 4.5 million.[6]

That's around one in five people – a ratio that Europe should have been embarrassed by.

Unable to reach Europe by legal routes, people therefore kept travelling by illegal ones. In response, European leaders flailed for a response that would create the appearance of solving the boat crisis, without doing anything that would actually make it more manageable. They ended full-scale rescue operations in the southern Mediterranean, arguing that their existence was the reason so many people were risking the sea routes. Then they reinstated them, once it was clear that people were coming anyway. Next, they settled on a far-fetched military strategy, promising to attack the Libyan smugglers with naval ships. Inevitably, it was a failure.

With each desperate scheme, politicians repeatedly ignored the reality of the situation – namely that, whether they are welcomed or not, people will keep coming. As a result, the politicians initially failed to realise that – unless we abandoned one of the seminal achievements of the post-Holocaust era, the 1951 UN Convention on refugee rights – there was no easy way of blocking the migrants' passage, only a means of managing it better. Had they created an organised system of mass resettlement from the Middle East in 2014 and 2015, and had this kind of scheme got going fast enough, and on a large enough scale, Europe might have been able to curb the most chaotic aspects of the crisis. Such a scheme would have given many migrants an incentive to stay put in the Middle East for the short term, and to place their faith in the formal processes of resettlement. This in turn would have allowed Europe to manage their arrival in a more methodical manner. It might have also persuaded Turkey to do more to stop people leaving its shores – both by finally giving migrants the right to work, and by guarding its borders better. But, throughout 2015, no programme of this kind was put in place – forcing hundreds of thousands of people to take the only option left to them: to sail to Greece by themselves. It was a perfect storm in which refugees had no reason to stay put; Middle Eastern countries had no reason to prevent them from leaving; and Europe no means of blocking their path.

The mess reached its nadir in the aftermath of the Paris attacks in November 2015. Two of the nine assailants were revealed to have probably arrived in Greece a month earlier in a boatload of refugees. Panicking, some commentators and politicians called for the door to be shut entirely on refugees, fearing that their arrival put the continent at risk. Such paranoia was understandable and predictable – but ultimately illogical. For a start, this was the reaction that the terrorists had hoped to spark: definitive 'proof' of the West's moral decay, and therefore a powerful recruiting tool for Isis. Second: the majority of the attackers were in fact European citizens.

There are obvious security concerns inherent in the passage of thousands of undocumented people to Greece. Short of ripping up the 1951 UN Refugee Convention, however, the only way of mitigating these concerns would have been, for the reasons outlined above, to provide legal, orderly entry to significant numbers of them. Such a move would have decreased the flow across the Aegean, and consequently could have made it easier to monitor and control who was entering Europe. But no one had the vision to think this far ahead. Instead, fear of social meltdown was used to excuse inertia – fear that became its own self-fulfilling prophecy.

In spring 2016, Europe finally did manage to substantially reduce arrival numbers, even if it did not eliminate them entirely – by effectively ripping up the 1951 Convention. The EU promised to pay Turkey €6 billion, in exchange for policing their borders better, and allowing Europe to deport greater numbers of refugees from Greece. The deal largely worked: migration numbers fell, even if they did not vanish completely. By midsummer, mere hundreds landed on the Greek islands every week, rather than the thousands who had landed in previous months. The isolationists claimed victory.

This apparent win nevertheless came at great humanitarian and moral cost, weakening the foundations of Europe's enlightened post-war settlement, and consigning millions of would-be migrants to a life of limbo. Those who had been successfully deterred by the EU–Turkey deal were now trapped in the Middle East, in countries where – despite recent legislative changes – refugees do not in practice have the right to work, where Syrians cannot afford to feed their children, and where hundreds of thousands of those children are therefore forced into child labour. And Europe had sealed their fate by abandoning the principles of the UN's 1951 Refugee Convention – the document that was drawn up in the aftermath of the Holocaust to ensure that refugees would never again be turned away from the borders of the western world. For some, Europe had been 'saved'. For others, this had only been achieved at the expense of much of what was worth saving in the first place: the values, standards and treaties that rebuilt Europe after the moral lapses of the 1930s, and the destruction of the Second World War.

And yet despite all this, migration continued. More than 25,000 people have still secretly made their way through Balkans between the EU declaring that route shut in March 2016, and my updates to this latest edition of the book in January 2017. Flows between Libya and Italy also hit a new record during that time, as did the death toll in the Mediterranean. More than 182,000 reached Italy in 2016, while 5,000 drowned.[7]

Just to reach the sea in the first place, most of them had already been on a journey that deserves to be considered a contemporary Odyssey. At a time when travel is for many easy and anodyne, their voyages through the Sahara, the Balkans, or across the Mediterranean – on foot, in the holds of wooden fishing boats, and on the backs of land cruisers – are almost as epic as that of classical heroes such as Aeneas and Odysseus. I'm wary of drawing too strong a link, but there are nevertheless obvious parallels. Just as both those ancient men fled a conflict in the Middle East and sailed across the Aegean – so too will many migrants today. Today's sirens are the smugglers with their empty promises of safe passage, the violent border guard a contemporary Cyclops. Three millennia after their classical forebears created the founding myths of the European continent, today's voyagers are writing a new narrative that will influence Europe, for better or worse, for years to come.

This book is about who these voyagers are. It's about why they keep coming, and how they do it. It's about the smugglers who help them on their way, and the coastguards who rescue them at the other end. The volunteers that feed them, the hoteliers that house them, and the border agents trying to keep them out. And the politicians looking the other way.

Based on interviews and encounters in seventeen countries across three continents, it tells the story of both the Mediterranean crossing and the crossing of what aid workers call Libya's second sea, the sea of the Sahara – and then the onwards march through Europe. It's reported from the hideouts of Berber smugglers, and the ports of Sicily; from the railways of western Europe, and the footpaths of the Balkans. Along the way, it's a critique of Europe's handling of the migration crisis, and an argument for how it could be handled better. The crisis will be with us in some form for several years to come; in this book, I want to recount what happened in 2015, the year that it reached unprecedented proportions, and what we can learn from it.

There's a bit of me in there too: towards the start of 2015, before migration became the year's defining European issue, my editor had the foresight to make me the *Guardian*'s first ever migration correspondent. We didn't know this at the time, but it was a role that would allow me to witness the migration crisis in more breadth and depth than most. It was a job of absurd privilege. In one memorable week I went from the Sahara desert to the middle of the Mediterranean to the border of Hungary. In another I crossed nine borders while up to 1,300 other people drowned trying to cross just one. In among everything else, this book will occasionally deal with my own unlikely migrations, as I follow those of others.

Above all, *The New Odyssey* is the story of someone else entirely: a Syrian called Hashem al-Souki. Every other chapter (or thereabouts) is about Hashem's quest for safety. His very personal narrative is juxtaposed with the narrative of the wider crisis, allowing us to cycle between the journey of an individual and that of the continent he passes through. Why Hashem in particular? He's no freedom fighter or superhero. He's just an ordinary Syrian. But that's why I want to tell his story. It's the story of an everyman, in whose footsteps any of us could one day tread.

Shivering in the vomit of others, tonight is just the latest indignity of Hashem's three-year odyssey. He's a bulky forty-year-old with a gentle smile, whose greying hair makes him seem older than he is. He first left his home in Damascus in April 2012, and all that remains of his house is the key in his pocket. The rest was blown up by the Syrian army.

He thinks of his children – Osama, Mohamed and Milad, far away in Egypt. He's doing this journey so they don't have to. So that his boys and their mum, Hayam, can be legally reunited with him if he reaches the other side – and if he later reaches Sweden.

His country destroyed, Hashem reckons his hopes and dreams are over. But his children's are still worth dying for. 'I'm risking my life for something bigger, for ambitions bigger than this,' he tells me before he leaves. 'If I fail, I fail alone. But, by risking this, I might achieve a dream for three children: my children – and maybe my grandchildren as well.'

He thinks especially of Osama, the oldest. Today, 15 April 2015, is Osama's birthday. Earlier this morning, Osama's fourteenth year began with his father crying, apologising for his imminent departure, and then leaving in the knowledge that the pair might never speak again.

1

A Birthday Interrupted

Hashem's flight from Syria

Sunday, 15 April 2012, 6 p.m.

Syria, Jordan and Egypt

Three years ago to the day, Hashem's journey begins. Again, it's Osama's birthday. And again, it is a birthday interrupted. Sunday's a working day in Syria, the first of the working week, and Hashem gets home around 6 p.m. He sits down briefly with his boys to watch some television. Hayam, a teacher two years younger than her husband, is already cooking dinner in the kitchen, and Hashem is procrastinating before popping out to collect a cake for Osama.

And then there's a knock at the door. More of a hammering, really – a hammering that Hashem never quite expected.

He isn't particularly political. He's just a thirty-seven-year-old civil servant at the regional water board. He runs the computer department, and it's his job to print the bills every month for the residents of Damascus and the surrounding countryside. He focuses on the water business, and minds his own.

But today, all that won't matter. The regime is going from house to house, rounding up all the men they find. Whether it's because they're Sunni, living in a country run by Alawites, an offshoot of the Shia, Hashem can only speculate. He has good reason to: Syria's civil war is increasingly being fought along sectarian lines.

Hashem's children watch him as he goes to open the door. Outside stand twenty men. Whether they're from the army, the police or a pro-regime militia, he doesn't know. But they're here for him, and half the people on his street.

The conflict had started far from here. A wave of anti-authoritarian protests erupted across the Arab world in late 2010 and early 2011, rippling through Tunisia, Egypt, Libya, Bahrain and Yemen. The demonstrations reached Syria in February 2011. The first was a protest in Damascus market, but the one everyone remembers best was a much smaller act of defiance in mid-March. A group of boys sprayed pro-democracy slogans across the wall of a school in Deraa, southern Syria. In the dictatorship of Bashar al-Assad, the former eye doctor who succeeded his father as president in 2000, such dissent wasn't tolerated. The boys were arrested and tortured. Their treatment sparked wider protests, which Assad's regime then met with gunfire, causing a number of deaths. At this point the demonstrations began to match the momentum in other Arab countries, where protests ultimately forced the departure of four presidents. Across Syria, outraged and increasingly fearless demonstrators gathered to demand Assad's resignation. As March went on, dozens were killed as hundreds of thousands protested throughout the country.

The repression failed to stop the uprising. Throughout the spring and summer, protestor numbers continued to swell across Syria, leading to a shockingly brutal crackdown that included military sieges and state-led massacres in several particularly restive towns. Horrified, soldiers began to defect from Assad's army. By the autumn, the defectors, largely united under the banner of the Free Syrian Army, increasingly resorted to guerrilla tactics to take on Assad, and the uprising began to take the shape of a war. By the start of 2012, the rebels controlled parts of the country.

Until April 2012 Haran al-Awamid, a few miles south-east of Damascus, had largely escaped the violence. Built around a row of ruined Roman pillars, it's a quiet place, which houses around 15,000 residents – many of them government employees. It used to be an agricultural town, but recent droughts and the construction of a nearby airport has seen many residents leaving farming for the public sector. At the weekends, families like Hashem's often spend their time in the local gardens, grilling meat under the pine trees. But, in recent days, tensions have been raised. Regime loyalists killed two young men, tied their corpses to a car, and dragged them around town. Not everyone dared to react, but the pair's friends and family did – they protested and chanted in the street.

And now, as Hashem is shoved into the back of a van, his children watching from the front room, the regime is getting its revenge. It's a long revenge, too. First, Hashem and his neighbours are taken to a secret network of cells, dug deep beneath Damascus airport. They're run by the powerful air-force intelligence, whose tentacles spread far beyond both aviation and civilian oversight. No prosecutor asks after Hashem's whereabouts, and neither he nor the others are charged or even interrogated. They're simply beaten, and kept locked up until enough men have been rounded up from the surrounding villages. Three days later, they're moved on – to the headquarters of aviation intelligence in Damascus itself.

Here, hundreds of men are crammed into single cells, deep underground. Every day, four or five of them are dragged to torture rooms. Single men are electrocuted with shocks to their genitals. Husbands like Hashem are sometimes spared that humiliation, but instead are hung from their wrists. Hashem spends twelve hours like this, the cords cutting into his skin. Others spend even longer and their hands later have to be amputated.

They are not anomalies. In fact, in some ways they are the lucky ones, since they have been allowed to live. It will later emerge that during this period between 2011 and 2013 at least 11,000 detainees were tortured and killed in Syrian dungeons like the one where Hashem finds himself. A cache of 55,000 photographs depicting the corpses of those detainees, smuggled from Syria by the photographer, code-named Caesar,[1] who was tasked by the government to document the bodies. The photographs bear witness to the regime's cruelty, showing many prisoners were beaten, strangled and electrocuted during their detention. Some have their eyes gouged out.

Hashem avoids such a fate, but his detention continues; after about three months he's moved to some kind of airport hangar. For now, he doesn't know where it is, though it later turns out to be Mazzeh airport, a military base used by the Assad family. The hangar is a vast space, capable of holding a few planes. There are nevertheless so many prisoners crammed in here that they have to take it in turns to lie down.

It isn't clear who rests by night and who by day. They were robbed of their watches when they were first arrested. There is no natural light in this echoing space, so time's passage can't be measured. Months pass. Maybe seasons, but who knows. Ramadan comes and goes, but the prisoners are none the wiser. All that's clear is that the beatings have decreased, as the guards grow bored of their violence. Still, for now, no one asks when they'll be released. They learn not to, for fear of another round of torture.

One day in late October, an officer comes to tell them that the president has decreed their release. The prisoners are driven in vans to the centre of Damascus, where they're tossed out into the street. It turns out to be Eid al-Adha, one of Islam's main religious festivals. They emerge blinking into the bright sunlight, wondering what kind of Syria awaits them after half a year of incarceration.

When Hashem was arrested, the rebellion against the regime was only a year old, and violence had mostly left Haran al-Awamid untouched. While he has been away things have changed. As a friend drives him home, he notices that they're going by an odd, circuitous route. What are we trying to avoid, Hashem asks. The front line, his friend replies. When he gets home, the news gets worse. Two of Hayam's brothers were shot by the same sniper on the same day. The second was trying to retrieve the corpse of the first.

The Red Cross has officially declared that the conflict should be termed a civil war. Bashar al-Assad has begun to use barrel bombs. Assad's Shia allies in Lebanon, the Hezbollah militia, have entered Syria to boost his defences – as the conflict takes a sectarian turn. The Kurdish minority had started to take control of northern parts of the country near the Turkish border. The Free Syrian Army and the regime are locked in conflict across most of the country. For Hashem, the future is bleak.

A month later, in the final weeks of 2012, the situation in his own town is untenable. Seeking safety, Hashem and

Hayam move their three boys on. First to Hozroma, a nearby village due east of Damascus. Then, when the bombs start dropping metres from his sons as they return from school one afternoon, it's clear that Hozroma is also no sanctuary. Within days, they up sticks again to a village called al-Tal, on the other side of Damascus.

All around them, their country is collapsing – and so, too, is their home. Literally so. Back in Haran al-Awamid, the regime wants to create a buffer zone around Damascus airport. So, in February 2013, they destroy Hashem's house, among hundreds of others. To this day, Hashem still carries the key. The door it once unlocked is gone.

With Hashem's family's home turned to rubble, Syria looks less and less like a place in which they can eke out an existence. They struggle on in al-Tal, before moving in May to Damascus itself. But that month they decide enough is enough: Syria can no longer be home. The rebels are increasingly dominated by jihadists, thanks in part to Assad's decision to release hundreds of Sunni extremists. Assad hopes they will subsequently infiltrate and radicalise the opposition, then stigmatise them in the eyes of any neutrals, and so increase the sectarian nature of the conflict – or at least this is what observers like Hashem conclude.[2] By spring 2013, this apparent plan starts to pay off. The group that would later call itself Islamic State begins to make significant advances in northern Syria.

By this point, the Soukis are sharing a two-room apartment in Damascus with three other displaced families. Recognising the futility of the situation, the Soukis apply for passports to leave Syria. In the short term, it's a disastrous decision. At the passport office, standing in front of his children, Hashem is again arrested and dragged to prison. Here he finds children and old men; some of them have languished in these cells for months. As usual, he's beaten, but there are fewer prisoners in this jail so the experience is marginally less traumatic than his first incarceration; he can at least lie down to sleep. His second stay also turns out to be far shorter than the first. While Hashem's locked up, investigators ask his former colleagues at the water board about his background, and one of them – an Alawi – sticks up for him. He's freed a few days later, and so with some trepidation he approaches the emigration office to try again for a passport. He approaches a policeman outside, and takes a chance. Am I, Hashem asks, still on any wanted list? The policeman sympathises with him, and goes inside the building to check. Several minutes later, the cop returns: Hashem's got the all-clear. So Hashem enters the office himself, reapplies for a passport – and, to his surprise, the application is granted.

It's an almost inexplicable moment of fortune, but he has no time to count his blessings. He needs to leave. But where can they go? Hayam and Hashem think about Jordan, where one in ten residents are now Syrian refugees, but they hear the conditions in the camps there are awful, and Syrians aren't allowed to work. Lebanon's another option, and now home to more than a million fellow Syrian refugees, who constitute a fifth of the total population. But the Soukis fear a backlash from Lebanon's Hezbollah supporters, who back Bashar al-Assad. There's another option, though: Egypt. At the time, in June 2013, the Egyptian government welcomes Syrians.

So Egypt it is – if they can find the money. With no home to sell, they lack savings to pay for plane tickets. Hayam sells her jewellery, everything but her wedding ring, but they still can't afford the airfare. A bus to Jordan is within reach, however, and so is an onwards ferry to Egypt. Around 11,000 Syrian pounds will take them in a Pullman coach to the Jordanian port of Aqaba. The boat from there to Egypt is about $65.

They're all set to leave – but there's just one person still to convince: Hashem's father. His mum understands why Hashem wants to take his family to safety, but his dad is distraught at the prospect. Who will look after him, if not Hashem?

'Why do you want to go and leave me?' his father asks him during one of their last meetings.

'Papa, I'm sorry,' Hashem replies. 'But it's unbearable here. I have to go – not for me, but for my children and my wife.'

At around midday on 26 June 2013, the family turns up at Marjeh Square in central Damascus. It is brimming with Syrians on the move. There are plenty of tourism companies in the area, and before the uprising they catered for holidaymakers. Today their clients, hundreds of them piling onto a line of buses, are all escaping a war.

Every seat on Hashem's family's bus is taken. The drive to Jordan takes them through a cross-section of the war they're fleeing. They pass through Deraa, the city where the uprising began, and which is still being contested. They pass through regime checkpoints, where the soldiers curse and mock them. 'Why', the soldiers scream, 'are you abandoning the nation?' Then it's the rebel checkpoints, and their reception there is coloured with the same disdain: 'You're leaving the country!' Only the jihadists of Jabhat al-Nusra, some of whose members would later form the Islamic State, have a different line. 'You're abandoning jihad,' they shout. 'You don't want to be mujahideen.'

Every checkpoint is an ordeal. At each one, each passenger has to haul his luggage from the bus, and present it for inspection. The process takes hours, and people's bags are often filched by those manning the checkpoint. The Soukis lose three suitcases. At one regime checkpoint, the troops want more than luggage: a young man on the bus turns out to be on a wanted list, so the soldiers grab him and march him off the bus. The other passengers are horrified – they know he'll probably be killed. So they turn to the driver, who drives this way every week. You know the soldiers here, they tell the driver: ask them how much they want to release him. The driver returns with a number: 2000 Syrian pounds. There is a whip-round, and everyone chips in some of their last savings. Hashem is now almost out of money. But the man's life is saved.

Perhaps the worst checkpoint is the last one: at Nasib, on the border with Jordan. It's 3 a.m. by the time they arrive, and the border officials want to check their details. But the computer system is down, and they must wait on the bus till it reboots. Will we ever leave Syria, Hashem wonders. The sun rises, but the computer does not. It isn't until six hours later that they finally cross into Jordan.

By the evening they're in the port of Aqaba on the Red Sea. Their ferry leaves at midnight, and at around 4 a.m. on 27 June they arrive in the harbour of Nuweiba, a little tourist town in Egypt's Sinai peninsular. The border shuts a few days later, and they're among the last Syrians to cross it.

Reaching safety, a dozen thoughts rush through Hashem's mind. He is relieved that his children have escaped a war zone, but he also can't forget the family and friends he has left behind. He might never see them, or hug them, again.

2

The Second Sea

The desert routes through the Sahara

Niger, August 2015

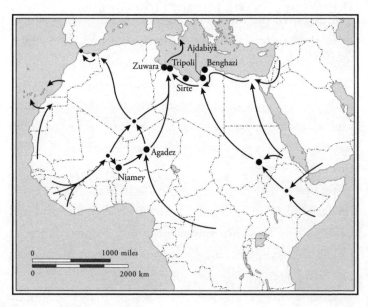

Desert Routes to Libya

You can't see the road from Agadez to Libya. You simply drive to the edge of the local airstrip, turn left, fork right, head past the one building on the horizon, a lonely police checkpoint. And that's it. There's no tarmac, just a few ruts in the sand. Only a select few local drivers know which dunes lead across the Sahara desert, and which ones lead to oblivion. And in three days of driving, there are plenty of wrong turnings to make.

Yet before they risk death in the Mediterranean sea, before they cross the battlegrounds of the Libyan civil war, and well before a tiny few of them reach the new security fences at Calais, this is the road most migrants from west Africa must pass. And along which many of them will die.

Europe's migration crisis is one predominantly driven by Syrians, Iraqis and Afghans fleeing war and religious extremism – people like Hashem al-Souki. Coverage of the crisis – and the suggested solutions to that crisis – focuses on these people. And it is true that the flow would ebb if wars in the Middle East suddenly reached a magical conclusion. But even a silver bullet as unlikely as this would not stop Eritreans from fleeing for Europe in their thousands, or Nigerians and Senegalese heading in the same direction, a few hundred miles to the west.

So to understand the crisis in all its forms, you have to follow this 'road' outside Agadez – the fabled mud-brick city in central Niger, and the main way station for west Africans en route to Libya, and the Mediterranean beyond. And you need to trace the similar trail that leads north from Khartoum, the capital of Sudan, carrying people from the Horn of Africa. We hear a lot about the dangers in the waters between Libya and Italy, where most of the shipwrecks happen. To grasp why people brave those dangers, we need first to digest what happens to them before they get to the coast.

'Think of Libya as having two seas,' one aid worker tells me in my first days as a migration correspondent. 'There is the Mediterranean. But in the south of Libya is the sea of the Sahara.'

Trying to figure out what he meant is what brings me to these few ruts in the sand, just north of Agadez, and to a young man I'll call Cisse, since he spoke to me only on the condition that I didn't reveal his real name. Cisse is twenty-five, and has a degree in geology. He is composed, articulate and smartly dressed. He worked briefly as a clerk in a uranium mine in northern Niger. For several years he took tourists on tours of the Sahara. And then, when the tourist industry vanished in the wake of a regional insurgency, Cisse turned to a third profession. People smuggling.

As a result, he's one of the comparatively few people who know how to navigate these invisible routes that lead to Libya. And he knows better than most the dangers that lie in the journey. It's a trek that Cisse makes once a week, along with thirty passengers in his pick-up. Each time the route looks different, thanks to regular sandstorms that change the shape of the desert. Cisse knows the Sahara 'like it's my bedroom'. But others don't, so they get lost in the maelstrom.

Once lost, they run out of fuel – and then water. 'And if there is no water,' says Cisse, 'you won't survive for more than three days.'

I experience one such sandstorm from the relative safety of Agadez. I'd seen a few in Cairo, where I lived for three years, but they're nothing compared to this. Agadez is a squat town, a warren of low clay buildings circling a single tall structure, a 27-metre-high minaret that looms above its surroundings like an adobe siege tower. But, in a sandstorm, you can't see the other side of the street, let alone the minaret. Clouds of sand swirl through the streets, vanishing whole shopfronts that were visible just seconds ago. The sand seeps through the frames of even tightly shut doors, smearing the insides of supposedly sealed rooms with a layer of coarse dust. Volley upon volley of sand hits the town like waves on a shoreline during a storm. But, unlike seawater, the sand doesn't then slope back to where it came from. It stays there, swirling in the air, smothering the local sultan's once visible palace in a fog of yellow. If you're caught in one of these in the desert itself, your car could be buried in an hour.

As well as this risk, there are the bandits: rival smugglers, jihadists, or simply opportunists looking to steal your car and leave you in the desert. One such ambush happened the fortnight I visit, and leaves a whole family dead. 'If you're lucky you will be rescued,' says Cisse. 'If you're not, they'll kill you and your passengers as well.'

No one knows how many have died in these varied ways. For every corpse discovered in the Sahara – at least forty were counted in 2015 – there may be another five or fifty that will never be found.[1] But, for one of Cisse's own passengers, the conclusion is nevertheless clear. 'In my opinion,' reckons Joel Gomez, a failed footballer from Cameroon, 'the Sahara is more dangerous than the Mediterranean.' And yet record numbers are still risking it.

It is late on an August night when I first meet Cisse and Joel, as they mill around one of Agadez's main bus stations. It's here on the southern cusp of the Sahara desert that hundreds of migrants arrive perfectly legally each night; in all of 2015, local officials estimated their numbers topped 100,000. This is the northernmost edge of what's called the Economic Community of Western African States, a Schengen-like visa-free swath of west Africa. Known informally as the Ecowas zone, within it anyone with means can take a bus from the coasts of Nigeria to the cusp of the Sahara desert in Niger. And it is here in Agadez that the bus drivers stop, and the people smugglers begin.

In the small hours of each morning, the buses arrive. The travellers totter out, often nauseous after a twenty-hour ride along bumpy roads, and smugglers like Cisse are waiting for them. Most have specific people to call – smugglers recommended by friends who've successfully made the trip in the past. Others don't, so they approach smugglers on arrival. And then they're all driven to the compounds.

Agadez has only a handful of multi-storey buildings. The main ones are the mosque and, next door to it, the palace of the Sultan of Aïr, who still retains a role in the local judicial system. But the houses overlooked by this pair are mostly single-storey courtyards, each enclosed by a windowless wall. These are the compounds, and perhaps fifty of them are used by smugglers – though no one knows the exact total. And that's the point: they're the perfect places to hide a hundred migrants until they head north to Libya.

Once inside, the haggling starts. The going rate between Agadez and Libya is thought to be about 150,000 West African francs (CFA), or £166. But one traveller said he paid as much as €500 (£363), while Cisse claims he charges each of his thirty passengers as little as 50,000 CFA (£55).

With such big numbers, it is no surprise that the business continues in full force despite a recent ban. In May 2015, following pressure from the EU, the Nigerien government banned people smuggling. In August, I pay a visit to the chief of police in Agadez, to ask whether the ban is enforceable. He proudly says it is, and that it has already been enforced. He rings a bell, and summons his lead anti-smuggling officer, who is told to tot up the number of smugglers he has arrested. Half an hour passes, and the officer finally produces a slip of paper. In three months, a handwritten calculation on the paper shows, his men have arrested a grand total of fourteen smugglers. Another was successfully encouraged to retire from the trade.

What about graft, I ask. Do smugglers still bribe policemen to let them through their checkpoints? 'Two years ago, what you said could be a reality,' claims the chief. 'But after that event' – he alludes to a two-year-old government report showing that policemen were routinely in the pay of smugglers – 'all the policemen who did that were sent elsewhere. And, because of that, the newcomers are very afraid. So now no vehicle goes by the checkpoint of the police.'

In these situations, you have to try not to laugh. Step outside the police chief's office and it is clear that many smugglers still operate under the police's protection. Cisse is a case in point. Since the law's implementation, he's been careful. When I ask to meet him a second time, and then a third, he fears it's a sting. The day after we first speak at the bus station, he tells me to meet him in the town's market, next to the linen stalls. Then he sends a man on ahead to check that I'm not with anyone strange.

But, tellingly, the chap who screens me is a plain-clothes policeman in Cisse's pay. 'Don't worry,' the cop tells Cisse on the phone. 'This guy's OK. I saw him at the police chief's office.'

This isn't the only policeman still taking bribes. At each of the three checkpoints before Libya, Cisse pays the police 10,000 CFA (£11) per passenger to let them pass. 'The law has changed nothing,' Cisse smiles. 'If you pay certain bribes to the police you can continue to operate the compounds.'

The town still very much beats to the rhythm of the smugglers' schedule. For most of the week, Agadez is subdued. As Monday approaches, the day that most smugglers leave together for protection, the town suddenly plunges into fast-forward. The smugglers' cars of choice are white Toyota pick-up trucks – usually the ones with blacked-out windows, and without any licence plates. Once the weekend begins, these Toyotas start to scurry around the streets in greater numbers. They're taken to the mechanics for any last-minute repairs. Then they're loaded with spare fuel and water; for each trip, Cisse buys 470 litres of the former and 250 of the latter. Dozens of other smugglers are doing the same. No one in the town seems phased.

On Monday afternoon, activities accelerate to a climax. Each smuggler gathers thirty passengers outside their compound, and crams them into the back of his Toyota. Sometimes the drivers come from Libya, and the profits are shared between him and the Nigerien compound owner. Other times it's Nigeriens, like Cisse, who do the driving themselves.

Either way, both methods see the smugglers try to squeeze every last drop of profit from their clients. The passengers are packed so tightly that those on the outside face outwards, with their legs dangling from the parapet. Once in position, they grip onto sticks attached to the car frame, to stop themselves falling out when the car picks up pace.

And then they're off, skidding past the airstrip, and out towards the lonely police checkpoint. Here, the drivers' colleagues linger by the policemen's hut to make sure the officers get their cut. One radios his colleagues back at the compound. 'Get a move on,' he says. 'The way is clear.' Minutes later, the smugglers' trucks hurtle past, and the policemen look the other way – more interested in my car's presence than that of a passing smuggler. The police chief's words ring hollow.

And it's not just the police who turn a blind eye. The reason the smugglers leave en masse on Monday is so that they can tag along with the weekly military convoy into the desert. Again, no one seems to mind. 'The army led us out of the town,' remembers one Nigerian migrant I meet further along the route. 'And the army didn't stop anyone.'

It's comments like this that help me grasp the scale of migration to Europe, the forces that facilitate it, and the futility of trying to stop it. In theory, you could end the war in Syria. Peace in Libya is also theoretically achievable, and with it an opportunity to curb smuggling along the Libyan coast. But you would still have 100,000 people piling through Niger every year – and no one particularly interested in stopping them. In one of the world's poorest countries, and in a town that has no other substantial industries, smuggling is a vital financial lifeline for many local people – and officials. Just look at the numbers. In a single trip, a smuggler might make as much as 4.5 million CFA (a little under £5000). In a year, he could take in as much as £250,000, in a country where the average annual household income is less than £500. In that time, the smugglers of Agadez will collectively make between £16 and £17 million. And that's before bribes worth, by my calculation, somewhere in the region of £1 million for the police.[2]

This money is particularly significant in a town that has many boarded-up travel agencies. Until as late as 2007, Agadez was a tourist town, and its little airstrip technically an international airport. Then a wave of local Berber rebellions, and the rise of a regional al-Qaeda franchise, halted the tourist trade. Even when things quietened down again, the tourists never really came back. The hotels are mostly empty and dilapidated. Even at the most famous one, the Auberge d'Azel, where visiting UN officials stay, the owner has started a sideline in engineering to stay afloat.

I want to chat to the sultan himself about all this, but the day we're meant to meet he has to leave town for a funeral. So I meet instead with his chief adviser, Mohamed Tuwara, and we sit in the shadow of the town's famous minaret.

Tuwara explains that the boom in smuggling has to be seen through the prism of the collapsed economy. 'This is part of what's happening,' sighs Tuwara. 'Because of the rebellions, the tourists won't come to Agadez any more, and the crafts-men don't sell their products. Many people have to change their work, so some of the craftsmen become gardeners. And there are some who become smugglers.'

As a phenomenon, this isn't new. For centuries, Agadez has been an important crossroads for travellers and traders trying to make it through the Sahara. In the Middle Ages, salt and gold merchants picking their way between Timbuktu and the Mediterranean often had to pass through the town. By the fifteenth century, Agadez had its own sultan, its famously imposing mosque, and a knot of winding streets that still exists today. The passage of people through those modern-day streets in one sense merely mimics a movement that has been going on for half a millennium. What makes today different is the scale. There are no good records of recent migration flows in Niger. But, given that ten years ago the rate of departures from Libya was a third of the current level, it follows that the footfall along one of the major routes to Libya at that time was also far lower than it is today. Back then, you could also reach Europe by heading from Senegal to the Canary Islands, or from Morocco to Spain's enclaves in north-west Africa. Those routes have now been cut off, due to greater security cooperation between those three countries, and in the process Agadez has acquired even greater importance as a migrant way station. 'Different people have always come here,' says Tuwara. 'But in the olden days we didn't know what migration was – it's only in the last four or five years that the word "migration" appeared in our speech.'

To understand the full horror of the Sahara, you have to trace the eastern route that runs from Sudan. People are often kidnapped and tortured by smugglers after leaving Agadez – but their experiences only hint at what happens in a more routine way to those who leave from Khartoum. This is the route taken by Eritreans fleeing the continent's most depraved dictatorship, Somalians fleeing civil war, and the victims of the Darfur genocide. The ordeals that await them in the desert are arguably more horrific than those they are trying to escape.

The week-long journey begins in a familiar way. Refugees are gathered in clay compounds in the district of Omdurman, a squat suburb that lies across the Nile from the centre of Khartoum. Then, in the small hours of the morning, they're crammed into lorries. Hundreds of people are squeezed into each vehicle, and then driven hundreds of miles through the desert to the Libyan border. Then the passengers are handed over to Libyan smugglers, who split them into the infamous Toyota pick-ups – thirty crammed into the tiny space at the back of the truck. Finally they're driven to Ajdabiya in north-east Libya, in a leg that's even longer than the previous one. And, according to several groups of Eritreans I meet, it's a journey worse than the sea itself.

Just as it is in Niger, it's very easy to get lost in the Sudanese Sahara, run out of fuel and die of thirst. You're packed like sardines into the back of the truck, so on most trips someone dies of dehydration, or falls off the side. One Eritrean I meet says eight people in his car died in the heat. Other interviewees say they suffered broken limbs after their car overturned – and still hadn't seen a doctor when they were rescued at sea several weeks later.

Then there are the bandits, militias and border guards. Adam, an Eritrean teenager, encountered the lot of them when he travelled through the desert, aged fifteen. I meet Adam in Sicily, a few days after he was rescued in the Mediterranean. He has a confident grin, and speaks in a lucid, fluid way that belies the horrors he describes, as well as the astonishingly young age at which he experienced them. He's barely five feet tall, more child than teenager, and in his desert journey from Eritrea he faced more traumas than most of us will in a lifetime. A skinny boy in a grey T-shirt, he could be on a day out with friends. Except he's been on the road for months.

The route on which he was taken passed close to the meeting point between the Sudanese, Libyan and Egyptian borders. As his convoy of thirteen Toyotas neared Egypt, Egyptian police fired at them. Veering from the route to avoid the Egyptians, Adam's convoy got lost, leading several of his friends to die of thirst. Further north, in Libya, they ran into a jihadist militia who hadn't been paid off by the smugglers – and who promptly fired on the convoy themselves. More migrants died – and a single smuggler.

After finally arriving in Ajdabiya, on the shores of the Mediterranean, Adam then fell victim to a game of politics. People smuggling is ignored and often even facilitated by the local militias who run Libya in the absence of a central government. But, on this day, both the main militia in Ajdabiya and the government in Sudan wanted to show the world that they were ready to tackle the scourge of migration. So Adam's group was unlucky enough to be returned to Sudan, as part of a deal between the authorities in Khartoum and Ajdabiya, and presented to a crowd of journalists at a televised press conference. The message was clear. Look: border enforcement.

Things could scarcely have got worse when Adam's group was imprisoned, and then sentenced to be deported back to Eritrea. By Adam's account, he was already in the process of being repatriated (to a likely jail term) when the UN finally stepped in and persuaded the Sudanese to uphold international law and deposit the refugees in a refugee camp near the Sudanese–Eritrean border. Having almost reached the Mediterranean, Adam was now nearly back at square one, after a return journey of over 4,500 kilometres.

But by far the most brutal part of Adam's journey came when he finally made it back to Ajdabiya several weeks later. While those travelling along the western route to Libya often avoid getting kidnapped and ransomed, it is a routine experience for most migrants who cross the eastern flank. Extortion does not happen by chance here. It is the primary business model for traffickers operating along the Sudanese route.

'It's become part of our culture,' an Eritrean refugee-rights activist tells me. 'We know where we are going to be tortured and what we will have to pay. We are prepared for that. We say it's normal.'

That normality goes like this: on arrival in Ajdabiya, you're locked in a compound until your extended family cobbles together the cash to pay the smugglers. Wherever your relatives are, be it Israel, Sudan or even the UK, the smugglers will have a contact your family can pay in person. No refugees will pay the money themselves before they reach Ajdabiya, because the smugglers might not take them all the way. And no one carries cash to pay on arrival, because it will be stolen. So your family will have to find $1,600 in retrospective payment for the desert journey. And if your family hasn't got that money, the smugglers torture you while your family listens on the phone. One Somalian interviewee was beaten in this fashion with a stick and a rifle butt every day for a month. Adam waited for six months, and as punishment he says he was made to stand in the blazing Libyan sun, on one leg, for twelve hours a day. It was at this point during our conversation in Sicily that Adam's grin folds into a grimace. He stops looking at me and my translator, Abdelfatah, and begins to stare at the ground. After a brief attempt to hold it all in, the young man begins to shake and then sob. We stop the interview, and Adam buries his head in Abdelfatah's shoulder. Sitting on a bench on a sunny coastal path in Sicily, it's difficult to compute all the horrors Adam has endured to get here. I think of what I would have been doing at his age – probably weighing up A levels, and looking ahead to university. Adam, by contrast, just wants somewhere to live.

In Ajdabiya, if and when your family pays, you're then entrusted to other smuggling gangs, and driven west to a range of towns, depending on your trafficker. Several groups of Eritreans I met were taken west to a place called Ben Walid, often driven inside sealed containers. As a result, most of these journeys left people dead from dehydration or suffocation.

There was a reason for that – the drive to Ben Walid is through Islamic State territory. If Isis fighters know there are refugees in the truck, they'll stop it, leave the Muslims and take the Christians. So that's why the smugglers use sealed vehicles such as oil tankers: it's harder to see inside.

I've met nine people who had the misfortune to travel in an open-top truck as they passed near Sirte, the Isis capital in Libya. They were easily spotted, and held for weeks in an Isis camp, until a bomb blast created enough confusion for the Eritreans to escape. One of them had tried to escape earlier – and was shot in the leg.

Life doesn't get better when you finally reach places like Ben Walid. There you're held in another smuggler's compound, and the same process follows: jail and torture until your family pays an associate of the smuggler back home. This time the price is $2000 – an advance payment for the luxury of the sea voyage. Once that's paid, you're moved to a third compound, known as a 'mazraa', near the sea. Again you wait in squalid conditions, usually for a week or more, but sometimes months. Food gets distributed just once a day, and again there are regular beatings. Women are often raped.

'All the suffering that a human can suffer happens in this mazraa,' says an Eritrean doctor called Tadese, when we meet in the middle of the Mediterranean. 'Of course, we knew about what it would be like before we got there. So why did we choose it?'

⊕

In Europe, many think they know the answer to this question: the boat people want to leech off our generous benefits system. In the most notorious summary of this argument, *Sun* columnist Katie Hopkins claimed those crossing the Mediterranean were cockroaches who would later turn British towns into 'festering sores, plagued by swarms of migrants and asylum seekers, shelling out benefits like Monopoly money'. Hopkins's outburst was widely condemned. But really it was just a brasher articulation of ideas promoted in a more genteel manner by government ministers. As the refugee crisis reached fever pitch in 2015, European politicians repeatedly fostered a sense that Mediterranean migrants were people with the specific goal of taking European resources, and perverting European culture. In a typically vicious remark, Miloš Zeman, the Czech president, warned that the influx of refugees would deprive Europeans 'of women's beauty since they will be shrouded in burkas from head to toe, including the face'.

In eastern and central Europe, leaders grew fond of the claim that 90 per cent of migrants were coming for economic reasons. In Britain, the government made similar arguments, though wisely avoided making up statistics that could easily be dispelled. Like Katie Hopkins, prime minister David Cameron described migrants as a 'swarm'. Foreign secretary Philip Hammond called them marauders bent on overrunning European civilisation. Home secretary Theresa May frequently scoffed at any suggestion that they might simply be seeking safety. Interviewed on *Today*, BBC radio's flagship current affairs programme, May said, 'People talk about refugees, but actually if you look at those crossing the central

Mediterranean, the largest number of people are those from countries such as Nigeria, Somalia and Eritrea. These are economic migrants.'

There are a number of reasons why this is a duplicitous argument. The first is that, in 2015, the central Mediterranean was no longer the primary route to Europe, having ceded that mantle to the waters between Turkey and Greece. The second is that, according to the UN, 84 per cent of people arriving in Europe by boat come from the world's top-ten refugee-producing countries.[3] The third, and most relevant to this chapter, is that, even in the central Mediterranean, the largest number of people come from countries from where there is good reason to flee.

May was right that Eritrea, Somalia and Nigeria are the three main sources of migrants crossing from Libya. But it is extraordinary to claim, as she implicitly does, that their citizens automatically have no right to protection under the 1951 Refugee Convention. Parts of Nigeria are safe. But in the country's north, where the Isis ally Boko Haram has waged an insurgency, over a million people have been forced from their homes. It's the same situation in Somalia. Some areas are increasingly stable, but in others the extremist group al-Shabaab is still fighting a civil war against the government – displacing another million civilians.

But neither Somalia nor Nigeria contribute even half as many migrants to Europe as Eritrea, which is the single biggest source of refugees from Africa. Of those migrants who crossed the Mediterranean in 2015, Eritreans formed the fourth-largest national group, behind Syrians, Afghans and Iraqis.[4] The proportion of Eritrean citizens to Eritrean refugees is higher than any other country in the world. The UN refugee agency reckons 5000 people leave every month, and that around 9 per cent of the country's 6 million have now fled.[5]

Why? What is it about this small, relatively new country perched on the Horn of Africa that is driving so many people to escape? Can it really be just about the benefits?

It's hard to tell from fleeting visits to the country. Journalists are rarely allowed in (I haven't managed it myself), and those resourceful enough to gain access find it difficult to delve into the situation in a particularly forensic way. It's very hard for visiting correspondents to do much more than note the rarity of their entry, speak to some government spokesmen, and comment on the capital's colonial-era Italian architecture (they're rarely allowed to stray beyond the city's limits, where living standards are far worse). The residents they interview are often too terrified to say anything controversial. Readers are left wondering: can it really be that bad?

To get a less varnished picture of what's happening inside Eritrea, you have to speak to the people who have escaped it. It's a good time to return to the story of Adam. Adam is in his mid-teens, but the events of his short life illustrate why so many Eritreans are fleeing their country. At fourteen, he became the oldest male member of his family still living at home; the others had been called up for indefinite military service.

With no father or older brother to look after his remaining siblings, Adam dropped out of school to help tend the family's land. No longer in education, he lost his right to a permit that allows Eritreans to move in public. Without it, he was soon arrested just for going outside. Still a fourteen-year-old child, he was then forced to become a military conscript – a fate that normally befalls Eritreans in their last year of school, and continues for the rest of their lives. But after six months of abuse and what amounts to slave labour, Adam escaped home. There he was arrested again, and spent three months in prison without trial before being returned to military service.

He escaped a second time, was caught a second time, returned to prison, and then sent for yet another spell of military service. By the time he finally fled to Sudan, aged fifteen, he had been jailed twice, and forced to become a child soldier three times. After being kidnapped and tortured by Libyan smugglers, he finally reached Italy by boat in May 2015.

'The day I arrived here, that's my new date of birth,' Adam tells me, after he steadies his voice and feels up to continuing the interview. 'The sixteen years I previously lived, they don't count. In Eritrea, I never used to think about the future – I never knew if I'd survive the day. But now I'm trying to do that.'

Dozens of Eritrean exiles I meet describe a totalitarian state where many citizens fear arrest at any moment and dare not speak to their neighbours, gather in groups or linger long outside their homes. Eritrea is not at war, but its first and only president, Isaias Afwerki, plays up the possibility of a return to conflict with neighbouring Ethiopia, which ruled the country until the early 1990s. This threat is used to justify the absence of a constitution, the destruction of the judicial system, and the implementation of indefinite national service that allows the government to treat each civilian as a modern-day serf for the duration of his or her life.

This indefinite national service is the defining feature of contemporary Eritrea, and the most obvious reason for its exodus. Through this system, the government controls almost every aspect of a civilian's life – male or female – from the age of sixteen or seventeen. Where you live, your daily routine, and how often you see your family – all this is decided by the government, thanks to the national service system.

'We are just like slaves for them,' says one twenty-four-year-old, who spent the entirety of his adult life as a conscript until his escape in late 2014. 'That's why we're leaving. It's become one big prison for us.'

Conscripts are technically paid. Different exiles report different monthly wages, but each fell between 500 and 750 nakfas (the local currency) – a negligible pay that equates to between £20 and £30. The amount is so low that it is virtually meaningless, former conscripts say. In exchange for this meagre salary, the government takes away almost all prospect of personal choice. Conscripts are posted where the government orders them, and remain there for months and often years without being allowed home. Fathers are sometimes away for so long that their children forget who they are. An Eritrean mother I met in Cairo, weeks after she fled her homeland, described her personal experience of this phenomenon, after I sounded sceptical about whether it was possible. 'It happened to my son and his cousin recently,' she said matter-of-factly. 'When they found my husband in the house, they said, "Who is he? Get him out!"'

The stories I heard were so far from our lived experience, and so far from the stated aims of the freedom fighters who liberated Eritrea after a decades-long struggle that lasted from the 1970s until the early 1990s, that I wanted to track down a former regime insider to see whether they were true. When Eritrea achieved independence, it did so after what was meant to be one of the most egalitarian liberation campaigns in history. The Eritrean resistance prided itself on the equal footing it gave to its male and female fighters, and the country founded by its members was meant to continue in that even-handed vein. Could it really have gone so badly wrong?

To answer this question, I speak to one of the highest-profile former freedom fighters, Andebrhan Welde Giorgis, who says: yes, it has. Once a key ally of Afwerki, Welde Giorgis is the former head of Eritrea's central bank, the country's ex-ambassador to the EU and the one-time president of Eritrea's only (and now disbanded) university. Until his defection in 2006, he was close to the regime's inner sanctum, and witnessed its descent into despotism at first hand.

It wasn't meant to end like this, Welde Giorgis says. In fact, 'The idea of national service was supposed to be along the same lines as that of Switzerland.' The premise seems almost comic now, but he says the period of service was meant to last for just eighteen months. The aim was both to safeguard the fragile new nation's security, and provide a temporary workforce to rebuild its war-shattered infrastructure and economy.

'It had a military aspect, a social aspect, an economic aspect, and also a cultural aspect,' says Welde Giorgis. 'But all of that was abused when it became indefinite. When it was proclaimed in 1994, people were in their late teens – and now they're in their early forties. How can they sustain families?

'The objective consequence is the destruction of the nuclear family. If you don't have a nuclear family, you don't have a community, and you don't have a society. It's modern-day servitude.'

Conscripts describe military service as a mixture of humiliation and tedium. 'It's not just about serving, it's about being tortured,' says one woman, who spent four years as a conscript before managing to escape. Exiles often refer to a torture position known as 'the eight', whereby a conscript lies on his front, has his hands and ankles tied together behind him, and is then hoisted into the air. One victim recalled hanging like this for days on end, as punishment for scuffling with a fellow conscript. When he was finally freed, it took weeks for him to regain control of his legs. Another commonly reported torture method involves the torturer mixing tea powder with sugar and water – and then spreading the resulting mixture across your naked skin, so that it attracts flies.

The serving part of military service provides cheap labour for the government. Another exile tells me, 'Sometimes they say, "Go to the mountains to quarry the stone." Sometimes they say, "Go to the forest to cut wood", and sometimes, "Go and clean the streets." Everything that the government might need doing, they use the conscripts as slaves.'

Unless they escape Eritrea, the unlucky majority of conscripts will stay in this limbo for their entire lives. But a minority will play out their national service in a partly civilian context. After their first year, which is a mixture of army training and classroom education, Eritreans take an exam. Those who do well are trained to fill a range of roles within the civil service – as teachers, nurses, or even newscasters within Eritrea's amateurish state television network, Eri-TV. The pay is as low as it is in the army, and most conscripts have no say in the positions they're assigned.

Some who end up within the civil workforce say they also had to fulfil military duties by night. In Sicily, I also meet Mehari, a twenty-two-year-old teacher. 'But when I say teacher, I mean that in the day I'd work as a teacher, but at night I would wait for orders from the army,' Mehari explains. 'At any time they can tell you to guard a building. It's very tiring. You end up slumped on your gun. All night you have to splash your face with water to keep awake – because if you're caught, you get in trouble.'

Mehari described his school as having an anarchic atmosphere. Most of the experienced teachers had already fled the country, so the staff was largely made up of young conscripts, whom the students had little respect for. 'Students mostly come to school to get permission to travel around the city,' Mehari said. 'No one wants to stay. They know that at the end of the day they will have to go to military service. So no one wants to learn. And the teachers know that. So the teachers don't want to teach.' Another exiled schoolmaster says that during his last year in the job his class of sixty-two dwindled to just seven because so many of the students had escaped the country.

Trying to escape is a dangerous business. Citizens cannot even move between districts without written permission – which for children is obtainable only from school. So if a child drops out of education in order to earn money for their family, then they – like Adam – run the risk of arrest.

The government has a wide web of informants, a network so extensive that some Eritreans claim they are wary even of speaking to their friends and family about politics. 'The distrust between people is very high,' one told the UN's Eritrea commission. 'You do not even trust your own brother; he could be part of the national security.' Some I speak to scoff at this level of paranoia, but others say it's justified. The housewife whose son no longer recognises his father, says, 'I wouldn't talk with anyone. You're afraid of anyone close to you, even your family. The government hires people to be their tools.'

Until the early 2000s, Eritrea had the semblance of a judicial system. But, for the past decade, multiple reports suggest police are simply locking people up without trial. One refugee I interview says he had not even heard of the concept of a lawyer until he reached Italy, while Welde Giorgis summarises the situation as follows: 'You're not brought before a court of law. You're not allowed to defend yourself. Your family has no rights of visitation, they don't know where you are, they don't know about the physical and mental condition you are in. Once you have disappeared you have one man acting as the accuser, the jailer, the judge and the executioner.'

Afraid of arbitrary arrest, some Eritreans say they try to avoid hanging around outdoors. In particular, people fear being caught up in what's known as a 'giffa' – a flash raid on a certain area by troops looking for truant conscripts. In a giffa, anything goes: the raiders can arrest people in the street or at home.

'They can get you anywhere,' says another Eritrean, who arrived in Italy in the summer of 2015. 'For me personally they came to get me when I was in bed with my wife. They searched all over the house – even under the bed. It's a very bad feeling, to think they can just enter your room like that.'

Beyond the fear, life is often dull. In the capital, Asmara, the presence of a small elite and the flow of remittances from relatives overseas allows for a more vibrant life. Asmarans can access foreign satellite networks – and as a result both Turkish soaps and a major Korean entertainment channel have become unlikely sources of entertainment. Residents regularly also watch Premier League football games in the city's old cinemas. But, outside the capital, people say streets are often empty and public spaces are almost lifeless. There is no private media. The only public meetings allowed are those of Afwerki's political party. Internet access is rare and several people said they had not heard of Facebook until they left Eritrea. People on active military service are barred from owning a mobile, while anyone else who wants one has to apply at a government office in the capital of their province.

The average Eritrean is now 'a helpless victim', Welde Giorgis summarises. 'And that's why you see these large numbers of Eritreans leaving the country at great risk to their lives. Many die from dehydration in the Sahara. Many have drowned in the Mediterranean. Many have become victim to organ harvesters in the Sinai. But nobody cares. Eritrea has become an earthly hell, an earthly inferno for its people – and that's why they are taking such huge risks to their personal lives to escape the situation. It's become unlivable.'

All of this helps answer the question posed earlier in this chapter by the Eritrean doctor, Tadese. Every Eritrean knows the risks of going to Libya. 'So why', he asks, 'did we choose it?' Because Eritrea is so much worse. And because neighbouring countries like Sudan – where Eritreans have few rights, and run the risk of being deported – aren't much better.

But what does this say about the people passing through Agadez? There aren't any Eritreans here. Apart from some of the Nigerians, most migrants travelling from west Africa aren't fleeing from a war. So why are they putting themselves through such a hell?

In one sense, the likes of Theresa May have it right. This minority of migrants – no more than a quarter of the 2015 total[6] – are after money, jobs and a better life. Back in the winding streets of Agadez, and further along the migration trail, I meet migrant after migrant who admits they're travelling simply to find work. There's the welder who had no welding to do in Senegal. There's the Nigerian engineer who could find no work in engineering. And his friend, Paul Ohioyah, a part-time pastor who's desperate for work as a plumber. All of these men have no right to sanctuary in Europe under the terms of the 1951 Refugee Convention – which enshrines the rights of those fleeing persecution but not poverty.

So the Theresa Mays of this world are correct: these particular people are not refugees. And by the same token, the UN refugee agency – which led liberal calls to distinguish between refugees and other kinds of migrants – is right to prioritise people who will automatically qualify for protection under international law. In a world where all types of migrants are viewed with suspicion, it makes sense in the short term for the UN to focus on the rights of the most vulnerable, even if it comes at the expense of people also in need of sympathy.

But for pragmatists on both sides of the debate, this very reductive picture of an economic migrant is ultimately not a particularly useful one. For a start, people who travel for so many miles through such horrific conditions in order to find work cannot accurately be portrayed as lazy benefit-scroungers. Ironically, they instead display qualities that would be prized in indigenous Europeans – the kind of on-yer-bike resourcefulness that conservatives wish was intrinsic to every native jobseeker. As Europe's population ages, there will be a place and even a need for such hardworking people, if their arrival can be coordinated in a coherent manner.

Second: while someone like the pastor plumber, Paul Ohioyah, may be best described as an economic migrant when he sets out from Nigeria, after a few weeks in Libya he will be someone more akin to a refugee. This will be explained in greater detail in the next chapter, but here is the situation in brief. The Libyan civil war, and the abominable treatment of most migrant workers there, means that migrants in the country are in danger almost as soon as they arrive. So somehow they need to leave again. And extraordinary though it might sound, a boat trip to Europe is often a slightly cheaper and marginally more likely means of reaching safety than another slog back through the desert, given all the risks of ambush, kidnap and death that the latter journey involves.

For me, the third and most compelling point is this: these kinds of people will keep on coming, whether Europe likes it not. Listen to the words of Paul Ohioyah, whom I meet after he was rescued from near death at sea by Tunisian coastguards. The UN is not going to help resettle you, I tell him, because you're fleeing from poverty not war. But Ohioyah doesn't care: we may dismiss him as an economic migrant, but in his desperation he sees himself as just as deserving as anyone. 'You have to issue us with papers,' he says. 'You need to tell us that we can have a future.' And, if not, Ohioyah promises a stark alternative: 'You can't escape us immigrants. We won't stop trying. We won't stop taking risks.'

The European right might wish they wouldn't take those risks. Those on the left, who delineate between good and bad migrants, might feel these people have less right to do so than those fleeing Syria. But, sooner or later, both camps will have to figure out how we can best absorb so-called economic migrants into our society. People who subject themselves to the horrors of the desert, the battlegrounds of Libya and the death boats of the Mediterranean are not doing so lightly, and are not people who will be easily stopped. They are people who genuinely believe it's better to die trying to get to Europe than live in poverty at home. Their desperation will ultimately prove stronger than our isolationism, particularly if climate change begins to force more and more people north, as some commentators have argued.[7]

Increased development in poorer countries is sometimes touted as a quick fix to economic migration. More jobs and investment in Africa, the argument goes, will persuade more Africans to stay put at home. Certainly, over several decades, prolonged economic growth often leads to a net decrease in emigration. But, as the work of the sociologist Hein de Haas has shown, in the short to medium term, a slight increase in GDP leads to a corresponding increase in emigration, since more people have the money to pay smugglers. De Haas cites statistics that show how it's only when annual salaries rise to around a quarter of the average salary in the developed world that a country's net migration levels start to decrease.[8] This kind of dynamic takes years to reach. It's no answer to the migration challenges of the early twenty-first century.

Many Western countries hope to contain the problem with other short-term solutions such as fences and naval patrols. But these tactics merely shift the migration flow to more porous borders – for example, from Morocco to Libya. Judging from the rhetoric of economic migrants, it'll take more than these comparatively minor obstacles to stop them from attempting the journey. Many even see it as their right.

Back in the bus station at Agadez, one of Cisse's passengers, Joel Gomez, points out that African migrants are merely mimicking a journey made by those who colonised Africa.

'The white man arrived in Africa by sea without a visa,' says the Cameroonian. 'And we have learned to travel from the white man.'

3

Trading in Souls

Smuggling networks on the north African coast

Libya, April 2015

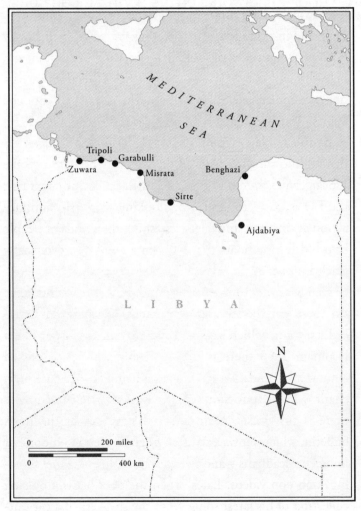

Desert Routes in Libya

On the night that Europe essentially declares war against him, Hajj couldn't care less. After hearing the news, Hajj simply lies down on his side, props his bare feet up on a cushion, and helps himself to two whole snapper fish. Then he downs a non-alcoholic bottle of Beck's beer. Then a plate of chopped apples. And after that a bowl of olives and cheese cubes.

In short, Hajj is unbothered. Unbothered by the TV behind him showing news of the latest attempts to end the Libyan civil war. And unbothered by the announcement that the EU is, as of tonight, now looking to pursue military action against the smugglers squashing thousands of people into old fishing boats that will, on a good day, eventually reach Europe.

Hajj has other things on his mind. First, there is his belly. An obese man, he takes some moments to arrange his extraordinary gut, which sags and flattens on the carpet like a beanbag. Then there is the moonshine, which is passed among his friends – a local poet, a haulier and a fuel merchant – in an innocuous plastic water bottle. And finally there is the music. Hajj casts a last glance at the news bulletin, which shows a stricken migrant boat – 'Not one of mine,' he deadpans – and switches to a jollier channel showing Arab pop videos. Later, when the poet blasts a pulsing collection of his latest songs from the speakers of a car outside, Hajj joins in with the singing.

'I'm not threatened,' Hajj says, once the festivities quieten down. 'It's been happening for years, these promises and threats. They'll move on.'

On the face of it, Hajj should feel concerned. It is approaching midnight on Monday, 20 April 2015, and just a few hours ago European leaders said they were planning to set their navies on Libyan smugglers. And here in Zuwara, the ground zero for people smuggling along the north African coast, that basically means Hajj. He's a thirty-three-year-old law graduate. And he's also the man locals say is responsible for over half the smuggling missions along this bit of the coast.

But, instead of feeling fearful, Hajj and his friends are amused. 'What are they going to do, put two frigates here?' Hajj chortles. 'Two warships? In Libyan waters? That's an invasion.'

They all scratch their heads. What on earth would military options look like against such a tangled, complex trade? A trade deeply rooted in not just the coastal economy, but in dozens of way stations across the northern half of the African continent. And one that is now reliant not just on a few experienced individuals but – thanks to the ongoing unrest sparked by Libya's 2011 revolution – on overlapping and informal networks that emerge, morph and fade by the week.

'Who? Where?' asks Hajj's friend, the haulier, when contemplating the potential targets of EU anti-smuggling operations. 'No one has the name "smuggler" written on their chest. Anyone here who has no money can sell their apartment, buy a boat, and organise a smuggling trip. By the time of the next trip you'd already have regained half the cost of the apartment. It's a very easy formula.'

Hajj has been smuggling people across the Mediterranean for a decade. But now newcomers are undercutting his prices, and competing to buy the same boats. 'Just go to the port,' says the haulier. 'Those boats are all for sale.'

Earlier in the evening, I'd done exactly that. I watch from the quay with one of Hajj's friends, another smuggler who promises to show me how the process works. Just as the light starts to dim, a blue wooden boat begins to slide slowly from the port in Zuwara. There is nothing to distinguish it from the dozens of other boats moored nearby, all wooden skiffs knocking against each other in the breeze. It looks like a fishing boat, and days earlier it had been one.

But the watching smuggler picks it out easily. Yesterday this boat might have carried hundreds of fish back to port. Tonight, he says, it will soon bear hundreds of refugees towards Italy. A day later up to 900 people drowned in nearby waters, yet another trip is following in its wake.

The smuggler has bought the boat off a local fisherman for somewhere between 80,000 and 160,000 dinar (£40,000–£80,000).[1] For up to another 25,000 dinar (£12,500) the local coastguard will allow the boat to leave port with a nudge and a wink. Its silent departure is a lesson in the intangible nature of the smuggling trade.

Smugglers don't have their own separate, independent harbour of clearly marked boats, ready to be targeted by EU airstrikes. They buy them from fishermen at a few days' notice. To destroy their pool of boats, you would have to destroy whole fishing ports.

'One of the reasons why fish is expensive is the lack of fishing boats going out to sea to fish,' Hajj says later. 'So many of [the boats] are being sold to smugglers.'

There has always been smuggling along the Libyan coast. Zuwara is infamous for it, and the Berber tribe that lives there – the Amazigh – is renowned for producing skilled smugglers. Long before the 2015 refugee crisis, Hajj was himself sending people to Europe. He started in 2006, a year after graduating from law school. He couldn't find work as a lawyer, so he turned to the traditional alternative: people smuggling. And over the next few years, Hajj gradually took more and more control of the market. Now he's so familiar with the process that he refers to the sea as a swimming pool.

Until 2011, the business was a comparatively low-level affair. In the middle of the first decade of the twenty-first century, the smugglers of Libya and Tunisia might collectively send around 40,000 people[2] each year to Lampedusa, the southernmost Italian island, and the Italian mainland beyond. Spain had built not one nor two but three fences around its pair of enclaves in north-west Africa, so Morocco was finally no longer the best option for those trying to reach Europe. The hop from west Africa to the Canary islands also became harder, due to security deals between Spain, Senegal and Mauritania. So migrants increasingly came to places like Libya instead. That flow nevertheless tailed off almost completely by around 2009, when Libya's then dictator, Muammar Gaddafi, signed an agreement with the Italians, promising to stem the flow. He was good at it. That year, the number of arrivals had dropped to just 4,500.[3]

Yet, a year after that, things changed once more. The Arab uprisings of 2011 began in Tunisia and reached Libya by February. In the security vacuum created by the toppling of Tunisia's president, some 30,000 Tunisians seized the opportunity to travel by boat to Italy.[4] Another 30,000 mainly sub-Saharan African migrants departed from Libya as Gaddafi struggled to keep his grip on power in the face of several armed uprisings and a NATO bombing campaign. Smugglers claim that Gaddafi was himself one of the reasons behind this sudden revival of the smuggling trade. Attempting to show NATO's members what they'd miss if they helped to topple the man who kept Fortress Europe safe from the south, Gaddafi is said to have personally ordered the departure of several migrant boats . Whatever the truth, 2011 was certainly a record year for people smugglers working the Italian route, with 64,000 migrants arriving on Italian shores by the end of December.[5]

There was another drop in 2012, when the level was as low as 15,900.[6] Smugglers argue this was because they, like everyone else, were mostly trying to make the new Libya work – and because they wanted to repay the 'favour' NATO and the EU had given the country the previous year (by helping to speed Gaddafi's departure). True or not, smuggling activity was back to normal in 2013, with 40,000 reaching Italy.[7]

The year 2014 was when things spiralled out of control – both in Libya's cities and on its coasts. After three years of simmering tensions between different clans and cities, and between Islamists and those of a marginally more secular bent, Libya fissured into full-scale civil war. A more Islamist-minded coalition, known as Libya Dawn, took control of Tripoli and the western smuggling ports. An Isis franchise emerged in Gaddafi's old home town, Sirte, at the centre of the Libyan coastline. And the internationally recognised government retreated to Tobruk, in the country's far east.

Complex as it seems, this description of a three-way civil war is itself a simplification. Within the two main factions were dozens of different militias, some of whom ran different geographic areas and even government institutions. Even within the main jurisdictions of Tripoli and Tobruk, there was no all-powerful central command. And, within this cantonised chaos, few had the ability or interest to restrict the work of people smugglers. The result was an astonishing spike in migration to Italy. More than 170,000 people reached the Italian coast in 2014, nearly triple the previous record.

The Syrian civil war played a significant role in this unprecedented increase: about a third of the passengers in 2014 were Syrians who'd reached Libya solely for the purpose of getting to the boats, and who hadn't yet heard of the easier route between Turkey and Greece. The rest were largely sub-Saharan Africans escaping the Libyan chaos, and taking advantage of the security vacuum to do so. A record number died in the attempt: around 3,200, though some think the figure was greater. In 2015, an even higher number died – at least 3,500 – although the total number crossing from Libya slightly dipped to 150,000.[8] But this was scarcely a victory for the European right: the level remained in the same ballpark despite the wholesale abandonment of the route by the Syrians, who switched en masse to the crossing between Turkey and Greece.

This spike in Libyan smuggling is due not only to the disappearance of a central government, and the subsequent inability of the militias to maintain control. It is also due to the participation in that smuggling trade by the militias. As the Libyan civil war dragged on, militias increasingly struggled to fund their operations. The UAE was alleged to have propped up parts of the Tobruk alliance, while some of those in Tripoli were allegedly backed by Turkey and Qatar. But their support wasn't enough – and some militia leaders seemed to realise they could make up much of the shortfall with money from the migration business. If 170,000 people cross the sea, and each pays, on average, around $1000 – then the potential profits are huge.

There is no definitive study of the militias' involvement. Some of them actively police the trade, perhaps hoping to curry favour with the international community. But my research, and that of colleagues,[9] suggests that other militias are doing the opposite. For some of them, it's a largely passive role. In exchange for allowing a smuggler to operate on their territory, a militia leader might demand a cut of his profits. A smuggler told me that the faction that controls Libya's eastern border with Egypt allows migrants to cross for a fee – and the same happens on the Egyptian side. On the coast, smugglers say they bribe the groups that control the ports.

Sometimes the militias' involvement seems more pro-active. Migrants I've interviewed in Italy said their trips were organised by the leader of one militia in north-west Libya, and they gave me his name. Others described a process whereby they were arrested by the militias that run some of Libya's migrant detention centres, and then detained within these camps. Those who could quickly come up with the cash were allowed to buy their freedom. Those who couldn't were sold on to different militias in other parts of the country, transferred to their detention camps – and then finally sold to smugglers. The smugglers would then get their money back through the migrants' families or fellow countrymen, who would be told to scrabble together a ransom.

I visit two of these camps, after officials from Libya Dawn organise access, and they are miserable places. One is a half-finished building that was meant to be a school. Now it houses 450 migrants, who sleep on the floors of urine-soaked classrooms, sixty to a room. Women and children are kept separate from the men, and the corridors between their cells echo with phlegmy coughs and the wails of babies. Around midday, everyone shuffles shoeless through the sandy central courtyard, queuing for their daily bowl of rice (and a potato). This time it is the men who sob, as they tell me their stories at the side of the yard. 'Why are we asked to pay a thousand dinar to leave?' asks one. 'Why?'

This is one of the topics that Hajj himself is more reluctant to talk about. Physically, he finds it hard to talk about any-thing – his heavy frame frequently leaves him wheezing. But he's at his quietest when controversial topics like the militias come up.

It is hard to get him to speak in the first place. For a start, there's the war. Zuwara is one of the last towns before the Tunisian border, and a few miles from the war's front line, so the fighting doesn't affect the town itself. The coastal road to Zuwara from Tripoli, however, is controlled by various different groups, and is frequently closed by fighting between militias from the Libya Dawn alliance and those who represent the official government. The night before I leave Tripoli, the area where I'm staying is the scene of a noisy gunfight, punctuated by several rounds of shelling, that lasts for several hours. While it's ongoing, it's unwise to make for Zuwara.

But the war in Tripoli comes and goes. Fighting can flare at a major roundabout in the morning. By the afternoon, the militias and their pick-up trucks will have disappeared, heavy civilian traffic will have returned, and the only reminder of the morning's battle will be a burned-out car or two. By midday, my translator, Yaseen, and I are on the road to Zuwara, ready to meet Hajj.

Now the problem is Hajj himself. I'm supposed to meet him on the day I arrive in his town. For weeks, a local bigwig has promised that our meeting is a done deal. In the end it almost doesn't happen. On that first night, Hajj doesn't show. Nor does he emerge the next day, so we spend it on the Zuwaran beachfront, peaking at the warehouses and unfinished houses where migrants are kept the night before they reach the boats. Then we head to the port, where oil smuggling happens in the open, with the smugglers funnelling stolen fuel into their boats without regard for who might be watching. On the third day, Hajj is also absent, so my host – a fuel smuggler – takes Yaseen and me on a tour of the town, which is much like any Libyan town of 80,000 people. Quiet, lots of concrete, and plenty of land cruisers. The thing that most denotes it is the Amazigh flag, a green-red-and-yellow tricolour that hangs from many buildings. It's a reminder to the visitor that this is an Amazigh (or Berber) town, not an Arab one. Zuwara's inhabitants speak their own language, view themselves as the original Libyans, and have long felt marginalised by their Arab usurpers.

By the evening, Hajj still hasn't emerged, so the fuel smuggler takes us back to the port to watch a people-smuggling boat silently leave port. Then the smuggler introduces us to the local coastguards (a telling connection), who inform us that even if they wanted to stop the smuggling, they can't: they and their colleagues down the coast have just three inflatable boats to patrol the entire coast of western Libya.

These are all interesting details, but my central question remains: where's Hajj? I am starting to lose patience when the fuel smuggler's flashy jeep takes a detour from the route home to halt outside one of the biggest mansions in town. An enormous man wearing a T-shirt and shorts plods out of the mansion's front gate. Without any introduction, he waits for Yaseen to hurry out of the front seat, before taking his place with a thud that rocks the whole car. Then we all drive back to our host's house in silence, and gather inside for dinner.

'Yes,' Hajj wheezes, once I find a way of asking if it's him I've come to meet. 'It's me.'

It is the prelude to two days of conversations that, coupled with a meeting with a smuggler in Tripoli, help build a picture of the Libyan people-smuggling industry.

It's a process that is hard to distil into a single narrative. A minority of migrants is brought to the Libyan coast by one continuous network – people like the Eritreans in the previous chapter. Hajj and his rival in Tripoli, however, say they aren't part of that kind of system. Their clients tend to be people who have been in Libya for some time. Perhaps they've been earning money with the specific aim of spending it on the boat voyage. Or perhaps they initially intended for Libya to be their final destination (it was a stable and lucrative place to work before the 2011 revolution) but changed their minds once the civil war made their lives untenable.

It's worth lingering slightly longer over this particular point. In Europe, it is often argued that the majority of the migrants from Libya are economic migrants, and therefore unworthy of sanctuary. In the case of Eritreans, this is demonstrably false. In the case of west Africans, this is also arguably wrong – but it takes a richer understanding of Libyan life to make this argument. It is nevertheless an obvious point once you consider the miserable existence of a foreigner in Libya. Even if they're never caught up in a gunfight or an explosion, the instability caused by the civil war means that a black African runs the daily risk of kidnap and extortion. To find work, most immigrants from the sub-Sahara gather daily at a few known intersections in Tripoli, and wait for rich Libyans to come and offer them a temporary job. It is a recipe for exploitation. Many say that once they're taken to someone's compound they're treated as slave labour – locked up and told to work for free. Others report that the exploitation is even starker than this. Omar Diawara, a Malian whose disastrous sea journey I describe later in the book, was simply kidnapped by two men who'd promised him a job – and told to raise a ransom. With no police force worthy of the name, and with many so-called policemen in on the act, migrants have no legal recourse and are therefore regarded as easy targets. One man I met says he was stabbed by a child in a provincial Libyan town, while the boy's father looked on and laughed.

In this climate, many migrants realise that their only real option is to leave Libya by sea. Without proper paperwork, they can't ask for help from their embassies – many of whose staff, in any case, have left the country while the hostilities continue. There's little point to returning the way they came – across the desert – because the cost and the risk of death is as great if not greater than crossing the sea. So the sea suddenly becomes the realist's choice.

It's at this point that people like Hajj come into play, at least indirectly. Hajj is in touch with various middlemen from the different migrant ethnic groups. Migrants approach the middlemen, and the middlemen bring the migrants to the smugglers. Some smugglers pay their middlemen a minuscule cut of their profits. Hajj doesn't – he leaves them to get their money from the migrants themselves. But the result is the same: a constant flow of customers, ready to set sail for Europe.

What each passenger pays depends on who they are. By Hajj's maths, at this point in spring 2015 a sub-Saharan African is expected to pay up to $1000, but usually a bit less. Syrians were scarce in Libya by this stage, but the few that remained would pay $2,500; everyone knows that the

Syrians have more money than the Africans. Due to the saturated market, prices overall are lower than usual – and as a result smugglers are trying to fill their ships with larger numbers, in order to make back the shortfall. 'It's ridiculous,' Hajj admits. 'Three hundred passengers is the maximum for a seventeen-metre boat. But people are sending out boats loaded with 350, 700, 800. They are being overloaded because the price of an individual has gone down.'

The more you pay, the less dangerous your journey. Since they pay less, the Africans are often shoved below decks. If the ship sinks, they'll almost certainly drown, and even if it doesn't they're more likely to suffocate in the hold. Since they pay more, Syrians travel on boats with slightly fewer passengers. And if they pay a lot more, they can supposedly travel alone. Hajj claims that one Syrian family paid him $100,000 to ensure they got to Italian waters, and so he sent them in an inflatable boat all to themselves.

The vast majority receive nothing like that level of service. They are instead crammed into warehouses or farmhouses, the mazraa, and told to wait their turn – which can be a long time coming. One Syrian I meet in Italy, days after he finally arrives there, spent four months in a mazraa near the town that lies just east of Zuwara. He was essentially there under duress: forbidden to leave, and refused access to the boats. Twice he was taken to the shore to board a vessel, and twice he was returned. A third time he reached the boat itself – but too late: there was no more space. It was only at the fourth attempt that he finally set sail. 'The four months that we stayed there . . .' he remembers. 'Do you know what death is like?'

Everyone I meet who's stayed in a mazraa says something similar. Whether they came through Zuwara, or ports to the east such as Sabratha, Tripoli or Garabulli, migrants speak of a hellish experience. Of being trapped along with up to a hundred people to a single tiny room. Of frequent beatings, and squalid conditions. Of mouldy bread, provided just once a day. And for the women, of rape. Bored and armed smugglers will choose a woman, and then sometimes beckon over some male migrants, so that they can see what's being done to their female companions. 'They want us to see them raping the women,' explains one Eritrean, who says the episode sparked in him a wave of self-loathing. 'You hate yourself. You hate that you are a human being.'

I have no proof of how Hajj treats his own customers. He wouldn't take me to his warehouses. It's therefore still possible that he is the only smuggler in Libya who treats his clients with respect. Certainly, that's the way he portrays it. Like all the people smugglers I've ever met, Hajj emphasises his own exceptionalism. There is a point in our conversation when Hajj falls silent for so long that I wonder if his contracting arteries have finally got the better of him. His eyes begin to well up. The moments pass. Then finally he speaks again, and it turns out that he was simply overcome by the memory of the only shipwreck for which he admits responsibility, way back in 2008. Or so he says. It's a hammy, unconvincing performance with an obvious subtext: I'm not like the others, and I care about my passengers. He'll admit there was – once – a rape at one of his warehouses. But generally they are peaceful, comfortable places, he says. Everyone has a PlayStation there, and torture 'has never happened',

Hajj claims. 'In ethical terms, they're people who have brought you a lot of money, so you can't treat them like that.'

I would like to believe Hajj, but I can't. I'd like to believe that he really does pace around anxiously, smoking his way through five packs of cigarettes, until word comes that his clients have safely reached Italy. I'd like to think he does send a rescue party out when he hears that one of his boats has run into difficulty. But I suspect these are things he says only because he knows it might impress an international journalist. He labours over these points for the same reason he asks to be known in my journalism by the nickname of Hajj; it's an honorific that describes someone who has made the pilgrimage to Mecca. He's a smuggler, yes. But he wants to be considered a smuggler with ethics. And perhaps in doing so, he protests too much.

That said, I don't subscribe to the way that smugglers are depicted by most politicians and media. In the common imagination, smugglers are seen as the root cause of migration to Europe, evil actors who created the demand, rather than unscrupulous businessmen who responded to it. True, there are some migrants who say they were forced onto their boats. But the vast majority depart of their own accord.

The politicians and their outriders in the media who suggest otherwise have good reason to do so. By elevating the role of smugglers you diminish the agency of their clients. In the process, you obscure the actual reasons why people might risk their life to cross the sea – the wars and dictators that forced them from their homes. By denying the existence of these real root causes you simultaneously absolve yourself from the duty of providing sanctuary to those fleeing from them. Acknowledging this duty would prove very problematic: it would be an admission that your own failure to do so previously was the reason why so many thousands then turned in their desperation to smugglers – and why so many of them then drowned in the ocean. It would be an admission that a Syrian boards a boat only when he realises that there's no realistic means of winning asylum from the Middle East. And an admission that Libya's current predicament is in part the result of NATO's (justifiable) airstrikes against Gaddafi in 2011 – and subsequent (and unjustifiable) failure to help Libya's post-Gaddafi transition.

The writer Jeremy Harding made this point best in 2000, writing in the *London Review of Books*: 'We think of agents, traffickers and facilitators as the worst abusers of refugees, but when they set out to extort from their clients, when they cheat them or dispatch them to their deaths, they are only enacting an entrepreneurial version of the disdain which refugees suffer at the hands of far more powerful enemies – those who terrorise them and those who are determined to keep them at arm's length. Human traffickers are simply vectors of the contempt which exists at the two poles of the asylum seeker's journey; they take their cue from the attitudes of warlords and dictators, on the one hand, and, on the other, of wealthy states whose citizens have learned to think of generosity as a vice.'[10]

Traffickers and smugglers are also a varied group – too big all to be tarred with the same muddy brush. For a start, there is a distinction between the two terms. People smugglers are those whom migrants pay to get them from one country to another. They might treat their clients roughly, or even cruelly – but their central role is one performed with the consent of the migrant. By contrast, traffickers smuggle their passengers without their consent, and with the intent of enslaving them, forcing them into prostitution, or imprisoning them until the repayment of a debt. In this respect, those Libyans who capture and trade migrants for profit, or who hold them for ransom, are clearly in the trafficking business. But those who put migrants on the boats, even after treating them with indignity, are usually best described as smugglers.

Among smugglers there are different shades of grey. The driver who delivers a taxi load of refugees between countries in the Balkans can't really be compared with someone who rapes his nominal clients in a camp on the Libyan coast. The Syrian who puts his countrymen into dinghies on the Turkish coast is putting them through less danger than the Libyan who shoves Senegalese teenagers into the hold of a boat off the coast of Tripoli.

I've met a dozen smugglers in five countries. Some are charming, and I enjoyed sparring with a couple of them. One was surprisingly sweet – we'll come to him later in the book. Most of them I didn't warm to. Most of them were untrustworthy – they didn't turn up to appointments, or they told blatant lies. More than any other group of sources, smugglers had to be persuaded that somehow an interview might be to their advantage. In Egypt and Turkey, I'd tell people I was interested in paying for a seat on the boat – but first I wanted to understand how the process worked. Another Egyptian smuggler, who had recently organised a trip that ended in a notorious shipwreck, thought an interview would give him the chance to restore his reputation, and revive his business.

Hajj himself believed our conversations could help shine a brighter light on the plight of his Amazigh minority, and so lead to greater financial aid from the West. This is how it is with smugglers – everything has to be framed in monetary terms. I feel a bit grubby just talking with them.

But ultimately I feel ambivalent about most of the smugglers I meet. Some of them have got very rich by stuffing people into leaking boats or packed land cruisers. But the majority admit they're ashamed of what they're doing. They've usually turned to smuggling because they've few other means of making an income. Smugglers often live in places – like Zuwara and Agadez – where the local economy has collapsed. Or they're people with no means of working legally. Because they, like the people they're smuggling, are refugees. If they weren't despatching the boats they'd be on their decks themselves.

Speaking of which, Libyan smugglers use three kinds of boats. The biggest are the rarest: the steel-hulled ships, capable of carrying numbers approaching a thousand. These are very rare: the Italian coastguards say they see only a couple of them a year. The second type are the wooden fishing sloops, which account for around a third of the smuggling missions, and are crammed with between 300 and 700 people. Finally, there are the inflatable dinghies, known as Zodiacs. About two-thirds of the boats that leave Libya are Zodiacs, but because they tend to carry between 100 and 150 passengers they are probably responsible for less than half the total number of migrants arriving in Italy. They should carry even fewer. These are boats that are designed for between twenty and thirty passengers, rather than five times that number. They're also meant for short trips, not inter-continental smuggling missions. The ones I've seen in person are very poorly made. They often have just one air pocket, rather than several, meaning that if any part of it springs a leak the whole boat will start to deflate. Aware that the set-up is a disaster waiting to happen, smugglers often fix wooden planks to the bottom of the Zodiac, to make it slightly more buoyant.

Smugglers don't agree about how dangerous these boats are. Some say the Zodiac is too dangerous for this kind of work. But Hajj says they're his preferred smuggling vessel, claiming they're safer than the wooden skiffs. To be fair, there is probably not that much in it; they are both floating coffins. There's no comparison, though, when it comes to the practicalities of getting the two types of boat to water. The rubber boats are much easier and cheaper to send to sea. You can launch and board them from the shore itself. The first ones were raided from Gaddafi's storehouses, but now you can import them fairly easily (though from where, no one will tell me). The wooden boats, on the other hand, have to be bought from local fishermen, and the process is more complicated.

The cost of a Zodiac remains steady, at around 11,000 dinar (£5,500). The fishing boats are becoming dearer. A few years ago, when fishermen could get a special loan from the government to subsidise the cost of a boat, a small wooden vessel, perhaps seventeen metres long, might have cost 80,000 dinar on the black market. But now the loan system has ended, and boats are slightly scarcer due to the rise in smuggling, fishermen want more money for their assets. As a result, Hajj is paying double what he used to. Boats aren't exactly running out, he says. However, the usual vendors have fewer and fewer boats for sale, so he's having to buy from fishermen who previously preferred not to get involved. And such people need to be offered rather more tempting amounts. 'Say 160,000 dinar, rather than 80,000,' Hajj estimates. 'If I want a boat, I will buy it at any price.'

That's because the profits on offer are so exorbitant. Hajj and Ahmed are evasive when I ask them to tot up their earnings. But, even without their help, it's easy to work out the ballpark total. At a conservative estimate, a Zodiac filled with just 100 passengers who each pay $1000 will create a turnover of $100,000. Subtract the cost of the boat itself, the engine, the cost of keeping the migrants alive in a warehouse for a fortnight – and you'd still be left with around $80,000, or £52,000. Even if half of that went towards keeping the local militia happy, the smuggling gang would then have at least £26,000 to share among themselves – from just one week's work. A wooden boat would reap even more. Once the boat, the engine and other expenses are paid for, a fishing trawler filled with 400 migrants would bring at least £180,000 to be shared between the smugglers and anyone who needed a bribe.

Getting the wooden boats out of port is a delicate matter, and smugglers approach it in different ways. The practice is rampant, but the smugglers still try not to be too obvious about it. Some smugglers ask the original owner to report the boat missing, even though it will still be moored in plain sight inside the port. Then they scrub off its name, so it can't be traced, and pay the coastguards 2000 dinar to look the other way when they sail it out to sea.

Hajj claims he pays 25,000 dinar for a similar privilege – but he won't explain why. Perhaps it's because he works from a different port. Perhaps it's because the fee includes money for a local militia. Or perhaps because his method is even more blatant: he doesn't bother to report the boat missing. His teams simply procure permission from the coastguards to take it out to sea for a three-day 'fishing' trip. And then they don't come back.

Instead, as night falls, they drop anchor at a safe distance out to sea. Then, in the darkness, the migrants emerge from their safe houses to a series of waiting Zodiacs. In Zuwara, some of these houses are warehouses, some of them beach huts and others unfinished villas. But they are all on or close to the beach. Then the migrants climb into the Zodiacs and a short ride later they're loaded onto the trawler. Sometimes the process takes several trips. Once everyone's on board, they're given a satellite phone, a GPS tracker, life jackets (at 15 dinar each, or roughly £7.50) and some food and water. Then each person is allocated a place to sit, and told to remain seated for the duration of the voyage. Hajj claims to keep numbers to acceptable levels on the boats. But, because he still packs so many on board, he admits the way they sit is important. 'We give them direct instructions not to move too much,' he says. 'If two or three start to do that, others want to do the same. That creates chaos that causes it to capsize.'

The hope is that the boats can last until international waters before anything like that happens. Once outside Libyan jurisdiction, the passengers call for help on their sat-phone. They won't be the only ones: smugglers with thousands of migrants waiting in their warehouses tend to release several boats at the same time, once or twice a week. In a rare instance of humanity, they wait for the best weather of the week and then release them in a flurry – partly to make the risk of sinking slightly smaller, and partly because a flotilla of boats is more likely to be noticed than a single vessel.

The crew often aren't smugglers themselves. In the inflatables, the driver is almost always just a co-opted migrant; someone who can hold the tiller steady. On the wooden boats, sometimes the crew is drawn from the passengers – people with a bit of nautical experience. But usually they're low-level members of the smugglers' wider networks: fishermen from Egypt, Tunisia or Libya who fancy a free trip to Europe. They're arrested on arrival in Italy (among a group of sub-Saharans, the Arabs are easy to spot), and the Italians trumpet their prosecutions as major developments. In reality, they're minor players who have been sent to sea for a reason: because they're expendable. Later in the summer, when I spend a week on a rescue vessel run by Médecins Sans Frontières, I talk with the pair of Libyan ship hands who were aboard a boat of Eritreans rescued by MSF. They seemed genuinely clueless about the whole operation – and I didn't feel this was a pretence. 'Two days?' one gasped, when I told him how long it would take for MSF's boat to reach Italy. 'In Libya they said it would take a few hours!'

Throughout the summer of 2015, European politicians and officials frequently speak about trying to smash these smuggling operations. Judging from the tenor of their rhetoric in April, when the idea is first mooted, they initially assume that this could be achieved through straightforward naval operations. Donald Tusk, the president of the European Council, talks of destroying the boats before they could be used. As I discover that night, smugglers like Hajj scoff at the idea – and they're later proved right. The summer draws on, the EU makes more and more noises about military action, but little actually happens. We're told that the operation has moved from one phase to another – from the planning phase to the observation phase, for instance – but the whole thing seems clownish. With great fanfare, the EU opens an intelligence-gathering headquarters in Sicily in June 2015, involving Frontex, the EU border agency, and Europol, the EU law-enforcement squad. Politicians including David Cameron hail this as the missing piece of the puzzle: the hub where Europe's spooks can glean key bits of intel from recent migrant arrivals, and then work out how to 'disrupt' the people who brought them there.

This fanciful plan seems to sum up Europe's whole approach to the migration crisis. Europe's political class hopes to get to grips with Libyan smuggling networks from the vantage point of Sicily, using all-but-useless information sourced from smugglers' clients, rather than the smugglers themselves. The set-up turns out to be even more farcical when I visit a few weeks later. The much vaunted hub turns out to be four people sitting in a makeshift office, around the corner from a disused car park where Sicily-based traffickers are guarding their quarries ahead of the onwards journey to northern Europe. The juxtaposition could scarcely be more symbolic.

Libya's peak smuggling season – August – comes and goes, the crucible of the crisis shifts eastwards to the shores of Greece, and the EU still has not started its military operation off the coast of Libya. Part of the problem is the lack of permission from both Libya itself, and from the UN. Both of Libya's rival governments view the potential naval operation as an invasion. As a result, several members of the UN Security Council refuse to give Europe the go-ahead. Finally, in October, six months after the idea was first raised, and just as the Libyan smuggling season begins to wind down, Libya's internationally recognised government relents. The UN gives the go-ahead to the mission – as long as it stays within international waters.

This makes for a fairly toothless operation. As I learned from Hajj several months before, the majority of boats – the inflatables – are sent into international waters on their own, without any smugglers on board. The wooden boats do tend to be accompanied by smugglers – but only low-level crew with little connection to or knowledge of the kingpins' movements. In any case, both types of smuggling trips are already intercepted by European rescue teams, and any smugglers found on board are already arrested on arrival in Italy.

The UN mandate does allow for one significant development. When smugglers' wooden ships are rescued by coastguards, their passengers are allowed to disembark, while the vessel itself is often left to drift in the sea. If it is damaged, the damage is often not enough to sink it. This allows teams of smugglers to enter international waters, track down the empty vessel, tow it back to the Libyan shore, and fix it up once again. A line of trawlers currently waiting for maintenance on the quay at Zuwara is testimony to this strategy. Hajj says it has allowed the same boat to be used four times in four separate migrant missions. In fact, it's he who first suggests that ending this cycle – by destroying the boats after they're evacuated – would go some way towards disrupting the smugglers' business model. Six months later, the UN mandate finally gives EU navies the right to do just that – as long as their arrests take place solely within international waters.

If such a strategy proved successful it would nevertheless only force smugglers to rely more heavily on inflatable boats. Once smugglers work out that they can't safely retrieve their wooden boats, it's natural that they will turn instead to Zodiacs, which are cheaper, and therefore more expendable. Sure enough, three weeks after the start of the operation in October, the second-in-command of the mission admits it's been a total failure.[11] No ships and no smugglers have been seized. I'd predicted as much to a Western diplomat, just before the operation's launch. Never mind, he responds cheerily, sooner or later we'll get permission to operate within Libyan waters.

Personally, I'm not so sure such a strategy will work either. To understand why, you have to return to the port at Zuwara, and look at the long line of blue fishing boats bobbing in the breeze. If Europe wants to use military force to smash Libya's smuggling trade, these are the boats that they will have to destroy. Every last one. For there is no way of telling which of them is about to be used by a smuggler, and which by a fisherman. Even after a smuggler buys one of them, the transition will be imperceptible to all but the few people aware of the transaction. Today's smuggling vessel was yesterday's fishing trawler – but, sitting in the port, the former still looks like the latter.

Watching the port's comings and goings by satellite or radar, a European spy would have little concrete indication that any particular fishing boat was leaving harbour for nefarious reasons. True, the smugglers' boats leave port in the early evening, an odd time for a fisherman to be going to work. In another telltale sign, the boats later drop anchor in deeper waters a few miles out to sea, as they wait for the migrants to arrive in inflatable dinghies. But nothing would seem certain until those boats start to be loaded with hundreds of passengers – too late for an intervention by any ethical navy.

More generally, it seems odd to discuss which naval tactics might be the best worst option when there are clearly much better ways of curbing the smugglers' trade. The message from refugees is clear: find us a safer route. When you're fleeing dictatorship, war or hunger at home, and faced with further conflict and exploitation in supposedly safer havens such as Libya, the smugglers are your single chance of safety. 'It is not our choice to penetrate the sea,' an Eritrean nurse tells me, locked inside a detention camp fifty miles east of Hajj's home. 'But if the government won't help us, if UNHCR won't help us, if no one can help us, then the only option is to go to the smugglers.'

A return to stability in Libya is also crucial. The Libyan civil war has left local law enforcement either unconcerned about, unable to deal with, or part of the problem in the first place. By April 2015, some coastguards say they haven't been paid for months, so it's little surprise that the gamekeepers have turned poachers in their quest to put food on the table. Only a reunified Libya can restore sanity to its institutions.

If and when that happens, smuggling communities will also need proper economic alternatives to a trade that some EU officials believe generates 50 per cent of the local economy.[12] Otherwise they'll keep smuggling to make ends meet.

There's always the chance that morality might prevail. In late August in Zuwara, a shipwreck sees dozens of bodies wash up on the main beach, prompting revulsion throughout the town – and dire publicity in the international media. One local militia decides that Zuwara has been shamed enough, and tells the smugglers to down tools. Most of them do so. An intermediary tells me that even Hajj has retired. (He's not a man who hands out phone numbers, so I never hear from Hajj himself.) A couple of foreign correspondents visit the town and talk to a few members of the militia. Articles are written. The word goes out: Zuwara is smuggler-free.

Will this last? It's hard to predict. In 2012, many smugglers including Hajj suspended their operations for a few months. By Hajj's account, they were waiting to see whether the EU would support a post-Gaddafi Libya, and in particular Zuwara. In his eyes, they didn't – so the smugglers went back to business. 'We wanted to return the favour to the EU because they stood with us against the tyrant,' he says. 'I reinitiated my project because I found out the EU was just taking us for a ride.'

It's possible that the latest suspension of smuggling in Zuwara will result in a similar relapse. When local money dries up, and residents realise that the fabled EU has little to offer Zuwarans in return for their good behaviour, the local campaign against the smugglers may ebb once again. 'If you're not protecting me, I will not protect you,' Hajj himself had warned the EU, back in April. 'I am the guard protecting your outer gate. If you neglect me, then anyone can get in.'

It's a slightly moot point, though – since Hajj is not the only guard, and Libya is not the only gate. Fly 500 miles east to Egypt, and you'll find a separate smuggling trade, flourishing for different reasons and in a different context. I first properly encounter its protagonists late one night in the autumn of 2014. It is about 10.30 p.m., and I'm having a drink at the end of the week with my translator, Manu, in a cramped old bar in the centre of Cairo. Suddenly one of our mobiles rings. To our surprise, it's a man called Nizar al-Baba, the second-in-command of one of the main smuggling networks in Egypt. He wonders if we could come to 6 October City, a town about an hour's drive from here, to meet him and his boss. When? Right now.

In the circumstances, it's a slightly surprising development. I've been chasing Nizar and his uncle and boss, Abu Hamada, for weeks. In September, an Egyptian boat had sunk in the Mediterranean, killing over 300 people in mysterious circumstances. Survivors said the ship had been rammed by another smuggler's vessel. Some of those who'd paid to get on the boat, but were instead arrested as they attempted to board it, claimed the smugglers had left them to the police. This was how I originally met Hashem; he'd been one of those caught on the beach, and once he and his family were released, I was put in touch with him by a small

Egyptian NGO that fights for detained refugees. During interviews, Hashem and his fellow survivors repeatedly mentioned the smuggler behind the trip, a man known by the nickname of Abu Hamada. His real name is Fouad al-Jamal, but everyone called him by his pseudonym, which means 'Father of Hamada'. To get to the bottom of what happened, Hamada's dad was clearly someone I needed to meet.

Despite my calling most days, neither Abu Hamada nor Nizar was very keen to reciprocate. Nizar answered some questions on the phone. But they both ducked out of a face-to-face interview. Once, Nizar agreed to meet on the waterfront in Alexandria, Egypt's main Mediterranean port. We hired a car for the three-hour drive, and were there half an hour early at the agreed hotel, next to one of the country's former royal palaces. But Nizar never showed, nor did Abu Hamada. We hadn't heard from him since – until this phone call.

So it is with some cynicism that we arrive, close to midnight, in 6 October City (in Egypt, a country with a penchant for naming places after dates, there are many towns and streets inspired by the day when Egypt began its glorious 1973 stalemate with Israel). For a start, this seems like an odd place for them to hold forth. Though 6 October is a hub for Syrian refugees, the pair's business is largely in Alexandria. Then there's their flakiness, and that of other smugglers – we're so used to being stood up that it seems somehow unlikely that they'll really be there. We arrive at the designated address, a cafe on a street that looks like most others in the town: two dull lines of beige apartment blocks. This one has one significant distinction. There's a small garden lined with hedges outside the cafe, a rarity in water-starved Egypt. And between these hedges we find another rare sight: a smuggler who keeps an appointment. It's Nizar al-Baba.

Nizar greets us like old friends, as if he hasn't been ignoring us for the past month, and turns out to be a frank conversationalist. We drink tea and chat until about one in the morning, discussing various topics including last month's shipwreck (not their fault) and whether he and Abu Hamada are profiting from the misery of others (absolutely false). Abu Hamada does not turn up. Or so I think, until the discussion turns to the subject of the ethics of Abu Hamada himself, and a man sitting at the next table behind us interrupts the conversation. He's a wiry older gentleman with a slim moustache, sipping tea in the darkness behind us. 'What's wrong with making a profit?' this man interjects. 'If I'm making money at the same time as helping my countrymen, what's the problem? I'm the only person people can trust in this business.' Here is Abu Hamada. He's been listening in all along.

It's particularly intriguing that Abu Hamada refers to his 'countrymen', since it sets him apart from the likes of Hajj in Libya, or Cisse in Niger. For Abu Hamada, as he reveals over the next hour, is no Egyptian career smuggler. He is, like many of the people he smuggles, a Syrian – or, more accurately, a Syrian Palestinian; someone of Palestinian ancestry whose family fled to Syria after the establishment of Israel in 1948. He was brought up in Yarmouk, the Damascus suburb whose obliteration came to embody the wanton destruction unleashed by the Syrian civil war. As an adult he worked as a power-station engineer, as did his nephew Nizar. Now, a generation after his parents fled their home, sixty-two-year-old Abu Hamada is a refugee again. And in the years since 2013, he has gradually become the go-to smuggler for Syrians trying to reach Italy from Egypt.

Egyptians have made the trip from Alexandria for decades, as have migrants from east Africa. There's a village in the province just south of Cairo where around 15 per cent of the residents now live in Turin. But, starting in 2013, Syrian refugees became one of the biggest groups leaving from the Egyptian coast, after the Egyptian state suddenly made it clear they were no longer welcome – and somehow Abu Hamada got mixed up in it all.

'At first it was just a service I offered to my friends,' Abu Hamada says, as the small hours get bigger. 'I would take a few people to the ship owners. Then my reputation increased because people trusted me, and the number went from a few to a thousand. And then I realised I was starting to make a profit.'

Abu Hamada's story is a useful counterpart to Hajj's. One of Hajj's main arguments is that greater investment in his region, and greater support for its institutions, will help to curb smuggling. What Abu Hamada's trajectory tells us is that while this may be true, such a strategy ultimately has its limits. Abu Hamada has not turned to smuggling because he desperately needs the money, or because the Egyptian state has collapsed. An accidental smuggler, he fell into the trade because the demand suddenly spiked in 2014, as Syrians realised that Egypt would never offer them the long-term future that they need. Providing alternatives to smuggling communities should be part of any sensible response to the migration crisis. But, in the end, where there is a demand for their services, there will always be smugglers.

In Egypt, their operations are smaller in scale than in Libya. No one knows exactly how many of those migrants who arrive in Italy originally set out from Egypt. But we know from the Italian coastguard that 62 boats reached Italy from Egypt in 2014.[13] Each of those ships would have carried between 300 and 500 people, meaning that Egypt-based smugglers were responsible for somewhere between 20,000 and 30,000 migrants that year – or around 15 per cent of the total to arrive in Italy. Of those, Abu Hamada's gang probably sent around half of them, judging from his and Nizar's calculations.

No single person controls every aspect of every trip. Foreign brokers such as Abu Hamada need Egyptian colleagues to carry out certain aspects of the operation, particularly at sea. But Abu Hamada is the central player in his network, the man through whom all money passes. Without him, his customers would not reach Italy.

The process starts far from the sea itself. Individual migrants approach one of Abu Hamada's Syrian brokers in their local neighbourhood, and fix a price. 'It's very easy to find someone – everyone knows a smuggler or two,' explains one Syrian refugee who reached Europe in 2014. 'In fact, you don't need to find them. They find you.'

Abu Hamada claims he charges a fixed price of $1,900 per person, but in reality the price fluctuates. Some pay as much as $3,500, some as low as $1,500, and the more you pay the sooner you get to the boat. All the money will eventually flow into a central fund controlled by Abu Hamada, from which he pays for the ship, the crew, his staff, transport costs and various other expenses. But first the migrant usually pays the money to a third party trusted by both sides. The third party releases the money to Abu Hamada only once the passenger sends word of his arrival in Italy. 'If the ship sinks,' says Nizar, 'we lose all the money.'

Methods change on a monthly basis, but when I first research the process it seems that the migrants must first reach the port of Alexandria, Egypt's second city, and the hub of the smuggling networks on the Egyptian coast. Abu Hamada's passengers are told a time and place to meet and, once in Alexandria, they are hustled into shabby apartments in the city's gloomier suburbs. Abu Hamada block-books dozens of flats there, all summer long, for use as a holding bay for his clients before they leave for the ships. At night, buses arrive. The migrants pile on, and then they're driven for several hours to remote spots along the Mediterranean coast. If all goes to plan, which it often doesn't, they then board dinghies at the beach. The dinghies take them to a larger vessel that carries them, with luck, to Italy within ten days. But few make the ship on the first attempt. The weather, the police and the coastguards can all force the buses to return to Alexandria for another night. One Syrian inter-viewee said she had thirty false starts, and after each attempt she was brought back to Alexandria.

The buses are organised by an Egyptian – known in the business as the 'monassek' or 'dalil', depending on who you talk to – and it is at this point that Abu Hamada's and Nizar's control of proceedings begins to loosen. As foreigners, they say their relationship with the Egyptian authorities is weak. But to get several busloads of illegal migrants to the shore, let alone to international waters, they say some level of government complicity is required. Which is where the monassek comes in. The monassek is paid by Abu Hamada – around £220 a passenger – to shepherd the migrants from the apartments to the large smuggling vessel that lies several miles off shore, and to deal with any government officials who might cause problems. 'We can't bring them ourselves,' says Nizar. 'So we're forced to go to the Egyptian middleman. He takes them from the apartments to the specific beaches, according to the deal with the government.'

Talk to most Egyptian middlemen and ship owners and they will deny they personally have a relationship with police and coastguards. Naturally, so does Egypt's interior ministry, whose spokesman says during a fiery phone call that the smugglers are lying about any corruption. But Nizar is adamant that, in his network at least, it is the monassek's job to ensure the complicity of relevant government officials. 'They just take care of one thing,' he says. 'They deal with the authorities.' In exchange for allowing smugglers to leave from certain points, Nizar claims, complicit officials are paid up to 100,000 Egyptian pounds (about £8,900) a trip. By agreement with the smugglers, police arrive after most of the migrants have managed to leave the beach. At that point, the remaining passengers are arrested and taken for a few days' detention in police cells, to maintain the pretence that Egypt is playing its part in ending the smuggling trade. 'It's normal that if I want to smuggle three hundred [migrants],' says Nizar, 'the authorities will take fifty and let two hundred and fifty go, to show the Italians that they are doing some work.'

Those who don't get arrested are taken by dinghy to a steel ship lurking several miles out to sea. This boat nominally belongs to Abu Hamada; every trip, he pays Egyptian associates – usually fishermen known by nicknames such as 'the Whale' and 'the Doctor' – to source a new one. As a Syrian, the ship cannot be listed in Abu Hamada's name and, in the eyes of the law, it still belongs to the Egyptian he 'buys' it from. Abu Hamada never sees the ship, and he does not choose its crew – who are usually out-of-work fishermen – nor when and where it leaves from. In coordination with the monassek, it is the boat owner who decides where a trip should leave from. 'The Syrian pays the money for the boat, but I handle everything else,' says one Egyptian boat owner who deals with Syrian gangs. 'I find and pay the captain, I find the boat, and it's my name on the boat documents.'

What this means is that Abu Hamada, exploiter of migrants, is sometimes exploited himself. The ship owner may claim to have bought a gleaming new vessel. But in reality the Egyptian fishermen often use old and faulty wooden ships instead. Sometimes they force the migrants to change ships, mid-voyage, so that their best boats aren't lost to the Italian coastguards. It's thought that one of these attempted transfers led to the shipwreck that killed 300, and which prompted me to look for Abu Hamada in the first place. Abu Hamada says he has no control of what happens at sea. But for the families of his clients, who've never heard of the Whale or the Doctor, it's Abu Hamada they blame. Their criticism is essentially the reason he agrees to this late-night interview: he thinks a profile in the Western press might help to get his side of the story out. It doesn't work. His reputation has taken an irreversible dip and so, the next spring, as the smuggling season begins again, the word goes out that Abu Hamada has retired. And as soon as he disappears a new Syrian smuggler appears on the scene – a woman nicknamed Umm Hossam, or Hossam's mother. Oddly, her right-hand man remains one Nizar al-Baba.

'Why is everyone attacking me?' Abu Hamada laments the night we meet, as 2 a.m. rolls past. 'You should be attacking the ship owners. If you want to say they're trading in souls, you'd be right.'

One of the most prominent Egyptian ship owners is a man nicknamed Abu Alaa, or Alaa's father. It's quite easy to get in touch with Abu Alaa. He has a Facebook page with all his contact numbers. As long as you're prepared to wait up past 11 p.m. – Abu Alaa is a late riser – he'll generally pick up his phone. He seems both to procure boats for other brokers and to run his own trips himself – so he has to be available to all callers. And for a while, those callers include Manu and me. We ring on a semi-regular basis, in a bid to get him to agree to an interview in person. We try this so many times that we establish a certain degree of familiarity. He butters me up by calling me the young Robert Fisk, which in the Middle East is still meant as a compliment. He also says he's read some of my articles – including the interview with Abu Hamada, which gnawed at his ego. In Abu Alaa's view, Abu Alaa is far more worthy of a profile than Abu Hamada. So, I ask, why not meet me in person? Because, he says, I can't let you see who I really am.

So a meeting never happens. But I do get a sense of the man from his Facebook page – and there's perhaps some merit in recounting some of its contents, since they help to show how a people smuggler has to market himself in the twenty-first century. You won't find many Libyan smugglers on Facebook. 3G connections are expensive in Libya, so the art of advertising your smuggling business on social media doesn't seem to have caught on. In Egypt and Turkey, however, dozens of smugglers have set up Facebook groups to drum up business. Once these were people contactable only through trusted third parties. Now they are openly publicising their phone numbers, prices and schedules on social media, in a bid to attract customers. The texts on some of their pages read like the website of a travel agency. 'A trip to Italy next week in a big fast tourist yacht,' says one smuggler's Facebook post, underneath a picture of a plush ocean liner. 'Two floors, air-conditioned, prepared for tourists. Recommended for families.'

Abu Alaa calls his group 'The Way to Europe', and illustrates it with an image of Moses parting the Red Sea. As if this isn't persuasive enough, Abu Alaa has uploaded other visuals to reel in the customers. One of the main images in his photo gallery is a picture of one of his boats, overlaid with the words: 'Vvvvvvery safe'. It looks old and rusty, but Abu Alaa uses this to his advantage. 'It may not look pretty, but it's perfect,' he continues. 'It's like a good suit you'd wear to a wedding. All its parts are made from iron.' Some would-be travellers aren't convinced. 'My brother,' writes one woman whose Facebook name is Azza, 'why would anyone use such a boat to travel?'

Abu Alaa takes no notice. He is only warming to his theme. He posts a picture of a luxury yacht, and tries to explain how a boat's aesthetic isn't any indication of its suitability. 'How beautiful and splendid,' he writes underneath the photo. 'But unfortunately it's not safe to use for long distances . . . It doesn't handle waves. So the look isn't important, my brothers. The insides are what count.'

Attempting to increase his credibility yet further, Abu Alaa sprinkles his page with occasional outbursts of religious devotion. 'I rely on God,' he writes at one point. 'God is our help.' Elsewhere he lists various types of boats and their costs, before giving his personal assessment of their safety record. He publishes weather forecasts, and accounts of trips that successfully made it to Italy. 'Bad luck to the fools who didn't go,' he quips. Then there's handy practical advice, ranging from conduct on board – 'don't use drinking water for other purposes; don't expose women and kids to the sun for long periods' – to the asylum process: 'Italy and the EU cannot deport refugees, whether they're Syrians, Somalians, Iraqis, or Eritreans. You can even ask the Pope in the Vatican.'

But Abu Alaa doesn't use his page only to advertise his trips. Once the trips themselves begin, he turns his page into a live blog about their progress, and in the process it becomes an unlikely news source for anxious families scanning Facebook for accurate information about their relatives' fate. In April 2015, Abu Alaa even seems to chronicle the journey of Hashem al-Souki, suggesting that he was the smuggler ultimately responsible for the boat that Hashem took to Italy. 'A trip from Egypt is on its way to Italy,' writes Abu Alaa on the day Hashem leaves for Europe. 'Now it's out of national waters and everyone is in good health.'

Two days later, Abu Alaa says the boat is a third of the way into its 900-mile journey. 'The Mediterranean is excellent at the moment,' he writes. 'The sea is very calm except the central part near Benghazi and Misrata.' He doesn't mention that the boat has turned back, for unknown reasons. But rumours swirl anyway: other Facebook groups and websites report that Abu Alaa's trip has run into difficulties, and his crew has abandoned ship. Relatives flood Abu Alaa's page to ask for confirmation. Abu Alaa responds indignantly, uploading recent Viber messages that he claims are from his passengers, and lashing out at the rumour mill. Few are convinced. One writes, 'Abu Alaa, they are saying the engine stopped. You are playing with our nerves, someone tell us if it's true.' Then another asks ominously, 'Please, is it true about many boats sinking?'

Reading this, I think immediately of Hashem.

4

SOS

Hashem's departure from Egypt, and his
sea voyage towards Italy

Monday, 20 April 2015, 12 noon

Egypt

In the middle of the Mediterranean sea, with no shore or ship in sight, a man on a boat puts a phone to his ear and listens to the ringing tone. It's about the only sound he can hear. The boat's engine has stopped. Hundreds of other people huddle on the deck around him, straining to hear what he is about to say. Hashem al-Souki is one of them.

The ringing tone ends. A woman picks up, an activist based in Sicily, and the Syrian begins to talk. 'We're in the middle of the Mediterranean,' he blurts out. 'We're about six hundred people – two hundred women, a hundred children. We've been without water for three days.'

The activist keeps calm. Nawal Soufi, a Moroccan-born Italian, has become a point of contact for Syrians trying to get to Italy by boat, and she takes several of these calls a week. Once migrant boats approach Italian waters, the passengers often call Soufi, and she then calls the coastguards.

The Syrian continues, 'The captain that was with us left us and ran away.'

It's a small lie, designed to help the crew escape punishment if and when the boat is rescued. But now is not the moment to quibble. On the day these refugees left Egypt, 400 fellow migrants drowned south of Italy. Yesterday, 800 more people died in what was the Mediterranean's most deadly modern-day shipwreck. There is a real risk that this boat will be the next to sink.

'For the love of god,' says the Syrian. 'There are women and children on the boat. We don't know what to do with them.'

Soufi begins to take charge. 'You're going to really concentrate on what I'm saying,' she says. She tells him to forget the coordinates the crew have told him to give her – they're often wrong. Instead Soufi asks him to look inside the phone's settings once they've ended the call, and then to text her the GPS location it gives. Once she's got that, she can call the coastguards.

'I want from you one thing,' she says. 'I want you to make sure that everyone on the boat wears a life jacket now, and whoever doesn't have one should open up someone else's life jacket and fit two people inside. Don't think that the sea is safe and that there's no problem. Drowning can happen at any moment, even when the boat is being rescued.'

For the hundreds crowding the deck, this is one of the defining moments of their lives. They left Egypt five days ago, but their journeys began far further afield. Some of them, like Hashem, have been on the move for years, and now they are finally within striking distance of Italy. This phone call is the moment both he and they discover whether it was all worth it.

When he first arrived in Egypt, Hashem didn't imagine he'd leave by boat. Egypt was supposed to be safe for Syrians – and at least when he first entered it, in late June 2013, it was. Syrians could easily access state schools and hospitals. The government was laissez-faire about their paperwork. Many were there illegally, but no official paid any attention.

But within days of Hashem's arrival all that stopped. On 3 July 2013, Egypt's first freely elected president, the Islamist Mohamed Morsi, was ousted by the army, after a week of mass protests against his rule. The state's attitude to Syrians changed overnight.[1]

The borders closed to Syrians without prior visas. Those without proper paperwork – and there were many – began to be arrested at checkpoints. Officials and their mouthpieces in the media began to claim that Syrians were terrorists, or supporters of Morsi. As the jihadist threat in Syria grew, Syrians in far-away Egypt were being tarred with the same brush.

One TV host, Youssef el-Husseini, told Syrians, 'If you interfere in Egypt, you will beaten by thirty shoes.' Another, Tawfik Okasha, told Egyptians to arrest any Syrians they found in public. Having left one civil war, Hashem and his family found themselves in a country that sometimes seemed to be on the brink of another.

Things didn't go well from the beginning. The family arrived early in the morning of 27 June, after their forty-eight-hour trek across Syria, Jordan, and then the Red Sea. By the time they arrived in the Egyptian port of Nuweiba, Hashem had about $100 left in his pockets. He'd spent everything else on the journey itself, and on the man whose life they'd saved at the regime checkpoint. Their luggage was in the hold somewhere – they hadn't been allowed to carry it with them on the ferry. Finding it took several hours. In the meantime, Hashem changed his dollars into the local currency, and got around 650 Egyptian pounds in return. As he hurried around, his exhausted sons slept on the stones of the pavement.

Hashem wanted to get to a town with the strange name of 10 Ramadan. He had little idea of where it was. But his friend Monther lived there – so, in the context, it was a better destination than most. The thing was, whenever he told a driver he wanted to go there, they either snorted – or demanded money he hadn't got. 10 Ramadan, it seemed, was hundreds of miles away, just east of Cairo.

Eventually someone said they'd take the family to Suez, the port that gave its name to the canal. It was still an hour from 10 Ramadan, but it was better than nothing. The other drivers wanted 1,500 pounds, whereas this man would take just 400 – on the understanding that he could take as many other passengers as he liked. They bumped their way to Suez, squashed between the car door and the thighs of strangers.

From Suez another driver took them to the edge of 10 Ramadan for the remainder of their savings, but refused to drive them any further. 'God judge you,' said Hashem. The driver simply shrugged, leaving them and what remained of their luggage at a roundabout, to the blare of a hundred car horns. They were penniless, and homeless.

The name of 10 Ramadan turned out to be the date of a victorious Egyptian offensive at the start of the 1973 war with Israel.[2] There was little triumphant about their own first few months there. With no money to pay rent, his family lived for four months in the storeroom of a tiny sewing sweatshop. The owner of the place let them stay for free. But, during the day, they shared the place with the seamstresses.

Even when they finally moved out, it was only to a cramped flat without furniture. They couldn't afford any. Visitors would sit on the floor to drink tea with them – not that many people visited.

It was a pretty dismal experience. Hayam couldn't find work as a teacher in 10 Ramadan, and there were no computing jobs for Hashem. So he joined a food company in the next town, wrapping vegetables, and later moved to a charcoal factory. He earned about $100 dollars a month. He missed his old work. He missed the sensation of being in an office, at his computer, sending emails. He would overhear snatches of songs by the great Lebanese diva, Fairouz, and remember listening to her music every morning during his drive to work in Syria. He missed his old lifestyle, his happy life with Hayam. On Fridays they would set down their picnic mats under the local apricot trees with their friends. Those were their happiest moments – when they would brew tea, eat lunch, and laugh. And then the war came, and they moved to Egypt where there were no apricot trees to sit under. Hashem missed the apricots, he missed his family, and he missed his friends. Ibrahim, Samer, Mohamed, Maher, Abdelsatar, Marwan and Hosny – one by one he lost touch with them. Their numbers changed. Maybe they all left Syria – Hashem never found out. The only people he kept in touch with were his parents. For the first few months, he spoke to his father as often as he could. Each time, both men would cry – until some time in the early autumn of 2013, when his father died.

It was a desperate period, both personally and politically. At around the time of his father's death, the US and the UK deliberated whether to target Assad. There were talks of a no-fly zone – a step that fell short of boots on the ground, but that would have stymied Assad's bombing campaigns. But amid memories of the disastrous Iraqi invasion in 2003, Syria's war was left to drag on without direct Western intervention. Hashem felt abandoned. To him, it was as if the world was condoning what Assad was doing – condoning the destruction of his home, and the bombs that had fallen near his children. As the war went on, he felt that the hand-wringing of the international community led to the arrival of Isis. The failure to support secular-leaning rebels such as the Free Syrian Army, the group that Hashem has most sympathy for, had created a vacuum in which psychopaths like Isis could prosper. The rise of Isis harmed Hashem, even as he lived in far-away Egypt. After the group's emergence, the owner of the local supermarket started to berate Hashem – as if the rise of the extremist group was all his fault. 'You're bringing Daesh here, you're from the Muslim Brotherhood,' he shouted, referencing both the local nickname for Isis, and then Morsi's political movement. 'Go back to your own country.' Officials were in on the act too. When Hayam went to the local administration to finalise their paperwork, the officer seemed revolted by her, a Syrian. 'Talk to me from over there,' he ordered when she dared to approach his desk.

Occasionally the humiliation took a more sinister form. One day after work, a man stopped beside Hashem in the street.

'ID,' the man said.

'I don't have one,' Hashem replied. 'I'm Syrian.'

'And I'm from state security.'

A chill ran through Hashem. Egypt's notorious state security bureau was feared and loathed by many Egyptians, who knew it as a brutal tool of government repression. The 2011 revolution had forced it to temper some of its worst excesses. The 2013 coup allowed it to re-exert its full authority again – and among its many targets were undocumented Syrians. But there was still a chance that Hashem's assailant was just an opportunist civilian. So Hashem returned fire.

'Where's your own ID, then?'

The man refused to produce it. But by this point it was all academic. A car drew up, and a second man got out. The pair grabbed him, and dragged him to the driver's window. The man at the wheel flashed his card: it said he was a police officer, Captain Sayed Abdelaty. And with that Hashem was shoved onto the back seat. Then the car screeched off into the darkness.

The captain started concocting an absurd story. He said that he and his team were investigating the robbery and murder of a local man. This man's killer had stolen a lot of money and property from the victim. Was Hashem the killer?

It was obvious that they were trying to extort Hashem – a vulnerable Syrian with no hope of institutional support should he later report these men to a higher authority. But unfortunately for Hashem, he had nothing to give these men – not that they believed him. The two men sandwiching him on the back seat began rummaging through his belongings. All the while, the car drove onwards, out of the town and into the desert. Hashem felt more and more desperate. The men carried on rummaging. Eventually, they gave up. They'd found just a ten-pound note.

What would they do now, Hashem wondered as the car cruised through the sand dunes. Shoot him? The car skidded to a halt. 'Get out,' said the captain.

Hashem got out. Would they kill him now? Instead the car drove off, leaving him in the darkness.

Then, in the summer of 2014, came a stroke of luck. A friend in Germany offered to put the money up for the family to go by boat to Europe – around $7000 for the five of them. Previously, they had dreamed of being resettled in America, via the UN's resettlement scheme. But they had heard nothing from the UN's refugee agency, not even about an interview, so they gave up hope in that. The dangerous journey to Europe was not something they chose happily, but it seemed the only way of winning their future back. If the US was not an option, then Sweden seemed like a good fallback; since late 2013, the Swedish government had promised to give permanent residency to any Syrians who claimed asylum on Swedish soil. First, though, you had to get there.

A smuggler was called. Their numbers are easy to come by in the Syrian community, and Hashem was put in touch with the lieutenants of Abu Hamada. A deal was struck, and on 20 August Hashem's family arrived by arrangement in Alexandria, Egypt's main Mediterranean port.

The centre of Alex, as it's nicknamed, is one of fading *fin-de-siècle* grandeur – villas and ruins, crowding an ancient harbour. But its poorer residents mostly live in the high-rise suburbs at its perimeter: forests of towerblocks, euphemistically given names like Miami and Palm Beach. They bear little resemblance to their namesakes. Hashem, Hayam,

Osama, Mohamed and Milad came to Miami, where Abu Hamada's men hustled them and hundreds of others into a set of gloomy flats.

Then they waited, a gnawing limbo in which they wondered if they'd been conned, if there really was a boat trip to Europe at the end of all this. A day went by, then another. Then a third and fourth. Finally, on the fifth day, the smugglers came again for them. And so began the daily grind of trying to get aboard boats. In the late afternoon, hundreds of them were picked up by four or five curtained coaches and driven westwards in search of the designated departure point. Masked smugglers drove cars in front and behind the convoy, and the drive went on for hours. But as they neared the beach, the smugglers suddenly said the weather was too bad. The trip was cancelled, so back they went to Alex, where they were taken to new flats in another area.

This abortive routine went on for days on end. The drop-off would sometimes be cancelled because of alleged police presence. At other times, it was bad weather – and, on one occasion, even a brief kidnap by Bedouin. Sometimes, one or two coaches would get delivered to the beach – typically the coaches that carried people who'd bribed the smugglers for special treatment. The rest would be taken back to Alex, and simply kept on the coaches until the next attempt – an exhausting and destabilising experience. Some were even left to the police.

Saturday, 6 September 2014, was the day the family finally – more than a fortnight after arriving in Alexandria – reached a beach. This time it was a beach far to the east of Alex, near a town called Gamasa. As ever, getting there wasn't easy. They stopped in a garage in southern Alexandria to change coaches. Then they drove eastwards into the night, before slowing down again when two smugglers got into an argument. The pair started shouting. The convoy lurched to a halt. Shots were fired. And then the coaches started moving again, the argument over as suddenly as it had begun.

Then they stopped at a roadside cafe for two hours. And then finally they were driven to a beach, and funnelled onto the shore through a gap in the fence. With three children, the Soukis were among the last to get squeezed through the hole.

As the family emerged onto the sands, dozens of refugees were already wading through the waves to reach two dinghies bobbing several metres from the shore. The water went up to their shoulders, causing some of them to hesitate. On the shoreline two men, seemingly smugglers, had little patience: anyone who stopped got a sharp shove in the back.

By the time the Soukis reached the water, the dinghies had already filled up, and were now ferrying people to a bigger boat that lay further out to sea. The Soukis, once again, had to wait their turn.

Their turn never came. Instead they heard the distant shout: 'Police, police.' Within moments, uniformed men appeared on the beach, firing weapons. Mysteriously, the two smugglers on the shoreline began to help the policemen round up the remaining migrants. Some made a run for it, and got hit by rifle butts for their trouble. Hashem's family stayed put, and they spent the next eight days in a police jail. It was an odd week. The police asked who had tried to smuggle them, and Hashem mentioned Abu Hamada. But the interrogators wrote down another name. And later that night, Nizar gave him a call on Viber. 'We know you told the police about us,' Nizar said. 'If you do it again, we'll kill you, your wife and your children. We can reach you wherever you are.'

There was just one silver lining to the whole experience. The boat they would have taken later sank, killing its 500 passengers. It was a tragedy that ended, Hashem would later say, 'one whole month of unfortunate events'.

And yet here Hashem is again, not eight months later, trying the whole saga again. 'If you were a refugee, living here, you would try again ten more times,' he says. He wears a life jacket, a gift from a friend. There's a small black bag on his back, containing just the essentials. A wheel of Président cheese. A blue jumper. A notebook. His identity papers and a Human Rights Watch report about the destruction of Haran al-Awamid hang from his neck in a waterproof pouch.

It's the same smugglers as last year – though, amusingly, they're trying to pretend they're a different outfit. This time the whole operation is supposedly masterminded by a woman called Umm Hossam, not Abu Hamada. Hashem even goes to meet her before paying for the trip – and Umm Hossam promises that she's just organising this trip as a one-off, to get her family to Europe. But once he's on the road Hashem realises it's the same gang as last September. He recognises Nizar, Abu Hamada's nephew, and a bunch of other drivers. They've just rebranded themselves in the wake of last year's PR disaster.

Hashem's going alone this time. He didn't dare put his family through the same trauma a second year running – though Sod's Law means this year is easier than last. Hashem and his fellow travellers are driven all the way from Cairo to Gamasa. No flats this year. No groundhog days along the north coast. First time lucky, they get to the beach – the same beach as last year, incidentally – and, first time lucky, they get to the dinghies.

Within an hour, Hashem's wondering if it was all worth it. He's already been soaked, tossed between several boats, and caked in vomit. By the time he reaches the third boat, the one that's supposed to take him to Italy, the night seems as if it will never end.

The boat is swaying, and his world is spinning. Hundreds of people are being loaded, tossed really, onto the ship. It takes hours – long, cold hours. Everyone is nauseous. Everyone is shivering. In front of him, children are turning blue.

Dawn breaks, at last. With it comes warmth, and with the warmth their clothes begin to dry. People look at each other properly for the first time. They share out seasickness pills and lemons, both meant to ward off nausea. The crew come round with the daily meal – a slip of brown bread for each traveller, and a sliver of processed pâté. But afternoon arrives, and everyone is still hungry. Hashem gets out his Président cheese, meant to last him the whole week, and gives it all to the children around him. People smile, and begin to talk. They're on their way.

Yet, as the sun begins to dip, there's yet another change of boats. The smugglers know they'll lose the ship that arrives in Italy, so they want to use a ship that they can afford to lose – something that's a bit older, a bit slower. No passenger is happy about it, but there's no point complaining. Last year's shipwreck, the one that Hashem narrowly avoided, reportedly happened after the migrants refused to move ships. The smugglers then rammed two boats together, to try to force the passengers of one to board the other. The first boat capsized.

Hashem makes the most of the move, and on the new boat finds a place next to the engine room. At least there it'll be warm. Others aren't so lucky: the Africans are mostly shoved downstairs. If this boat capsizes, they'll be the first to drown.

Night falls, and Hashem tries to sleep. It's hard on the boat. There's no space to lie down, so people sleep while sitting, hunched over their laps – or they take it in turns to stretch out on their backs. But whatever physical contortion they find themselves in, sleep is often hard to come by. The wails of nearby babies make it elusive.

Friday comes and goes, and people settle into the rhythm of the boat. For the first time, there are queues for the bathroom. There are conversations, and the first hints of friendships. Hashem meets Emad, another Syrian who fled Damascus. Emad tried to open a shop in Egypt, but it failed. So here he is, on the way to Europe instead.

Saturday morning, their third on the boat, is the brightest and hottest yet. It's a morning of good omens. The sun is so warm that the passengers take off their winter clothes. They gaze out to sea. And then, in the waters in the middle distance, they see something glistening in the sunlight. Whatever it is, there's more than one of it. The excitement draws a crowd to the side of the boat. People squint, and then cheer. There, leaping in waves, are four dolphins.

The crew hustle people back to their places – they don't

want the boat to overbalance. But people are smiling now. It's given them something to inspire them. Hashem strikes up a conversation with Walid, a twelve-year-old from Eritrea, one of the world's worst dictatorships. Walid wants to train to be a pilot in Europe, and something about that dream strikes a chord with Hashem.

'Walid reminds me of my kids,' Hashem writes in his diary. 'I miss them and their dreams.'

All around him, the mood of the boat is upbeat. They've been three days on the boat, and the crew seems to think they'll get to Italy soon. A Syrian, the same man who later calls the Sicilian activist, is asked by the sailors to shout out a set of instructions. When the coastguards arrive, he says, everyone must remain calm, and they shouldn't rat on the crew. Everyone's thoughts turn to Europe, the promised land.

Hashem feels conflicted. He's still thinking about his wife, and his kids, and he knows a long road still lies ahead. 'Everyone is happy but I have mixed feelings,' he writes, as the sun begins to set. 'I long for my family – I'll be away from them for a year. But some things give me comfort, most importantly the fact that I'll be achieving the dreams of my children.' If he can just get to Sweden, he can apply for them to join him. If he can get to Sweden, they'll have a future.

It's a beautiful sunset, he tells his diary: 'Just us, the sea, the sun, and nothing else.' Hashem gets out his phone to capture the scene. But as he looks at the sun through the screen he notices something odd. Aren't they heading west? And doesn't the sun set in the west? And if so, why is the boat heading away from it?

Hashem raises it with his neighbours. Look at the sun, he

says. Are we heading back to Egypt?

People begin to nod, and the news spreads throughout the ship. Suddenly there's uproar. They've come too far to turn back, and they're furious. The captain emerges from the bridge. Tough, he says, his bosses want to cram thirty more people on board. Thirty more? 'Yes,' says the captain. 'They're worth $60,000.'

It's bad news, exhausting news – but it's not as awful as they first feared. The extra thirty are already on their way in another boat, and in the end they meet halfway, in international waters. The new arrivals bring new supplies – cigarettes for the adults, nappies for the babies. Tempers calm, and people drift off to sleep.

Sunday arrives. More and more, the talk turns to the future, to Europe. One Syrian woman hopes it'll mark the end of fifty years of migration. As a child, she fled the Golan Heights after the Israeli occupation in 1967. 'Today I'm emigrating with my daughters to Europe, and god knows if my grandchildren will emigrate too,' she tells her new friends. 'I hope that won't happen, our whole life is migration after migration.'

Where Hashem sits, in an area of exposed decking at the back of the boat, a real camaraderie has been built. 'The ship looks like a complete community, with families and individuals, young and old, white and black,' he writes that day. 'It's a small mixed community where everyone cooperates with everyone else.'

Another night passes and, at dawn on Monday, the crew again promises that they're nearly in Italian waters. Again, they're told how to act once the coastguards arrive. Stay calm, don't identify the smugglers, don't move about in the boat. Around noon, the captain switches the engine off. The passengers stop talking. The Syrian with the loudest voice is handed a satellite phone. There's a number he has to ring to reach an activist in Sicily. She'll call the coastguards once she finds out where they are.

The ringing tone starts. Nawal Soufi picks up. She talks the Syrian through the SOS call, and then the conversation ends. Job done, the whole boat sits and waits. An hour, maybe two. The crew leaves the bridge and scatters among the passengers. Here we go, thinks Hashem: the trip is over.

And so everyone thinks – until an aircraft flies low overhead, taking pictures as it goes. The captain looks up. That's a Greek reconnaissance plane, he says, not an Italian one.

People turn their heads. A Greek plane? Are they still in Greek waters? It's another cruel setback. Greek waters mean Greek coastguards and a Greek rescue mission, and no one wants to go to Greece. As absurd as it sounds in retrospect, given the thousands of refugees who would arrive in the Greek islands later in the summer, Greece is still largely an unknown route for Syrians, full of potential pitfalls. To get to Germany from Greece would mean walking through two countries that lie outside the EU (Macedonia and Serbia) and then a third that is in the EU but behaves as if it isn't (Hungary).

The passengers begin to shout. They paid for Italy, not for Greece, and they want the engines restarted. Nothing doing, says the captain. The coastguards have been called, and the die is cast. But no one will stand for it, and eventually he backs down. The captain fires up the engines, and the boat moves faster than ever towards Italy.

Night falls, and the mood is fraught. The sea is rough, probably too rough for the speed they are cruising at. But no one wants to slow down, in case the Greek coastguard catches them before they're within Italian jurisdiction. So they plough on – until suddenly the engine judders to a halt. A tense two hours follow, as the crew attempts to fix things while there's still time.

With no momentum of its own, the boat rocks in the heaving waves. People scream, and for the first time since the first night they genuinely fear being drowned. Hashem is almost too exhausted to notice. He's been standing on one leg for hours, to give other people more room to sleep. Eventually, the engine gets going again, and at four in the morning another passenger allows Hashem to sleep in his place. He collapses, shattered, into a deep sleep.

He's shaken awake the next day to the news he's waited for all week: the Italians have arrived. He blinks, and peers over the side. Sure enough, four huge red inflatable boats are circling their ship. Each has a white cabin painted with the words 'GUARDIA COSTIERA'. He smiles. They're still a day from Italy, but they're almost there. It's over. The journey is over.

Two of the Italian boats draw alongside, and they begin to transfer people to a larger steel-hulled ship. It's women and children first, and the process takes a couple of hours, but no one minds. The atmosphere is joyous. People clap and chant with gratitude. 'Italia!' they cheer. 'Italia, Italia, Italia!'

5

Shipwreck

How people drown at sea, and how
they are saved

The middle of the Mediterranean, April 2015

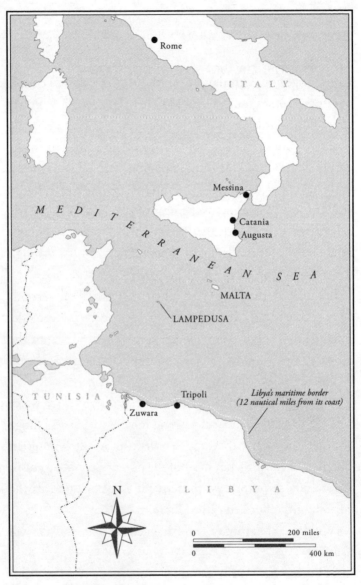

Southern Mediterranean

Late at night on Saturday, 18 April 2015, in waters a couple of hundred miles south-west of Hashem, another boat slowly chugs northwards towards Italy. Below decks, Ibrahim Mbalo is one of hundreds of mainly African men squashed in the darkness. Ibrahim and his companions left Libya eighteen hours ago, and have spent the interim period coughing on engine fumes, sweating in the heat of the hold. Now, nearly a day after their departure, Ibrahim thinks this ordeal might be about to end: the Tunisian captain has just burst through the cabin, telling everyone to prepare for a rescue.

But instead, there is a crash. Then a silence. Then, seconds later, another crash. Finally the boat starts to keel to the side. Trapped in a cabin below decks, seventeen miles from the Libyan shore, Ibrahim Mbalo and hundreds of others begin to sink below the surface of the sea.

The salt water gushes in. The cabin becomes a huge water tank, filled with drenched, gasping men who flail and lunge at what they can. Ibrahim, a twenty-year-old Gambian labourer, can swim – but most of the others can't. One grasps at Ibrahim, gripping his trousers, pulling him towards the bottom of the flooded cabin. Ibrahim is stuck.

'Will I die?' he thinks as he's dragged downwards. 'Or will I survive?'

So begins the Mediterranean's worst modern shipwreck:[1] in the coming minutes up to 900 humans will drown after their smuggler's boat capsizes. We don't know who most of them are – there are only twenty-eight survivors, three of whom I later meet in a reception centre in Sicily.

Ibrahim Mbalo arrived in Tripoli in September 2014, after a six-month stop-start odyssey from his home on Banjul island. In happier times, he used to spend his weekends swimming in the sea. But after his father stopped working, and could no longer pay for his education, Ibrahim dropped out of school, and went to Libya to make money.

The other survivors I met were both abused by their Libyan employers. One was kidnapped by his, and held for ransom – which he couldn't pay. The other simply went unpaid for months on end. Ibrahim, though, was lucky. He found work with a man who paid him a daily wage, and treated him with relative respect. But, even then, Ibrahim found Libya a nightmare: it's a country in the throes of a civil war. So, after a few months, he told his boss he wanted to leave. He would have returned home if he could. But having experienced the trauma of the desert journey once on the way up, Ibrahim wasn't keen to try it again. 'If you're going to Gambia, maybe the smugglers will take you in the desert and throw you there to die,' Ibrahim says. 'That's why a lot of people won't go back.'

Instead, Ibrahim's boss, Moussa, drove him to Garabulli, a known smuggling hub on the Libyan coast that lies east of Tripoli. There Moussa paid a smuggler 700 dinar (around £350) to put Ibrahim on a boat. And then, like the others, Ibrahim was taken to a holding house, where he was shoved in a room already packed with fellow migrants. By chance he was reunited with his friend Haroun, with whom he'd shared the journey north from Gambia. One night two weeks later, they finally made the short drive to the sea. Or, as Ibrahim calls it, 'the river'.

On the beach, he finds hundreds of other people waiting in the darkness. There are those from west Africa – Senegal, Sierra Leone and Mali – and those from the east: Somalia, and Eritrea. Some are even from as far away as Bangladesh. Armed with guns, the smugglers divide them up into eight or nine groups of up to a hundred migrants each. And then a series of large rubber dinghies arrives.

Ibrahim is scared. 'Either I will die', he remembers thinking, 'or I will go to Italy. Or [Libyan coastguards] will arrest me and take me to prison, and I will pay 500 dinar to get out.'

The smugglers herd each group onto a separate dinghy, and tell them on pain of death to remain seated. According to Italian prosecutors, one man who does stand up is thrown by smugglers into the sea to drown. Each boat takes twenty minutes to reach a larger ship moored a mile or so out to sea. The overwhelming majority of ships that go from Libya to Italy are either wooden fishing sloops or inflatable dinghies. This one is a huge steel-hulled merchant ship.

The loading of the ship takes several hours, and lasts until the small hours of the following morning. Armed men direct each migrant to a specific place on the boat, so that its cargo is equally spread. The survivors' descriptions of the boat's layout do not completely align, but they reckon there are at least three levels: one at the bottom next to the engine, a second in the middle with windows, and a third at the top that was open to the elements. Ibrahim is forced down to the lowest tier.

Up top, seasick passengers vomit across each other. Down below, things are even worse for Ibrahim. The heat of the engine makes the experience unbearable. But the armed smugglers arranging the rows of migrants will not let Ibrahim move. 'I couldn't go out,' he says later. 'If I'd tried they would have killed me.'

Eventually, not long before dawn, most of the smugglers disembark. According to Italian prosecutors, they leave only a Tunisian to steer the ship, and a Syrian to act as his mate. Arrested in Italy later, the Tunisian stands accused of mass murder, but his lawyer says he was merely a passenger.

As the boat moves off, Ibrahim is now free to move. So he picks his way through the other passengers to the middle level, where he sits next to his friend Haroun. It is a decision that will later help save his life.

For around eighteen hours the boat heads west without incident, and then tacks north. Every so often the Syrian mate would descend from the bridge to the engine room, to check it was still running smoothly. The boat travels slowly, and by around 11 p.m. on Saturday, 18 April, it is still only seventeen miles from the Libyan coast, and 130 miles from Lampedusa, the southernmost Italian island.

But boats heading north to Italy don't always need to reach Italian waters. Sometimes, they sail until they reach international waters, and then call Italian coastguards for assistance, and wait for the nearest European boat to rescue them. And that's what happens in this case. Using a satellite phone, the Tunisian calls the coastguards in Rome. In turn they call for assistance from the closest commercial boat – a Madeiran cargo ship called the *King Jacob*, a vast vessel 146 metres long. One hundred metres from the migrant boat, its sailors later report, the *King Jacob* slows to a halt.

Over on the smaller boat, Ibrahim remembers one of the two crew members then descending to the lower decks. 'The big boat is coming,' he tells the migrants, reminding them to avoid sudden movements in case they overbalance the boat. 'Everybody sit still, and go one by one to the big boat.'

Quite what happens next may never be properly understood. Ibrahim is below decks, unable to see much out of the windows. Sitting seasick on the deck, another survivor I meet is drifting in and out of consciousness, unaware of an impending rescue. A third survivor is awake and outside, but like everyone else could not see what the captain was doing at the wheel.

What seems clear is that as the migrant boat approaches the *King Jacob* it suddenly speeds up. The reasons why, and how, may ultimately be known only to the man at the wheel. But the result is the mother of all T-bone collisions as the boat hits the side of the *King Jacob*. According to one survivor, the boat's bow then swings ninety degrees to the left, until the two ships are parallel. Then it starts to capsize.

Trapped inside the hull of the migrants' boat, Ibrahim feels the crash, feels the boat begin to tip, and realises what is happening. So too do the hundreds of other passengers stuck inside with him, who all try to escape at the same time. But with so many people swarming the handful of exits, very few make it outside. Most are still inside as the boat dips below the surface and the water floods in. Many can't swim, so they grab onto whatever is to hand. One man finds Ibrahim's trouser leg and drags him downwards.

'Will I die?' Ibrahim wonders. 'Or will I survive?'

Life in Gambia was what had driven him to this wretched point. But as he struggled beneath the surface, his upbringing is also what saves him. All those weekends in the sea off Banjul island have made him a strong swimmer, and as a big man with big lungs he has become used to swimming for long periods underwater.

So when his neighbour grips his leg and won't let go Ibrahim doesn't panic. He says he unzips his trousers, wriggles free, rips off his shirt, pushes through a mass of flailing bodies to the top of the cabin – before forcing his way through an open window, and struggling to the surface of the sea.

Then he gasps. His friend Haroun has drowned. So have some 900 others. But after being submerged underwater for three or four minutes, Ibrahim has survived.

But the trauma does not end here. The *King Jacob* by this point is some distance away, and every time Ibrahim puts in a burst to try to reach it he feels as if the waves push him even further away. 'I tried and tried – and then I saw another boat,' Ibrahim says later. 'I followed that boat. I followed and followed. And then they saw me coming.'

The crew flings him a lifeline, and with his last grains of energy Ibrahim grabs it and holds on until they tug him to the deck. He stands up. And then he falls to the floor.

There are those who thought they could stop the boats. In the autumn of 2014, Italy ended its Mediterranean rescue operation – a full-on navy mission called Operation Mare Nostrum that saved over 100,000 migrants from drowning that year. Its closure wasn't a completely callous decision: the Italians did it grudgingly. But they didn't see why they should continue to run Mare Nostrum on their own. People crossing from Libya want to get to Europe, not just Italy. So Italy hoped the rest of Europe would help save their lives.

But the rest of Europe didn't want to help. European politicians believed that the continuation of a rescue mission would make things worse – encouraging more migrants to risk the journey. A British minister of state, Baroness Anelay, summed up the prevailing feeling. Justifying the decision not to replace Mare Nostrum, she said in late 2014 that the mission had created 'an unintended "pull factor", encouraging more migrants to attempt the dangerous sea crossing and thereby leading to more tragic and unnecessary deaths'.

This belief, tragically, turned out to be completely wrong. In the spring that followed the end of Mare Nostrum, more people attempted to cross the Mediterranean from Libya than during the equivalent period in 2014, which itself was a record year. And around eighteen times as many people died. Between January and April 2015, 28,028 people tried to reach Italy from Libya, according to the International Organization for Migration – compared with 26,740 in the first four months of 2014.[2] And more than 1,800 died, compared with 96 the year before. The week that Ibrahim Mbalo and Hashem al-Souki survived the Mediterranean, as many as 1,300 drowned. The decision to let people drown in the Mediterranean had not convinced people to stay put. Instead, it had led to more deaths than ever before.

This would have been obvious to any diplomat who'd actually done some research. Talk to most smugglers and migrants and they'll tell you they either hadn't heard of Mare Nostrum in the first place – or did know of it, but didn't place much importance in its existence. Certainly the smugglers understood the laws of the sea, and abused them to their advantage. They knew that if they sent boats out into international waters, and if those boats called for help, passing merchant ships would be obliged by maritime law to rescue them.

But such a strategy works with or without Mare Nostrum. So the smugglers were unbothered by whether it existed or not. And several didn't recognise its name. 'I've not heard of that,' said one Libyan smuggler, a former oil-rig technician, when we had coffee on a beach in Tripoli. 'What is that – [a mission] from 2009?'

It was just as small a factor in the decisions of the refugees themselves. Take the Ghanaian refugee I meet in a Tripoli suburb a few days before Ibrahim's boat sank, and the day after 400 others drowned in a separate incident. Abdo, thirty-two, knows all about what happened. But he says most people will still risk the journey, Mare Nostrum or no Mare Nostrum, because they feel it's the least worst option.

'We follow the news in the African TV and the BBC. We know what's going on,' says Abdo. 'We call each other, we say, "Eh, man, you see what's happening?" But you know in French we say, "Cabri mort n'a pas peur du couteau."' A dead goat doesn't fear the butcher's knife.

You can find similar sentiments down the coastline in Egypt. 'Let me tell you something,' a thirty-five-year-old Syrian explains one afternoon in a city just west of Cairo. 'Even if there was a [European] decision to drown the migrant boats, there will still be people going by boat because the individual considers himself dead already. Right now Syrians consider themselves dead. Maybe not physically, but psychologically and socially [a Syrian] is a destroyed human being, he's reached the point of death. So I don't think that even if they decided to bomb migrant boats it would change people's decision to go.'

This man's own story is instructive of why people trust the sea more than the lands they're coming from. He's a former army officer from Syria who fled to Egypt in the early days of the 2011 uprising, after he refused to kill unarmed protesters. Because of this, he's still a wanted man; assassins tried to kill him in Cairo not long after he arrived. Back at home, the Syrian state won't give his mother the cancer treatment she needs – all because he's her son. As a result, he's asked to be identified here only by the nickname of Abu Jana, which means 'Jana's dad'.

When Mohamed Morsi was ousted, Syrians suddenly needed proper paperwork to live in Egypt. A round-up began of those without legal residency. But to qualify for residency you had to have a valid Syrian passport. And many Syrians had only expired ones. To get a new one required a trip to the Syrian embassy in Cairo. But they wouldn't give any out if you were meant to be in military service, or if you'd claimed asylum through the UN refugee agency. Or if, like Abu Jana, you were a wanted man in Damascus.

So Abu Jana was one of the many who became stuck in legal limbo following the 2013 coup in Egypt. For a time, he actually did have the right paperwork – given to him during a more lax era. But, in the autumn of 2014, it expired. And with no means of renewing his passport, he couldn't renew his residency.

The first time we meet is late on a September night. Abu Jana lives in a windowless flat in an unremarkable suburban street. It takes me and my translator, Manu, a while to find the place, so it is around 11.30 p.m. by the time we arrive. We talk first about his recent attempt to get on a boat to Italy. After twenty minutes or so, we turn to why he wanted to leave in the first place. The reason is pretty simple: this was his last day as a legal immigrant to Egypt. 'In ten minutes, I won't be allowed to live here,' Abu Jana says. 'If I'm caught at any checkpoint I'll be sent back to Syria.'

Then he looks down at his watch. 'Nine minutes now. It's like Cinderella: at midnight, the dream will end.'

We return to discussing his failed attempt to get to Italy. Egyptian policemen arrested him and his family on the beach, as they attempted to reach the dinghies that ferry people to the smuggling boat itself. They then spent days stuck in a police cell. But despite that trauma, says Abu Jana, he's resigned to trying again when the weather improves in the spring.

His fate seems all the more obvious once midnight comes and goes. Abu Jana is now at risk of being deported to his death. 'Why do we keep going by sea?' Abu Jana asks me. 'Because we trust god's mercy more than the mercy of people here.'

We meet again the following spring, in April 2015, when he's preparing to cross the sea for a second time. He's managed to keep his head down for the interim period – but it has been a soul-destroying wait. He seems more dour, yet simultaneously more impulsive. His wife worries about giving an interview, but Abu Jana shrugs. What more could go wrong?

Hiding in his flat, Abu Jana is able to stay alive. But it isn't much of a life. Without residency, he can neither travel legally, nor find work in Egypt, nor enrol at a university. It also means he can't get a proper rental contract. And it isn't just Abu Jana left in a bureaucratic no-man's-land: his two young daughters are also in limbo. Without valid paperwork, Abu Jana cannot procure them birth certificates, so they legally don't exist. When the time comes, they will find it hard to start school.

'For all these reasons, I decided to leave,' Abu Jana says during this second meeting. 'I want to go by sea.'

As we talk, he packs his bag for the trip. Of all the bits and bobs he crams inside, little says as much about his trip as the laser pen. The lemons suggest he expects to get seasick: his wife reckons the bitter juice will ward off the worst of the nausea. The plastic bag and the roll of tape mean he expects to get splashed: together they'll make a watertight pocket to hold his documents.

But the laser pen shows that he knows he faces being drowned. In the dead of night, bobbing around in the waves, he wants passing ships to be able to find him – which is where a green laser might come in useful. 'Maybe someone can see it, and could help us,' he says.

Abu Jana certainly understands the dangers of going to sea. A friend of his drowned last year in the attempt. But Abu Jana does not care whether or not Mare Nostrum exists.

'I don't think the rescue mission has any effect on my decision or others' decision to go by sea,' Abu Jana says. 'At the very core of the decision to go there is risk. So the decision to go by boat won't be changed for, let's say, a 10 per cent increase in risk.'

This is something that Europe's chief border guard refuses to grasp. Fabrice Leggeri is the head of Frontex, the agency that patrols the borders of the European Union. Frontex sends agents to some of the land borders, and patrol boats to the maritime ones. A square-jawed former head of the French frontier police, Leggeri is ideal for the job.

When the EU decided not to replace Mare Nostrum in October 2014, it claimed that Leggeri's teams were more than able to pick up the slack in the southern Mediterranean, thanks to a Frontex operation there known by its codename of 'Triton'. This was an inspired piece of window dressing. Unlike Mare Nostrum, Triton's mandate was not to search for and rescue people. Its role was merely to patrol the continent's nautical borders – in waters far to the north of where Italian ships used to station themselves during Mare Nostrum. It had fewer ships at its disposal, and a budget that was just a third of its predecessor's. The assumption was that a smaller-scale border-patrol mission would indirectly save more lives.

I speak to Leggeri from Libya, at the end of a week in which 1,300 people drowned in waters not far to the north. It's the perfect time to ask Leggeri whether he thinks the EU's assumption is still valid, six months after it was first made. The events of the last few days have undermined the concept of the pull factor, I suggest to Leggeri over a crackly Skype line. Not only have more people embarked from Libya than ever before – but a record number have now drowned. Shouldn't Frontex now be doing more than just border patrol?

At first Leggeri spends twenty minutes dodging the question, saying it's a discussion for his superiors in the European Union. But, after one direct question too many, he puts his cards on the table. And he plays the same hand that European politicians have played since they ended rescue missions in October 2014.

'We should not support and fuel the business of traffickers,' Leggeri says. 'What happened in the past was that if smugglers are sure that European boats are patrolling very close to the Libyan coast, then traffickers might use this opportunity to advertise, and say to potential irregular migrants, "You will be sure to reach the European coast. It's very easy, European boats are patrolling not far from the Libyan coast, so let's jump into the sea and you'll see European boats very soon."'

As a result, he says, 'Triton cannot be a search-and-rescue operation.'

It is a staggering claim to make, days after the deadliest shipwreck in modern Mediterranean history.

Fortunately not all of Europe's top brass respond in the same blinkered way. The deaths spark a brief but fierce outcry in Europe, forcing politicians to at least pay lip service to saving lives. Though Leggeri is not himself so keen, several European politicians entrust him and Frontex with several more navy ships. It's still no Mare Nostrum operation. And the primary mandate of these boats is still not search and rescue. But the fact that they are being loaned to Frontex at this time suggests that their mission is implicitly a rescue one.

A few weeks after this call in April 2015, I visit the headquarters of the Italian coastguards in Rome, to see how the new system is working. Whenever a migrant boat gets rescued in the Mediterranean, it's the Italian coastguards who run the show. They may not carry out the rescue themselves; sometimes they call the navy, or Frontex, or a passing merchant ship – or one of the boats run by charities like Médecins Sans Frontières. But it's the coastguards who field the SOS calls, and it's they who then decide who is going to carry out the rescue. That's why their offices are known as the Maritime Rescue Coordination Centre (MRCC).

From the outside, those offices don't seem like the nerve centre of one of the world's biggest ever maritime rescue operations. The coastguards live in the middle of the EUR district of southern Rome, a bland administrative quarter begun by Mussolini in the 1930s. The building itself is far from the coast, and looks like any anonymous office block.

But up on one of the higher floors is a windowless room where hundreds of thousands of lives are decided. Even inside its walls, there is little hint of its purpose. Were it not for the wooden wheel hanging in one corner, ripped from an old-fashioned sailing boat, or the digital map of the Mediterranean projected onto the wall, you might conclude from the bank of telephones that this is simply some sort of call centre.

These phones certainly ring. The year before I visit, they must have rung at least 827 times – that's the number of migrant rescues the coastguards here coordinated in 2014. So far in 2015 they've organised a mere 257.

Two captains show me around – Captain Leopoldo Manna, a lean man, and Captain Paolo Cafaro, who is short and squat. Manna runs the emergency room itself, while Cafaro plans for future operations. They look and sound different: Manna speaks English with the vowels of an Italian; Cafaro has the drawl of someone from the American Deep South, and his elongated pronunciation of 'buuuut' occasionally gives me the giggles. Together this unlikely duo organise the rescue of the hundreds of thousands of migrants in the southern Mediterranean.

It all starts with a phone call. Sometimes it's from an activist like Nawal Soufi. Father Mussie Zerai is another: he's an Eritrean priest who has become the main point of contact for his compatriots. Both Soufi and Zerai then call Manna's team and give them the boat's coordinates.

Sometimes the migrants call themselves, using a satellite phone provided by the smugglers in a rare piece of customer service. A messy conversation usually unfolds. Manna's colleagues will first ask for the coordinates on the sat-phone. Often the migrants can't decipher what's on the screen – or the Italians don't catch what they're saying.

'Usually they are confused, they're not clear,' says Cafaro. 'They have very poor English, they're difficult to understand. What they say is: we are in danger, there's water on board, children, women, pregnant women, please help us. It's quite difficult for us to get them to read exactly the position that's displayed.' Occasionally, the coastguards simply have to call up the telephone's manufacturers to ask them to trace the coordinates of that particular handset.

Once that's known, then the coastguards can begin the rescue. Across one whole wall in the operations room is a huge computerised map of the Mediterranean. It shows the coastguards the location of all the boats in the sea, with the exception of the ones that have switched off their tracking devices. 'When you talk about smugglers, when you talk about rubber boats and wooden boats with immigrants, generally they don't have any [active] automatic identification system,' Manna sighs. 'We only know where they are when they call us.'

Fortunately, at this point Manna needs to know only where the legal boats are. He's looking for the merchant ships, the NGO rescue missions and the naval vessels that are in the region of the stricken migrant boats. Once one has been identified, he calls it to order it to carry out a rescue. And under the laws of the sea it has to oblige.

Sitting here in Rome, coordinating every single rescue mission, Manna and Cafaro have a bird's-eye view of what's going on in the waters between Libya and Italy. It gives them an insight into the crisis that few can match. They can tell you the proportion of wooden boats to inflatables used by smugglers – in 2015, rubber dinghies became the boat of choice for traffickers running out of wooden fishing sloops. They can scotch rumours that jihadists are sending boats from Libya to Europe. There have been no boats from Benghazi, a jihadi stronghold, since last summer, says Cafaro. And what about Derna, an Isis toehold in eastern Libya? 'No.' And Sirte, Isis's Libyan capital? 'Absolutely not.' It's possible to send individual militants amid a boatload of innocents, as two of the participants in the Paris bombings in November 2015 seem to have demonstrated. But it's less likely that the jihadists themselves are running the show. In December 2015, Isis fighters allegedly made a brief incursion into Sabratha, one of the western smuggling hubs, but at the time of writing they do not control the ports that send the migrants.

Cafaro also has strong views on the proposal to bomb smugglers' boats, an idea that is all the rage when we meet in May 2015. 'The problem of migration, of desperate people, will not be solved with these [military] measures,' he says. 'It will assume other forms, they will try to find other ways.' And ending rescue missions won't put them off, he adds. 'The famous pull factor? We are dealing with people in deep misery. We are dealing with people coming from civil wars. They are desperate. They will leave their countries anyway, with Mare Nostrum or not.'

The coastguards have been 'suffering' since Mare Nostrum ended, Cafaro continues. Even during the quieter winter months, they needed more boats at their disposal. Following the twin April fiascos that killed the 1,300 migrants, European governments have given Frontex more ships to patrol with – and these in turn can be turned over to Cafaro and Manna if and when there is an emergency. Politicians such as David Cameron, the British prime minister, trumpet this as an example of Europe's commitment to saving lives. But for the coastguards the system isn't working yet.

These new ships often aren't being deployed in the most effectual places, says Manna, since he is allowed to direct them only once he receives an emergency call. In his control room Manna points at a weather map of the Mediterranean, highlighting how sunshine seems set to reach the Libyan coast again after a stormy period. Experience tells him that this means a new wave of migrant boats will arrive in the coming days, since the smugglers tend to send out twenty all at once, rather than in dribs and drabs.

It's a development Manna would ideally pre-empt by directing a boat such as Britain's HMS *Bulwark* towards the likely crisis area. Instead, *Bulwark*, outside his management remit, is returning to Palermo just at the time when it is needed most. A German boat that is currently deployed in the right area will soon have to leave to fetch some supplies.

Manna points at the map, and waves his hand over the waters closest to Libya. 'The German ship is here – it's not under my orders. It voluntarily stays here, it's a very good help, and I appreciate it so much. But I don't have the ability to decide if she stays or if she goes. At the moment, I would have decided to not keep this vessel here. It is not useful here. I would have said: go inside the harbour, have a rest, pick up food and water, then wait two days.'

As a result, when the surge does come, Manna won't have the boats he needs to prevent a disaster. It's a problem that I'll get to witness first hand a few months later.

On a merchant ship around thirty miles north of Libya Gordie Hatt hurries up the stairs to the bridge, his long white hair tied back in a ponytail. 'Where is everyone?' says the sixty-three-year-old Canadian, bursting from the staircase. 'It's just Amani and me down on deck, and we have a thousand people trying to find a place to sleep.'

Hatt has a point. This is the bridge of the *Bourbon Argos*, one of three merchant ships hired by Médecins Sans Frontières to rescue stricken refugees from the waters north of Libya, in the absence of full-scale EU rescue operations. Earlier on this morning in August 2015 the crew rescued two boats in quick succession, a pair of operations that brought 1,001 refugees aboard the *Argos*, almost all of them Eritreans. The boat is supposed to take only 500, so Hatt needs all the help he can get on deck.

But what he doesn't know is that an even bigger problem is unravelling on the waters in front of the boat, consuming his colleagues' attention. In this bit of the southern Mediterranean there are nine rescue operations in progress, involving MSF's boats, the Italian coastguards and a few warships from European navies. But it's not enough. Here on the bridge, Hatt's colleagues can see two more flimsy refugee boats on the water. And only one of them is getting rescued. It's a vivid example of what Manna had warned me about months earlier: even with the new boats given to Frontex back in May, the coastguards in Rome don't have enough boats to work with.

Here on the *Argos*, the decks are already full up. They cannot safely squeeze aboard any more passengers – so MSF's Norwegian second-in-command stands by the radar monitor looking grim. 'We can't help them,' says the Norwegian number two. 'The only difference would be if they started sinking and we had to rescue them.'

The situation is already tense enough when his boss, Lindis Hurum, picks up the bridge telephone and radios another rescue ship in the area. 'Does your boat have a gynaecologist?' she asks. 'We have a very pregnant woman on board who needs to deliver within twenty-four hours.'

This is the regular reality in the southern Mediterranean, at the height of the 2015 smuggling season. Since May, the EU has stepped up its search-and-rescue missions in the region. But, as the coastguards in Rome warned, they haven't done it in the most efficient way. The operations are still understaffed, as this week's incident shows, and overly reliant on private groups, including the Migrant Offshore Aid Station (MOAS) and MSF, who have been left to pick up the pieces. Sometimes literally so: in July MRCC asked the *Argos* to rescue a refugee boat in distress several nautical miles away. But, by the time it arrived a few hours later, the boat had vanished into the water, leaving just a few dozen life jackets bobbing on the surface.

The team pray they'll avoid a repeat today. For most of them, the action starts at 6.19 a.m., when Hurum knocks on the doors to their tiny four-berth cabins. A veteran of MSF's ebola mission in west Africa, she herself has been up all night monitoring the situation. Her vigilance pays off at dawn, when MRCC radios to say that a refugee boat just outside Libyan waters has called for help, using a satellite phone given to the refugees by smugglers.

'You have thirty minutes,' Hurum tells the ten-strong team as she wakes them up. There's a frenzy of rustling and stumbling as they reach for their life jackets and helmets. They gather downstairs in the calm of the mess room, where the muffled blare of the ship's huge engine sounds like the throb of a distant bass note. The loudest is Hatt, a former navy technician, whose job is to fix, build or invent any contraption that the team might need. And the quietest is Amani, an Eritrean interpreter, who himself braved the sea voyage thirteen years ago, and has returned to the same waters to help rescue the people following in his wake. Hurum tells them all to be ready for more than one rescue. 'MRCC wants to know: how many can we take?'

Around the MSF team, the ship's sailors are donning overalls and gas masks. At times, it's been a bit of a culture clash. MSF hires the boat from a merchant fleet called Bourbon, which employs the boat's all-Ukrainian officers, and all-Filipino seamen. They're men who stick to strict timetables and hierarchies, while MSF's multinational team pride themselves on their flexibility and egalitarianism. And they're used to transporting fuel and anchors, not traumatised refugees with scabies and head lice.

At mealtimes, the Ukrainians insist on sitting apart from the MSF team. In the tiny mess there are two tables, one a metre from the other. In such a cramped space it would make sense to let anyone sit anywhere. But in keeping with maritime tradition, the Ukrainian officers don't want to mix with their clients from MSF.

At first, this physical division was also an ideological one. The MSF team like to refer to the refugees as 'guests', and attempt to appear as welcoming as possible. 'We're like the character in Dante's *Inferno* who takes Virgil to the other side of the river Styx,' says the team's communications officer, before realising he should flesh out the metaphor. 'We are the parentheses of normality between a very hard situation in Libya, and another one in Europe, a period of safety and rest and dignity in which they're considered human beings.'

The Ukrainians haven't always completely shared these lofty goals. They're worried about catching diseases from those 'guests', and initially wore intimidating gas masks when they were in their midst. Early on, they also didn't seem to agree completely with the mission's objective. 'Lindis, you can't save the whole of Africa,' Hurum was told by one officer when she first joined the ship. Another still fears that some of the refugees will turn out to be Isis terrorists, with explosives strapped to their chests.

But gradually most of them have warmed to this unusual job. After weeks rescuing refugees, the first mate now bristles when he sees them numbered on arrival in Italy. 'They're people not numbers,' the mate says one morning.

Then there's Captain Ruslan Voznyuk. When I first board the ship, I feel sure he'll have some conflicted views about what he's been contracted to do. Every day Voznyuk wears the same black T-shirt emblazoned with the logo of the Right Sector, a nationalist party in Ukraine. He even admits he isn't certain about immigration. But one day we happen to be the only people eating breakfast in the mess, sitting awkwardly at the two separate tables that lie just a metre apart. To break the silence, I ask what he thinks of all this. To my surprise, he says he is proud of his mission, and enthusiastic about the aid workers on his ship. 'This job must be done,' he says in his abrupt English. 'In the sea there must be no sinking. God gives life so people must live.'

On this particular morning, with a rescue imminent, the crew dash around to put their captain's words into action. Most things are ready – the portable cabin that houses the makeshift hospital is already pristine. The mini-morgue that will house any corpses is already cold. The toilets are clean. Now the ship's dinghy needs to be winched into the water, and a rope ladder put in position.

Up on the forecastle, Hurum and her deputy scan the sea through their binoculars for the first signs of the boat. For a while, they just see the red morning sun, edging over the horizon. But then there it is, a distant black sliver between the water and the sky. It edges closer and closer, until you can see a few flecks of orange against the black – the life jackets of those on board.

Finally, the boat's contours emerge more clearly. It is a blue boat, one of the wooden skiffs, with a white line running along its side. And soon it's so close that you can see the passengers' faces. They're mostly Eritrean. One is crying, others are smiling, and some are singing with joy. In the openings that lead to the hold, men peer from the darkness. Up on deck people eat bananas, and at the ship's stern lounge two lone Libyans. 'They seem calm,' says a relieved MSF translator. 'It should be an easy rescue.'

But in a rescue like this things are never simple. As the *Argos* glides to a halt alongside the refugees, shielding the smaller boat from the waves, the crew can see that the Eritreans are using a bucket to bail out the hold. How long the boat will last is unclear. The passengers packed inside the hold are also a concern. The lack of ventilation, coupled with the fumes of the engine, often suffocates people trapped in their hundreds below deck. Over fifty died last month like this.

Then there's the possibility of panic. By this point in other rescues passengers have been known to try to sink their own boat, to make sure their saviours don't give up on them. Last week, Amani explains, 600 refugees ignored the instruction to leave the boat one by one, and instead piled onto the *Argos* in any way they could.

It's Amani's role to avoid a repeat of that. He raises the loudhailer. 'Stay calm,' he says in Tigrinya, the most widely spoken Eritrean language. 'Stay where you are. We have enough places for you all. But please come one by one.' Ropes are thrown, and the ladder is lowered. And then the rescue begins.

One by one, they totter uncertainly up the ladder and onto the deck of the *Argos*. Some can barely walk, their legs cramped and numb from hours of sitting in the same position, trapped between their neighbours. Some are covered in vomit, after choking on the fumes in the hold. As they step on the deck, and Hatt extends a hand and a hello, relief blooms across their faces. 'I must thank you,' says Lingo, a thirty-five-year-old Eritrean geography teacher. 'When we saw you, we automatically changed from animals into humans.'

The rescue takes about an hour. There are around 350 mainly Eritreans on board, a few Somalis, and a couple of Libyan deckhands – and they've all got to come aboard one at a time. This time there is no panic, and everyone boards safely. For a few people the relief is bittersweet: they were separated from their relatives before they left Libya. Now it's a waiting game, to see if their husbands or brothers were also put on a boat – and if that boat was also rescued.

For the majority, this is a time to rejoice. Seemingly without discussion they organise themselves in neat rows on the packed deck. One man rises from their midst, stands before them, and begins to sing. Then the hundreds sitting below him join in unison – they all know the words. A series of Christian hymns wafts over the waters of the Mediterranean. Minutes after being rescued, this huge crowd of Eritreans are thanking God for letting them live.

The MSF team can't relax though. Their work has just begun: forty minutes away another boat is in difficulty, this one a bigger steel one, with perhaps 650 people on board.

When you first draw alongside a boat like this nothing quite prepares you for the shock. I've seen hundreds of photos of this kind of boat before. I've even just witnessed a smaller rescue. But a boat of 650 refugees, crammed onto every last plank of the deck, and into every last space in the hold, is an overwhelming sight, however many photos you've previously looked at. As we draw near, I realise that pictures never quite convey the epic scale of the situation – this swaying boat, set against the vastness of the sea that surrounds it. This knot of lives, only ever a few moments from death.

It also makes me wonder how many of those boats are never discovered; how many simply disappear without trace. Up close like this, the boat looks big. But thirty minutes ago we could barely see it through the binoculars. It amazes and frightens me how easy it would have been to cruise on past it, completely oblivious to its drift towards oblivion.

The closer we get, the more vulnerable things look. The sky-blue paint is rusting, and the hull sits low in the water, weighed down by a cargo too large for the size of the vessel. The faces become clearer, some petrified, some smiling. But whatever their faces are doing, their bodies are almost all motionless. If anyone moves it could overbalance the boat. The boat teeters, even on these placid waters. Just a slight turn in the weather would probably prove catastrophic.

This boat is one of the lucky ones. Then there are the boats that sink, like Ibrahim Mbalo's. And there are the boats that neither sink nor get rescued – but just drift in limbo for days until they run aground in Tunisia or Libya. Or get picked up by the Libyans that call themselves coastguards. I've met the survivors of two such boats, and I was left wondering whether, short of drowning, there are any maritime experiences that are as horrifying.

Both boats were inflatable dinghies, packed with over a hundred migrants. That's possibly why they didn't get spotted: it's easier to spot the metal boats on the radar. But the inflatables need an eagle-eyed sailor to notice them, particularly at night. So these two just drifted for days.

The first trauma lies in the lack of a compass. If you still have fuel in your engine, no one will agree on where to point the boat. 'Everyone had an idea, everyone was trying to drive the boat,' one man tells me after he spent days adrift in April. 'We were just following the sun.'

The second trauma arrives when the fuel runs out. And then the food and water. You're left drifting at the whim of the winds and the waves, without any means of deciding your own fate. The only agency you have is in the decision to keep still. When people are that tightly packed, sudden movements can cause the boat to capsize. With nowhere to move, those in the middle of the boat simply shit themselves, and urinate onto their neighbours. 'They pissed on all our clothes,' says a Malian woman from the same boat. 'I was sick of the scent.'

At the edge of the boat, two men overbalanced, fell into the water, and drowned. A third seemed to be overwhelmed by the situation, or the thirst, and tried to sabotage the boat. 'So the other boys', says the Malian woman, 'put him over the side.'

I hear a similar story from a group of Nigerians a few months later. They were cast adrift, and they had to toss one of their group into the water. It was chilling to hear their various justifications for it. One said the murdered man had simply gone mad and was endangering the lives of the rest. He started to bite people (one survivor had human bite marks on his leg), so the only option was to kill him. But other survivors could not reconcile themselves to his murder, and so appeared to have concocted an elaborate alternative justification. Not only had the man bitten people, but he was possessed by the devil – and then committed suicide. 'He turned himself into a vampire and started to bite people in the leg,' one thirty-three-year-old claims. 'The rescue boats came but the vampire covered the eyes of the rescuers using witchcraft, so that they could not see us. Then the vampire ran into the sea and killed himself.' The vampire admitted this, said another survivor. 'Before he flew into the sea, he told us he had bewitched the rescuers.'

Back on board the *Argos*, there is one man who knows all too well what it's like to drift for days in the Mediterranean.

When the team draw up alongside the two boats this morning, it's an emotional moment for them all. But, for Amani, the experience is particularly personal. He was once one of those in need of rescue.

Thirteen years ago, Amani escaped Eritrea, after being arrested for his political activism. Then he survived an epic trek through the Sahara to Libya, where he was then held against his will by smugglers. Finally, after two failed attempts, he crossed the Mediterranean to Italy. It was in a flimsy fishing boat very similar to the ones he now helps to rescue.

'I came the same way,' Amani tells me, in a quiet moment. 'I know all the risks they face in the Sahara and the Mediterranean, the problems they face from the Libyan smugglers.' Doing this job summons up 'flashes of bad memories' of similar experiences. He remembers emerging from the desert crossing, covered in sand. He remembers waiting to board the boat from Libya, and being forced to watch smugglers rape some of the women who hoped to travel with him.

'I saw the same bad things, and I even have some family members who've drowned in this way,' says Amani. 'So helping these people is really a pleasure.'

He's been in their boat, almost literally. But their plight still has the capacity to stun him because in some ways it is worse than what he endured. 'I was so shocked,' Amani says, of the first time he approached a refugee boat as a rescuer. 'When I saw the women and children packed like chickens, everywhere full, I was really shocked. Now they are putting almost double the number of people on board than when I did it.'

But, overall, Amani reckons the people following in his wake are marginally safer – because his boat had to go further than theirs. 'They are lucky because the rescue missions now come so close,' he says. 'We had no rescue. If big ships saw us they thought we were fishermen, and nobody cared about us.'

Over a decade later, Amani has been able to move on. He won asylum in the UK, and then worked as a translator in the NHS, and as a care worker with the elderly and with autistic children. He's now married, with three kids of his own – and for that reason his latest voyage in the Mediterranean has packed a different kind of emotional punch than it did the first time.

In particular, he cites the example of a young mother who recently died of dehydration, along with four others, before the *Bourbon Argos* could reach her. 'It was the most emotional time in my life,' he says. 'I tried to convince myself that they died naturally. But there was a mum of three young children. And I am a father of three children. So I wondered if that was my wife, and they were my children, how hard that would be.'

As an Eritrean, Amani has an easy connection with this particular set of passengers. But one of them seems more relieved to see him than most. It's Lingo, the geography teacher. 'Remember me?' Lingo asks him, once everyone is safely on board. At first, Amani doesn't. This guy looks old. His beard is grey, his skin is wrinkled. Amani can't place him.

But Lingo remembers Amani. For they are in fact the same age: thirty-five. They were contemporaries at university, in the days when Eritrea still had one. They attended the same student protests back in 2002. After they were arrested for their activism, they were taken to the same underground prison. And here they both are again, meeting thirteen years later in the middle of the Mediterranean. Amani's eyes widen, once he realises who Lingo is. 'He looks so much older,' Amani later tells me. 'That's what Eritrea does to you.'

But Amani has also changed, says Lingo. 'He's put on a bit of weight,' Lingo laughs. 'All that European cooking.'

It is a poignant moment amid a scene of chaos. The intense drama of the morning has died down. The pregnant woman has been evacuated to an Italian navy ship, later to give birth in Malta. The *Argos* is now on its way to Italy. On deck, confusion reigns. There are more than 1000 people here in a space meant for no more than 500. The captain has grudgingly opened the foredeck, but still there is not enough space for everyone to sit in comfort. Some don't mind. This is the safest place they have been in months, and so they've just lain down on the floor, shut their eyes, and slept.

But most people are moving around, half delighted to be safe, half anxious about what happens next. Where are they going? How long to Italy? Will there be any food? Is there any more water? Are there any cigarettes? There's always something going wrong. The toilets are blocked, or a bit of the deck is flooded.

It's a slightly awkward place to report from. There's barely any space to stand, and I find myself interviewing people while squatting between sleeping migrants. The MSF team could do with an extra hand on deck, rather than someone asking endless questions. On a few occasions I put down my notebook and start behaving like a human being – helping to answer questions from the Arabic speakers, and then distributing sheets of gold foil that the Eritreans fold around themselves to keep warm at night. Once everyone's wrapped up, it makes for a grand sight: more like a throng of carnival-goers in their glinting fancy dress than a deck of refugees.

Handing out food is the biggest headache. One thousand people tend not to form very orderly queues. Amani and his colleagues desperately try to create some sort of process. But with so many people, and in such a confined space, ultimately they have to let people organise themselves.

Gordie Hatt breathes in the air. 'The smell of humanity,' he says. 'That smell is something that will stick with me the longest. The smell of people who have had fear going through them for a long time – that fear has a smell of its own.'

Inside the makeshift hospital the medical team gets the best understanding of where that fear comes from. All day people queue outside for the chance of seeing a doctor for the first time in months. Many have been beaten, during three separate stints inside the compounds of Libya's traffickers. Several of them have broken limbs, untreated since their pick-up rolled over in the Sahara. One has a bullet wound courtesy of his time at the hands of Isis, who shot and kidnapped him earlier in the summer. A woman has a bruised vagina, after concealing around $400 inside it. In Libya, if you keep your money in such a thing as a wallet, it will be stolen within hours.

And many women have had experiences even darker than this. 'Never enter without knocking,' one of the nurses warns me. 'You don't know if there is woman inside telling me that she has been raped.'

The clinical staff's role is sometimes as pastoral as it is medical. The team places the families and the unaccompanied children outside the hospital door, so that they can keep an eye on their most vulnerable passengers. On this particular trip there are seventy children without parents – most escaping Eritrea's slave state, which turns all minors into child soldiers. The nurses try to give them more attention: some of them are just ten or twelve.

Others set out with their mothers, but their mums died en route. 'There was one father with three boys, and their mum died, and the boys didn't realise it,' says one of the nurses, recalling a previous trip. 'But the closer we got to Italy, the more they realised. And then they asked us: could you be our mother?'

On this trip, it takes two days and two nights to reach Italy. Most get sent to Sicily, where the biggest reception centres are. But it's late August – Libya's peak smuggling season – so Sicily is full, and the *Argos* is sent instead to Crotone, a port on the heel of Italy.

It's a bittersweet moment, easing into port to find a waiting gaggle of doctors, coastguards, Frontex officials and journalists. On the one hand, this is cause for huge celebration. It marks the end of a traumatic ordeal that has seen most of these people trek through a desert, subject themselves to repeated torture and humiliation in Libya, and then a terrifying sea voyage. Kids gathered in a line near the gangway grin with delight and expectation. Behind them, a trainee priest from Eritrea is welling up. 'I don't believe I'm actually nearly there after all we went through in the Sahara,' says the would-be pastor, his eyes reddening. 'It's a dream come true, and sometimes when things feel like a dream, you can't believe them.'

But in some respects, this man is right to temper his emotions. He has arrived in Europe, and the worst is over. But a long and confusing asylum process is now about to begin – a process most have little preparation for. 'Can I work on this ship?' asks another Eritrean passenger, as the gangway is lowered to the quay. 'Have you got an email for the people I should contact?'

The bureaucracy starts even before anyone has even left the boat. As soon as the gangway touches the quayside, a trio of Frontex agents scamper up it and onto the deck. This is one part of the EU's ham-fisted attempt to smash the smuggling networks. Among these thousand refugees, the three officials hope to find some smugglers. None of the trio speak Tigrinya, but one knows Arabic – so they separate the few Eritrean Arabic speakers from the rest. The Eritreans eagerly follow them – they think they're about to get fast-tracked through the system. What they don't know is that they're instead due for hours of pointless questions about Libyan smuggling, a process they have been victim to, but have little understanding of.

Lindis Hurum seethes at the soullessness of it all. After a couple of days in which the refugees have been treated like humans, they're about to become mere statistics again. As they disembark they're immediately stickered with a number, and then taken to waiting buses, ready to be taken to camps. I walk down the gangway myself at one point, and for a moment the waiting officials think I'm a migrant. It's a briefly alienating experience – hidden behind his face mask, a man lunges towards me with his stickers, and another points a gun-shaped thermometer at my temple. Suddenly, they realise their mistake, and everyone has a laugh. For the real migrants, it's not so funny. Those with scabies are forced to lower their trousers there and then on the quayside. Their clothes are later burned.

'On the boat we're trying to see them as people with a story,' Hurum says, wincing while she watches. 'But the minute they step on the shore, they're just seen as a statistic, and everyone's wearing a mask again.'

But when everyone is disembarked, four hours later, Hurum is able to reflect on what is fundamentally a triumph of humanity. Last year she led a team trying to stop the ebola epidemic in west Africa. It was one of the most dispiriting experiences of her life. She and her team had to wear white spacesuits, protecting them from infection, but preventing them from meaningful interaction with patients. Almost all of whom died.

But here in the Mediterranean, lives are largely being saved. 'This is the perfect mission to recover from a mission as dark as ebola,' Hurum says. 'It's the complete opposite of ebola. In the past few weeks, five people have died, but we've saved thousands.

'And we've been able to hug them.'

6

Promised Land?

Hashem's first steps in Europe

Sunday, 26 April 2015, 11.30 a.m.

Western Europe

A kilometre inside the French border, Hashem al-Souki wonders whether he can leave the toilet yet. He went there to escape the police, but that was ten minutes ago. Have they left yet? And, if not, will they bother to check this bathroom?

Hashem hasn't planned for this. The hard bit of the journey was supposed to be the boat, not the onward odyssey through Europe. But five days after getting off the ship, he now finds himself having to overcome yet more hurdles that he hadn't really thought about until he arrived in Italy. Train timetables. Border crossings. Policemen.

Right now, the police are the most pressing concern. A group of French gendarmes entered this train at Menton, the first station inside France. They're looking for people like Hashem – refugees trying to leave Italy. As he ducks into the toilet, just in time, they arrest two Eritreans in the same carriage. The pair had been sitting only a few seats away. They'll be sent back to the Italian border, where they should be fingerprinted by the police there – a formal process that means they'll have to claim asylum in Italy.

And that is exactly what Hashem wants to avoid. Now he's in Europe, he can claim asylum anywhere. According to the EU's Dublin regulation, he's supposed to do it in Italy, the first European country he came to. But if he does so, it might be a long time before he sees his wife and children again. The process of applying for family reunification in Italy is seen as comparatively slow – and France is no faster. So the goal is to get at least to Germany, where the process is considered more streamlined, without getting finger-printed. But it's still several months before Germany promises to welcome any Syrian, regardless of whether they've previously registered and been fingerprinted in any other EU country, so for Hashem the best-case scenario is Sweden, where Syrians are allowed indefinite leave to re-main. And for Hashem that's the ultimate prize: a long-term future in a place where his kids can settle without fear of hav-ing, yet again, to move on.

But, first, he has to make it through France. To this day Sweden will still expel you if you've been fingerprinted in another EU country. So if he's caught in France, and forced to claim asylum there, he won't be able to make either of his preferred destinations. At the moment, with the French policemen pacing the corridor outside, he might not even step safely onto French soil in the first place. He waits it out. That's all he needs to do: wait till they leave. He waits. He thinks. He reasons with himself. They won't check everyone – just the people who look out of place. Eventually they'll get bored and leave. Won't they?

Hashem begins to panic. Maybe this wasn't the best way to come. At first, he'd wanted to take the train directly from Milan to Munich – the quickest way to Germany. But others had warned him that he risked arrest by Austrian police once the train crossed into Austria. On the other hand, they said, the slow train to Nice in the south of France doesn't get checked by police. How wrong had they been.

Minutes pass. The train doesn't move. Surely the police are in another carriage by now? They must have left, Hashem decides. It's been too long. So he thumbs the lock, takes a deep breath, opens the door, and leaves the toilet. It's yet another make-or-break moment, the kind that could decide not just his life but that of his wife and their children.

He re-enters his carriage. He looks up. There, blocking the aisle ahead of him, is a French policeman.

Five days earlier, he'd been so glad to see the authorities. The Italian frigate took about a day to reach Catania, a port in Sicily, and throughout the journey the migrants couldn't stop thanking their rescuers. People stayed up late, talking about their plans – who wanted to go to Sweden, who wanted to reach Germany. They finally arrived at the Sicilian coast on the morning of Wednesday, 22 April.

The police got on before anyone got off. The officers picked their way through the crowds, and identified the Egyptian crew members. It was as if they'd been tipped off: they knew them all by sight. Then they asked a few migrants themselves: are these the smugglers? To a man, the migrants denied it. The smugglers left in a rubber dinghy before the boat was rescued, they claimed. But the police didn't seem to buy it, and the Egyptians were escorted away.

Then the passengers started to disembark. First children, then women, then the men. Finally Hashem walks down the gangway and sets foot for the first time on Italian soil. It's a feeling of immense relief. He thinks first of his family, so far away. For some reason, he then imagines the sole of a foot. If his family's future could be characterised as a sole pricked by thorns, then Hashem's just plucked out the pointiest one.

He's taken to a Red Cross tent, where doctors give him a medical check-up. He's handed a bottle of water, an apple and a sandwich. And then a convoy of buses turns up, and they're all piled inside.

No one knows where they're going, but the assumption is a camp for asylum seekers. But night falls, and the bus keeps on driving. Someone asks the driver: where are we off to? Venice, he says.

Those with phones look up Venice on a map. Is it in Sicily? To their surprise, it's not. It's at the opposite end of the country. Everyone's delighted. They all wanted to move northwards, and now the Italians are doing it for them.

Eighteen hours later, at lunchtime on Thursday, the buses arrive in the mainland part of Venice. The canals and gondolas will have to wait till another day. A volunteer takes them to a centre where they can wash and charge their phones. He explains to them how they can get to Milan, the springboard for journeys to northern Europe. Using the man's instructions, they make for a nearby station called Mestre, where they spend the night sleeping on the station benches. Early the next day they take the train onwards to Milan, arriving at its main terminus in the middle of the morning.

It's quite a juxtaposition, Milan central station. The building was first begun early in the twentieth century, a vast, Romanesque palace that looms over the surrounding piazza. Inside its columns is a chic shopping mall, with branches of Zara, Mango and Swarovski that spread over three floors. In the main concourse, old men in tailored suits sip on their espressos in the cafes, watching well-coiffed businessmen glide through the glass doors to the platforms.

Yet just down a set of stone steps, in the station's echoing atrium, is another world. Here, on a stone mezzanine, Hashem joins hundreds of migrants who gather daily to contemplate their next step. For months it's a scene that's been part of the station's rhythm – so much so that local police have even permanently cordoned off a bit of floor space for migrants to occupy. Surrounded by a blur of oblivious Italians, here are Syrians, Iraqis, Eritreans and Somalians – some of them still sunburned from the sea. Every few hours there's a new wave of arrivals, the latest boatload from Sicily. Some set out from Libya, some from Egypt. And they're all mingling in this grand atrium in Milan.

Hashem looks around in a state of wonder. He's surrounded by statues and friezes, ornate lamps and marble plaques. For a few minutes the station feels like a beautiful castle, built for the migrants. There are volunteers from local charities, here to hand out water and food. There are people from the local authority, trying to find them beds for the night. It's a far cry from the treatment many of them experienced only days earlier. Sitting on a marble bench, another Syrian recounts how he was essentially kept hostage for the past four months on the Libyan coast. Whereas, here in Milan station, there's even WiFi. Hashem makes use of it, switching on his WhatsApp for the first time since Egypt. A wave of unread messages floods his inbox.

Despite Hashem's relief at being here, the new continent nevertheless brings a new set of problems. How on earth is he going to wriggle through mainland Europe to Sweden? He hadn't really contemplated it before. He'd assumed it would be straightforward. But now there are complex choices to be made, borders to be navigated, police to be dodged. He needs money, but he hasn't got enough. He needs to know the train lines, but he doesn't understand them. In the concourse he looks up at the departures board. It reads like hieroglyphics.

'The sea was easy!' Hashem smiles, only half joking. 'It was direct to Italy. No changes, no police, no stations. No fingerprints.'

The volunteers advise people to take a train to Verona, and then another one to Germany, before heading north to Scandinavia. But Hashem's not sure. So he calls a friend of a friend – a Syrian called Mehyar who made the boat trip last year, and who's now safely in Germany. How on earth did he do it?

Don't go directly to Germany, Mehyar advises. The trains between Italy and Germany have to transit through Switzerland and Austria, and the police in both countries often board the carriages. Instead, he should take a roundabout route along the coast to France, past the Piedmontese hills and onwards to Nice. That's the way Mehyar went, and there were no police at the border.

But the decision can wait another day. Hashem wants his first solid night's sleep in ten days. He wants to wash, to feel clean. After ten days in the same clothes, he doesn't feel comfortable in his own skin. So he waits for the Milanese authorities to allocate him a place at one of their migrant camps. Families get taken first, so he's the last priority. Day turns into night, and the station starts to lose its appeal. With nowhere to sleep, even this grand place is just another reminder of a migrant's rough lot.

Eighteen hours since their last proper meal, the last few refugees turn increasingly delirious. One of them bangs his head against a hoarding. Another lashes out in frustration: 'We have been treated like cattle wherever we went – in Libya, in Sicily, and now here.' Local volunteers doggedly stay with Hashem and the others – some of them will stay all night. But not everyone is so welcoming. A passer-by's voice echoes around the hall: 'Why are you helping these immigrants? Aren't there enough poor in this country already?'

Finally, at well past nine at night, the local officials return. There's some space for the last few migrants at a place a few miles away. They're driven westwards in a minibus, to a suburb called Certosa where they're billeted in a converted school. Their beds are among hundreds lined up in rows inside what used to be a green-floored basketball court. They're just camp beds, nothing special – but after sleeping on the floor for so long, it almost feels like a luxury.

On Saturday, he and his group muddle their way through the metro back to the station. It's a short but confusing journey, and one that makes him question whether Europe's infinitely more complex railway networks are the best method of getting to Sweden. And there's worse news waiting for him. Of the Syrians who tried to reach Germany yesterday, all but two of them were apparently arrested – and they include people who tried to go through France. It's a disaster, and Hashem loses all confidence in the railway as a route out of Italy.

The other option is the car. At the centre last night people were sharing numbers for smugglers who, for a fee, will drive people north. It's a safer option: no one stops cars at

European borders, and you don't have to constantly navigate a rail system you don't understand. There are various different smugglers for hire. There's someone in Malmö, Sweden, who says he can drive four people to Sweden for €875 each. For €750 someone else will drive you to Copenhagen. A third man offers a ride to Ulm in southern Germany. Some smugglers take a dozen people in vans; these chaps drive small cars.

But even this route has its problems. The chap in Malmö is just that – in Malmö. He wants half the money up front before he drives down to Italy. But what if he pockets the cash and stays put? It's a lot of money – far more than the trains. The guy in Copenhagen hardly wants less, and he won't take you all the way. And really Ulm is useful only if you want to end up in Germany. Hashem doesn't. Plus there's the risk of something more morbid. It isn't unknown for smugglers to promise their clients a car seat – but then force them into the back of an unventilated lorry. People have suffocated that way.

For now, though, this debate is academic: at the moment, Hashem has no money to pay for either route. He's still waiting for his brother-in-law – Ehsan, an economist who claimed asylum in Sweden last year – to wire him something to tide him over. Around lunchtime that payment is made, so Hashem queues up at the Western Union in the station to pick it up. In the queue are several familiar faces: he's not the only refugee in need of a helping hand.

There are endless forms to fill in, and Hashem doesn't understand half of what the man is saying behind the glass screen. Pickupthepen. What? Pickupthepen. What? PICK.

UP. THE. PEN. He picks up the pen. He signs a bit of paper. The money is shoved underneath the glass. It comes to just over €500.

Today's the day he thought he'd be moving on. And now he can: with the money he now has in total, Hashem's got just enough for a car to Denmark. But is that the best option? He hasn't a clue by this point. He's come so far, but with his next move he could still blow it all. Then the news comes through that, actually, no one got arrested on the French border yesterday – the guys were detained in Austria. All of a sudden the railway becomes more palatable. And so, instead of moving on today, he traipses back to the metro with his friends. There's a train to Nice at seven the next morning. Tonight, he'll make his mind up whether or not to take it.

In the end, he does. Both the car and the train seem to have their risks, but at least the train is cheaper. And his friends from the boat, the ones who were keenest about the car, are still dithering – whereas Hashem is keen to crack on. The sooner he reaches Sweden, the sooner he sees his family. So the 7 a.m. to Nice it is, along a railway line that hugs the coast as it heads west past the hills of Piedmont. He carries almost nothing – just the waterproof pouch with his money and a few key documents. His stinking blue jumper, the one that kept him warm on the boat, he chucks in a bin. It's an almost triumphant moment. He's in Italy now, and he doesn't need his sea clothes.

There is a nervous moment, minutes after he first boards the train. The conductor suddenly looms above him and says something he can't understand. Hashem freezes. The conductor repeats himself, more aggressively. Is he asking for

Hashem's passport? Thankfully someone intervenes: Hashem's simply in the wrong carriage.

He finds his correct seat, and the train soon eases out of Milan. It flits in and out of tunnels to give him alternating glimpses of pastel-coloured streets, and steep wooded hill-sides. Often, though, all he sees is the sea, and that sight floods him with dread. He just can't get away from the Mediterranean. The best he can do is shift in his seat and turn the other way. He wants a smoke to calm his nerves, but he knows in Europe you can't do that on a train. It'll be a recurring tension.

Everything goes wrong at Menton, the first station after the French border. That's where Hashem finds himself, heart pounding, in the toilet. And that's where he emerges pre-maturely to find a policeman still blocking the aisle next to his seat.

Hashem gulps. Is this it, then? He thinks about turning around, but that'll make him a person of interest. Whereas if he strides forward with purpose, he might get away with it. The policeman isn't checking everyone. And if you don't look too hard at Hashem's clothes, don't notice the dandruff caking his collar, or the whiff of unwashed socks, perhaps, just perhaps, he could be a Frenchman.

At least that's what Hashem hopes as he puts his head down and marches along the aisle. The gendarme looks up. Hashem nods at him. The policeman blinks. And then lets him pass.

So Hashem escapes this time, but the whole encounter gives him a scare. By the time the train draws into Nice ten minutes before noon, his mind is scrambled. If this is what it's like at every border, then is there even any point in trying for Sweden? Maybe his best bet now is just to go to Calais, and try to break into a lorry bound for the UK. Maybe that's as good a route as any.

To make matters worse, no train bound for Paris has a seat free for six hours. They're all booked up. So Hashem has an afternoon to kill in a city that he fears might be the end of him. Buying new tickets is ordeal enough. He doesn't understand the self-service machines, so he's constantly cancelling his transaction and starting again. In the queue behind him people tut and shift noisily from one foot to the other. Can't he get a move on?

The screeching machine spits out the right ticket eventually – by which time he's killed half an hour. But now what? Should he stay in the station? No, not while there's so many other Syrians here. If he can spot them from fifty metres, so too can the police. But he can't just go and sit in a cafe either. He doesn't want to spend any money. He tries strolling around, but a blister on his foot, which got infected during the sea crossing, gives him hell. What about the beach? Not now – he's sick of the sea. He tries a bench on a quiet street next to a grocer's – but the grocer wants to talk. He moves on. Five hours to go.

The wait gnaws at him. Should he have gone by car? Could he go by car now? Or bus? Once in Paris, should he go via Belgium? Or stick to Germany? Hashem can't think straight, and every time he sees a policeman he feels a rush of panic. He clicks his teeth. His nerves are shot.

He finds a small public garden next to a railway bridge. In one half of the enclosure, a group of men play boule. In the other, children run around. He sits here for a while, and again thinks of his own kids. 'My children,' he mutters. 'Where are *my* children?'

For a moment, he could be back in Haran al-Awamid, grilling kebabs on the barbecue under the fruit trees on a Friday. He remembers his now destroyed home as it was before the war – quiet and full of greenery. He pictures the public gardens, the three ancient columns at the centre of the town. He imagines the boys running around. He sees serious Osama, who loves space and science; cheeky Mohamed, who loves cameras; and little Milad, who's at the age when he just likes to have fun. And then he thinks of Hayam, so many miles away from him. They grew up together on the same street, and went to the same school. In 2001, he secretly proposed to her even before he had asked her family's permission. This is one of the longest times he's spent away from her, and definitely the furthest distance.

He sends Hayam a message, telling her he's in France. She's confused – she thought he might be in Germany by now – and replies with a sad-faced emoticon. He regrets telling her, since her angst makes him more stressed himself. Three hours to go.

Hashem moves on. He thinks of buying a better phone-card, one that'll work across Europe. He tries one shop, then a second, then a third – but no one has something like that. He gives up. He finds a busier part of town, where all the tourists are. Here he gives in, and has a coffee at a cafe. An evening chill is setting in, and he shivers. He watches the trams bustle to and fro along the street before him, and for a moment he wishes he could board one. Tourists stroll past.

It's funny to see people here on holiday, for the beach and the sun, at a time when he's fleeing for a safer life. Two hours to go.

He wanders into a church and takes a pew halfway towards the altar. Somewhere to sit down again. At the sides of the church, under the stained-glass windows, people pay a few euros to light a candle. The place reminds him of a church in Syria – a monastery in Saidnaya that is perched on a craggy hilltop. Hashem's a Muslim but, every once in a while, he would go to Saidnaya to light a candle and enjoy the view. How far away that all seems.

At 7 p.m., with an hour to go till the train to Paris, Hashem limps back to the station. Three soldiers amble around in circles near the station entrance, giving him pangs of panic. He's destroyed all the sundry tickets and receipts he had from Italy, meaning that if he's caught now he won't be sent back to Italy: there's no proof he was ever there. But, even so, France isn't a place he wants to settle in. His family can't join him here – not for a couple of years at least.

In the newsagent's at the station, he gets a French newspaper, something to make him blend into a crowd. He plumps for *Le Monde*. By coincidence, its journalists have written about Hashem's country today. Or rather they've translated work by *Der Spiegel* – a long report into the origins of Isis. On another page there's a picture of Ségolène Royal. She used to be the partner of the president, right? Hashem knows a bit about European politics.

Le Monde does the trick: the ticket inspector greets him in French on the platform. Hashem nods awkwardly, and hurries to his seat. He eases it back – on these French night trains, he notes with admiration, the leather seats almost fold flat – and tries to sleep. The sun sets, and a couple of hours later the whole carriage is gently snoring. Some of them are backpackers who snooze with jackets placed over their faces; others are elderly tourists from Italy who've come prepared with eye masks. Hashem is the exception. The tension keeps him wide awake all night. All he can think of is the German border.

Hashem looks out of the window, and he realises he still hasn't parted ways with the sea. There's the coast, its beaches and its waves. The sight of it all sickens him, but he has to endure it while the train follows the seafront round to Marseilles. Only then does it leave the coast. Finally it snakes slowly up through France, going first from east to west, and then west to east, turning back on itself like the winding queue for an airport check-in desk. Every few minutes it stops at some new, half-lit platform. Or at least, that's what it seems like to Hashem, who's awake for every one, listening to the creak of the seats, and the occasional cough or sneeze from a stirring passenger. He needs a smoke, but he can't while he's on the train, and he's too scared to hop off for a quick cigarette on a provincial platform.

Dawn finally comes, revealing flatter countryside just south of Paris. A short while later, nearly twelve hours after it left Nice, the train eventually arrives in the capital itself at twenty to eight on the morning of Monday, 27 April. It's the twelfth morning since Egypt. A short metro ride takes him from Gare d'Austerlitz to Gare de l'Est, and now he's one train journey from Germany. In fact, he could be in Sweden by the early hours of tomorrow. In Paris he can buy tickets to Hamburg, via Frankfurt. From Hamburg, another series of trains will bring him to Copenhagen. And from Copenhagen, it's just a half-hour hop across the Øresund Bridge to Sweden.

But, first, he has an hour to kill in Gare de l'Est. It's funny to be flitting through some of Europe's finest cities, but to see them only through their stations. Gare de l'Est isn't the biggest of them, but to Hashem it still feels vast – more of an airport than a station. 'Who are all these people?' he wonders at the commuters, marching past him into the city. 'They're all going to work, these people?' They seem far more frenzied than he ever was during his morning commute in Syria, listening to Fairouz on his car stereo.

He goes to the ticket office to buy a ticket to Hamburg. The price is over €250. Hashem blinks – 250? Did he hear that right? That's a third of what he might have paid to get from Milan to Copenhagen by car. But then he shrugs. By now, he has no other choice.

Waiting for the train, Hashem shivers in the cold – partly because of the temperature, but also because he hasn't slept or eaten since yesterday lunchtime. He goes to a little cafe beside the platforms. He looks at the sandwiches on display. Which of them are halal? That one? No, he realises. It's got pork in it.

Just after nine he boards the train to Frankfurt. Two hours twenty minutes to the border, and the anxiety rises in him once again. He doesn't want to stop in Germany, but if he can at least get there he'll eventually be reunited with his family. And that's what matters.

Hayam messages him. Where are you now? Hashem doesn't answer – not yet. He doesn't want to jinx it.

At 9.10 a.m. the train to Frankfurt eases out of Paris. Europe's railways never stop impressing him. This one has carriages with two floors, and huge seats that seem more like armchairs than anything Hashem's used to on a train.

He goes for a shave while he still has time. He bought a little razor in Gare de l'Est – or rather, he bought a whole packet of them because he couldn't find a single one for sale on its own. But it's worth the expense. If a policeman does get on in Saarbrücken, the first town in Germany, Hashem knows that appearances matter.

He returns from the bathroom, and spots a copy of *Charlie Hebdo* lying on the table. He picks it up. The cover cartoon shows something like Kate Winslet rising out of a boat of migrants. 'Un *Titanic* par semaine,' it says. 'A *Titanic* every week.' Hashem doesn't quite get it. Who on earth is that woman? But he smiles, regardless. It's about refugees like him.

At 11.30 the train scuds over the German border, and slows down as it approaches Saarbrücken. Another moment of reckoning awaits. Hashem busies himself with hiding in plain sight. He dusts off his dandruff, plugs in some head-phones, and buries himself in a copy of the *Süddeutsche Zeitung* that he bought in Paris. He can't read a word of it, but he hopes no one will test him.

The train crosses a bridge over a river that cuts through a lush bit of greenery. It's a pretty sight, and Hashem moment-arily loses himself. 'Manzar gameel,' he says loudly, over the top of the music blaring in his ears. 'Lovely view.'

The whole carriage flinches. A few people turn and stare. And then the train stops in Saarbrücken.

7

Between the Woods and the Water

The beginnings of the Balkan route

*Greece, Turkey, Macedonia, Serbia and Hungary,
early summer 2015*

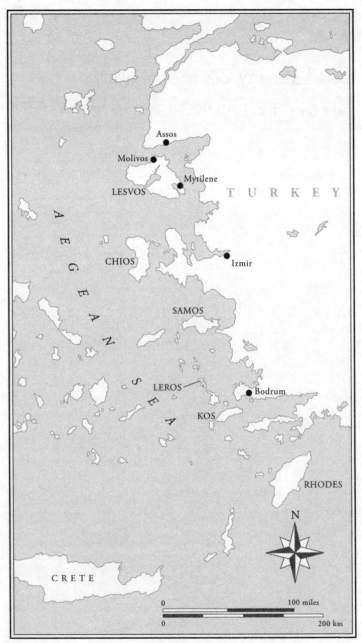

Turkish West Coast

1 Hashem and his wife, Hayam, and three children, Milad, Mohamed and Osama.

2 The contents of Hashem's backpack (clockwise from top left): his diary, in which he hoped to record his sea journey; Syrian ID cards, and a print-out of the Human Rights Watch report into the destruction of his home town; Syrian passport; life jacket; family documentation; wheel of cheese, to last him the duration of the boat journey; sea-sickness tablets; baseball cap, to keep his skin from burning on deck. Not shown: the key to his destroyed home in Syria.

3 Migrants leave the city of Agadez ahead of the treacherous trip across the Sahara – a journey many see as even deadlier than the sea.

4 The 'road' through the Sahara. It's no more than a few ruts in the sand – meaning that smugglers and their passengers often get lost, break down, and die of thirst.

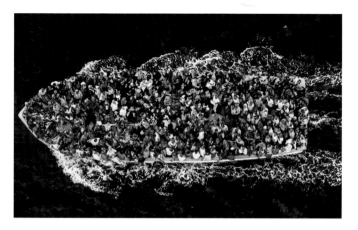

5 A refugee boat from Libya.

6 A boat in trouble – refugees land on the Greek coast.

7 Refugees try to reach the Greek coast in a dangerously packed dinghy.

8 A smuggler advertises his services on Facebook. His boats almost certainly don't look like this one.

9 A shopfront, Izmir, Turkey. Retailers swapped their usual stock for life jackets. Many were fake.

10 Captain Leopoldo Manna, a senior Italian coastguard, coordinates rescue operations near Libya from a control room in suburban Rome.

11 Eritrean refugees relax on the deck of the Médecins Sans Frontières boat, the *Bourbon Argos*, after being rescued off the Libyan coast hours earlier.

12 MSF aid workers prepare to rescue a stricken refugee boat off the coast of Libya.

13 The Greece–Macedonia border – a father carries his child through the Balkans.

14 Hungarian police allow a refugee family to cross the country's border.

15 Scared that her unborn baby might be dead, Fattemah (with Nasser and Hammouda) walks towards Macedonia through the Balkans.

16 Eric Kempson, a volunteer on Lesvos, scans the distant Turkish coastline for refugee boats.

17 Hans Breuer, Austria's last wandering shepherd, drove several refugee families to safety during the summer of 2015.

18, 19 Hashem hides behind a copy of *Süddeutsche Zeitung*, shortly before crossing the French-German border, and celebrates moments after crossing into Sweden.

20 Hashem's diary of his journey and a passage written on the boat.

Squinting across the water, Eric Kempson has spotted something. He stands high on a cliff, gazing over the six-mile strait between the Greek island of Lesvos, where he lives, and the Turkish mainland, which looms in the distance. 'See that?' he says, handing me the binoculars. I stare into them, but I can't see much. It's just before 6 a.m. one morning in June 2015, and the sun is coming up. A grapefruit blur rises from behind the dark Turkish cliffs in the distance, and the sky has begun to brighten. But the sea still looks murky, especially on the Turkish side, and all I can really make out is a black speck, perhaps two or three miles away.

Eric, however, is a connoisseur of such specks. Every morning now, he gets up before dawn with his wife Philippa, and together they go to watch for them. Sometimes there are five or six specks on this stretch of the water. This morning, there's just this one – and Eric knows all too well what it is. 'That's a boat of refugees,' he says, taking back the binoculars, 'and it'll arrive on this side in about fifteen minutes.'

It seems like too optimistic an ETA for something we can't even see properly. And yet, as two other correspondents and I hurtle around the winding coastline in a rented car, bent on meeting the boat's passengers as they land in Europe, it turns out that Eric's judged it just right. The speck makes quick progress, and within ten minutes it's morphed into an inflatable dinghy. From the windows of the car, we can see the outline of perhaps fifty passengers packed tightly inside the boat's black rubber rim. And they can see us. As their boat reaches the final stretch, our car bumps down the road that runs along the cliff above them – and a few of them begin to wave. Their faces begin to gain definition, and what was previously just a speck and then a silhouette now changes again into a tangle of humans and bright orange life jackets.

We lose sight of them again as we rush from the car and scramble down a steep bit of scree to the shore. By the time we reach the bottom they've already landed. Some of them are ripping off their life jackets and throwing them on the narrow strip of sand. One man stabs holes in the boat's tubing, causing it to deflate, and then throws his knife into the water. There's a rumour among the refugees that if their boats are still seaworthy the Greeks will send them back. Right now they have a more pressing concern: how to leave thisbeach. It's an unfortunate place to land. Ahead of them, the scree blocks their path. To the sides, the beach doesn't seem to go anywhere. Small groups try to see where it leads, but they quickly return. With no other exit, they start to scramble up the rocks, grabbing the branches of nearby bushes, and heaving themselves up. Occasionally, they tread on loose pebbles, and a stone or two tumbles down the slope behind them.

Unusually, this group contains just one Syrian family. The majority of those coming from Turkey to Greece in 2015 are Syrians. But most of the passengers on this boat are Afghans, and the rest hail from Somalia, ripped apart by civil war, and Pakistan, where over a million people have been displaced by insurgencies in the north of the country. Collectively, they are a bizarre sight – a mixture of the surprising and the banal. Some must have lost their clothes in the recent past, and have had to make do with baggy items that are almost comically too big for them. One child wears a huge suit jacket, with sleeves that hang down to his ankles. But some of the Afghan teenagers are dressed as if they're off to meet friends at the mall, wearing fake Ray-Bans and skinny denim breeches. One old man has a flat cap on his head, an old brown jacket over his shoulders, and a staff in his hand. As he reaches the top of the scree, and then limps down the country lane at the top, he could be an elderly French farmer on an afternoon ramble in Provence.

I'd expected these moments to feel like a watershed for these travellers, the moment they reached the comparative safety of the European Union. Instead, most of them don't even stop, let alone celebrate. At the top of the slope one or two of the natty teenagers take selfies. But the majority simply pause to check if they've still got any Turkish reception on their phones; if they do, they can decipher their location on Google Maps. When they realise they don't, they shrug, put their children on their shoulders, pick a direction, and start walking down the lane. Many of them don't even know what island they're on, but they know they've got to keep walking. Reaching Greece is not quite a footnote in their quest. But it isn't the panacea I'd previously imagined it would be.

True, they've all come a long way to get here. Many of the Afghans will have escaped areas controlled by the Taliban and Isis, walked for days over the border to Iran, then made a similar trek into Turkey, before a long coach ride to the western

Turkish coast. But, even now, they still have miles to go before they sleep. First they've got to walk forty miles to the main port at Lesvos – the government refuses to provide transport. Then there's the hike through northern Greece to Macedonia. And then another one through Macedonia to Serbia and Hungary. Finally, they'll face a risky car ride or train journey through the more hospitable countries of northern Europe beyond. 'Me, Sweden!' grins an Afghan called Navid, before turning on his heels, and marching down the lane.

The last family up the slope is the Syrian one, a family of six from the countryside outside Damascus. They left Syria for Lebanon two months ago, and Lebanon for Turkey two days ago. They're all still wearing their life jackets, and the mum is wearing incongruously chunky heels. Her elegant grey overcoat is soaked from the sea. The last thing they want to do is stop and talk: they're tired, they've been up all night, and they have relatives still in danger back home. Maher, the dad, simply hoists his youngest child on his back, holds two of the others by the hand, and off they march into the long shadows of the Greek sunrise.

Not for the last time, I'm reminded of the classical heroes I used to read about at school. This sight in particular summons up images of Aeneas, the Trojan who fled a burning Troy, voyaged around the Mediterranean for years, before eventually settling in Italy and starting the dynasty that would eventually build the Roman empire. As Aeneas leaves Troy, he has a lion's pelt on his back, his dad Anchises on his shoulders, and his little son Iulus tugging on his hand. Tall, upright and stoic, Maher looks like Aeneas today. Except that instead of lion's fur, Maher wears a plastic life jacket. And instead of just one child, Maher has four. Toddling behind him, one of them happily blows into his deflating armband. It's a moment of incongruous innocence. Wrapped in concentration, the little boy puffs into the shoot of the armband, only for a whoosh of air to rush out again a second later. I glance at my colleague Sima Diab, a Syrian photo-journalist who used to run a centre for Syrian refugees in Cairo. She lowers her lens to reveal a pair of tear-stained cheeks.

It is still June, so the situation is viewed in the media as a footnote to the bigger phenomenon off the coast of Libya. Yet even now it is clear that this sliver of sea between Turkey and the Greek islands will soon become the new epicentre of Europe's migration crisis. The previous year, in 2014, roughly 40,000 people moved from Turkey to Greece. By this point in 2015, twice that number have already made the same journey, more than two-thirds of them Syrians (and we're not even into the peak months of July, August, September and October, when the level grew to more than 750,000). The flow of people leaving Libya for Italy is at the same record level as last year. But it's about to be overtaken exponentially by the flow from Turkey to Greece. The Syrians have discovered the Aegean.

Lesvos, the island most affected by the crisis, has become the Greek Lampedusa. Even by this early point in the summer, over 1000 refugees arrive here daily, and on its beaches sunloungers lie cheek by jowl with abandoned life jackets. The Greek authorities, already struggling to deal with an economic crisis, cannot cope with the influx. So with many of the boats arriving just metres from their front door, the Kempsons try to fill the humanitarian vacuum.

Eric is an unexpected authority on Aegean smuggling networks. He's originally from Windsor, and spent his first life looking after baboons and big cats. Then he and Philippa – a former nurse – moved to the north coast of Lesvos sixteen years ago, and began renting a plot of land a hundred metres from the shore. Eric turns sixty this summer, and has a mane of long straight hair that is part 1980s rocker, part 1970s mullet. A talented craftsman, he pays the rent by selling an eccentric range of homemade wooden carvings – New-Agey bracelets, ornate grottos, macabre sculptures that nod to Munch's *Scream*. From a set of speakers in the shop next to his house he plays music by his only child, fifteen-year-old Eleni. Out in his garden, beyond the tomato patch and the olive grove, he's laid out a wide circle of stones for meditation.

I first encounter Eric on his YouTube channel. In the early weeks of the summer, it is the only regular source of news about what's happening on the north coast of Lesvos. Undeterred by his triple- or sometimes double-digit viewing figures, Eric churns out video diaries about his experiences of the refugee crisis, often more than once a day. The videos usually have slightly oblique titles, punctuated by several exclamation marks. 'Pampers expert!!', 'Octopus!!!' and 'If Only They Knew!!' are all representative of the genre. Sometimes, the contents of the videos are also a little inscrutable. Early on in the summer, Eric occasionally uses the surreal technique of pointing the camera at an obscure bit of shrubbery, and then holding the essentially abstract shot for the duration of the video. Something about this style reminds me of the opening shot of Michael Haneke's *Hidden*, where the director aims his camera at an almost static street scene, and then just leaves it rolling. The techniques diverge, however, when Eric begins talking over his videos in his distinctly un-Haneke-like burr, and recounts the day's events. At one point he starts to cry as he remembers how a boat sank before his eyes.

Migrants have landed in dribs and drabs in this area for as long as the Kempsons have lived here – but never in such high numbers, and never so many women and children. 'So a few months ago we loaded up the car and started helping them,' Eric explains when we meet. 'When you see two-week-old children, people with cut feet and people who haven't eaten for days – you can't do nothing.'

In the absence of any aid agencies or government assistance, the couple have become the area's first responders. Every day they wake before sunrise to be ready for the dawn landings, and I join them for two days in June. Their routine starts on top of a nearby hill, from where they can scan the opposite shore for any departures. Eric soon works out the inlets from where the boats emerge on the Turkish side, and where they generally end up on the Greek side. If all goes to plan two black inflatables will set out just before dawn, mostly full of Afghans. As the morning goes on, they'll be followed by three grey boats, usually full of Syrians. The fifth and last boat is the one that tends to be full of women and children – and this is the one that the Kempsons aim to help first. Once they've identified it, they scoot down to the likely landing point, and hand out water, dry clothes and food to the most vulnerable arrivals. And there are a lot of them: pregnant women, paralysed people in wheelchairs, a man with burn wounds so recent that flesh was 'hanging off his hands', Eric says. 'I hadn't cried in twenty years, and I am a hard bastard. But I've cried so much in the last four months.'

Initial reporting on the island's crisis centred on how the wave of migrants, sharing beaches with wealthy holiday-makers, had incensed foreigners and residents alike. There is certainly an awkward juxtaposition. On one nearby beach, tourists sunbathe metres from an Angry Birds armband left on the sand by an infant refugee. And there are certainly attempts to stoke tensions. A right-wing website reports, erroneously of course, that Muslim migrants are shitting in Christian churches. Eric's been personally targeted for his work. Neighbours sometimes accost him on the beach, worried that Eric's charity is what's drawing the refugees to Lesvos. While we speak in his workshop, an unknown caller breathes silently down his phone, and Eric concludes that this is someone else trying to intimidate him. Elsewhere in the Greek islands, other activists have been physically attacked, and local politicians are fanning the flames. The mayor of one famous island – Kos – says the Greek state shouldn't help migrants with anything, not even a cup of water. For most of the summer, the law is to some extent on his side. The government won't provide transport for migrants walking between the landing beaches and the registration centres, leaving them to traipse the forty miles in the heat. For now, it's also illegal for sympathetic Greeks to drive them instead. Three Greeks are arrested for giving lifts, while Eric himself gets a warning from a local policeman, who tells him to stop helping migrants on the beaches, lest he be prosecuted for people smuggling. In protest at the legislation, forty-one drivers organise a convoy from Molyvos to the island's capital, Mytilene, each car carrying a family of refugees in full violation of the law.* Sure it's illegal, says one of the drivers, who also runs her own camp for refugees in the south of the island. 'But on the other hand we cannot stay watching hundreds of people with their children – walking, lying in the streets – and let them die there under the sun. It's impossible. That's also a crime, to let someone die in the street.'

The Kempsons are the first link in a chain of volunteers who are determined not to let that happen. After they greet and count the day's arrivals on the beaches, Eric calls an Australian who runs a restaurant in Molyvos, the nearest village. With no governmental reception centre in this part of the island, Melanie McRostie has turned a slip of land behind her well-known quayside restaurant – the Captain's Table – into a makeshift migrant campsite. As soon as Kempson sends her the day's head count, McRostie's kitchen team start preparing meals for the island's newest guests, largely using food and supplies donated by locals and tourists alike. In fact, it's hard to find the antipathy I'd read about in the British tabloids. A few weeks earlier, the *Daily Mail* had run a piece about British holidaymakers, distressed at being watched by refugees as they ate their lunch. But the tourists I meet on Lesvos are either oblivious to what's going on, or they want to help. There's the German nurse who abandoned her sunbathing to help out at McRostie's migrant campsite. The British couple who fly in to assist the Kempsons. And the Belgian lab technician who spends his

* This law is rescinded later in 2015.

days driving Syrian families to the port in the south of the island, so that they don't have to walk the forty miles in the forty-degree heat. 'In the beginning I was worried – I thought should I do this or not?' he says. 'But when you pass them and see the women and children, you think, yes, I should. I must do something.'

I try to seek out the island's xenophobes. I make a beeline for the owner of a hot spring, who I've been assured will have some unpleasant arguments to make. But she says all the right things. I chat to the manager of a hotel whose beach is strewn with migrant boats. She, too, expresses warmth and sympathy. McRostie's neighbour is grumpy: he fears the migrants camped behind her restaurant will deter punters from eating at his new kebab shop. But in general, one pharmacist explains, there is a lot of sympathy and even empathy here for the refugees. After all, he says, their fate isn't so different from that of his own parents' generation. Many of Lesvos's current residents, as well as those on the surrounding islands, are descendants of Greeks who fled Asia Minor in similarly traumatic circumstances in 1922. 'We're not angry and we're not scared,' the pharmacist tells me. 'Our grandfathers were forced out of Turkey themselves.'

Back on the beaches, I find a Greek man in a tracksuit solemnly cutting up the rubber boats, dragging the debris to his pick-up truck. A scavenger? Perhaps he's one of the vulture-like locals people whisper about, who creep up and down the shores, gather the engines and debris from abandoned migrant boats, and then sell them on to scrapyards. But no: 'I'm the village president,' reveals Thanassis Andreotis, who does his bit by keeping the beaches tidy. This year, he sighs, it's turned from a weekly to a daily task. Aha, I think. Perhaps he's annoyed about the extra hassle? Again, no: Andreotis is fairly sympathetic to the island's new arrivals. 'They're hunted by their government and they're running everywhere from horrible things,' Andreotis concludes with sympathy, hauling the latest slice of inflatable up from the shore. A former policeman, Andreotis didn't imagine he'd spend his retirement like this. Nor did he expect to become an expert on all three of the Dublin conventions. But such is life in northern Lesvos in 2015.

How and why did this happen? It's a question that I'm asked increasingly as 2015 wears on, and the answer lies mainly in Syria. Refugees from other countries, not least Afghanistan and Iraq, do form a sizeable part of the flow, particularly once winter arrives. In their wake there is a far smaller percentage of so-called economic migrants from places including Bangladesh, Morocco and Senegal – and their numbers seem to rise once it becomes clear what a free-for-all this route is. Nevertheless, according to the UN, 66 per cent of the arrivals in Greece in the first ten months of 2015 are Syrians. Even if there are concerns about the accuracy of the UN's data (which I'll come to later), it's clear that Syrians are the people who first led the surge. In one sense, that's strange. The Syrian war has raged since 2011, and yet this drastic spike in arrivals to Europe is occurring only four years later. Why now, nearly half a decade on? And why here in Greece, rather than Italy?

There's no exhaustive study on this, but in conversations with Syrians throughout 2015 a few themes repeatedly crop up. The first is that the war in Syria shows no signs of ending – and even if it does within a few years, the post-war country that emerges from the ruins will likely be a cantonised one, ripe for bitter recriminations. Faced with this prospect, Syrians have quite naturally realised they need to move to find long-term safety. The threat of Isis dominates the Western media, and certainly its rise is one reason why many Syrians have fled their homes. But Isis mostly control Syria's unpopulated deserts. In the more populous areas run by more moderate rebel groups, the threat of Assad's regular barrel bombs and Russian airstrikes are a much more pressing danger. In regions where the fighting and airstrikes haven't yet become a daily fact of life, residents have the quite reasonable expectation that their homes won't remain un-touched for long. In Assad's own strongholds, the fear of compulsory conscription is forcing out the many people who don't want to fight for the dictator's depraved army – while rebel rockets are also a regular danger. For the first two or three years of the war, most believed they could wait all this out, with many taking shelter in the houses of relatives and friends. But no longer. If your children haven't been to school in several years, and if your home was destroyed in 2012, but it's still not safe to return to rebuild it, it's time for you to leave.

The year 2015 also marked the point when it became both easier and harder to leave in the first place. In 2014, when 'only' 125,000 Syrians claimed asylum in the EU,[1] the biggest proportion of them came through Libya. By 2015, it was increasingly difficult to get there. By now, Libya's eastern and western neighbours – Algeria and Egypt – had banned Syrians from entry, meaning that it was much harder for Syrians to use both latter countries as an access point for the former. The war in Libya also made the country less appealing as a springboard, as did smugglers' brutal treatment of their customers, the dangerous nature of their methods at sea, and the expense of getting to Libya in the first place.

Simultaneously, the word spread about an easier and cheaper route between Turkey and the Balkans. Migrants have for decades trodden this path, sailing boats between Izmir and the Greek islands, or walking over the land borders with Bulgaria and Greece. In recent years, the EU has strengthened its defences along the land borders, helping the Bulgarians and Greeks to build fences, and sending more border guards to patrol them. But Turkey's maritime border with Greece is harder to police, and some time in the second half of 2014, a bunch of Syrians discovered that it was comparatively easy to cross. Instead of trekking to Libya, and then risking the 187 miles to Italy, you could instead cross Syria's border with Turkey, reach the Turkish coast within a day, and be on an inflatable boat chugging towards a Greek island within another. You'd still have the Balkans to march through – but, with GPS on your phone, this was now something you could do on your own, without the help of smugglers. And, as more and more people opted for such a tactic, the more information each of them published on social media, and the more widely the route became known. Once the first few trailblazers had successfully navigated it, they wrote down their experiences and tips on Facebook, and set up WhatsApp groups that allowed anyone to find out how to follow in their footsteps.

By April 2015, these pages were all over Facebook. The most detailed one I found at that time – 'The Safe and Free Route to Asylum for Syrians' – already had several thousand members. Its founder explained in precise steps how any refugee could get from Athens to Hungary, setting out everything from how to buy tickets, and how much to pay for them, to what people should wear ('nice clothes, hair gel, and deodorant'), and what they should carry in their backpacks ('an international SIM card, creams for allergies, 100 per cent cotton underwear'). Until the Hungarians slammed shut their border in mid-September, the methods described by this anonymous guide are almost exactly the one that hundreds of thousands would subsequently use during the course of 2015. I would later follow much of it, and it was uncanny to tread a route that I recognised instantly from the Facebook description. When leaving Greece for Macedonia, the page advises, 'Leave from behind the Hara hotel in the early hours of the morning, open your GPS and walk. You'll find the river. Cross the bridge across the river, fast. Then walk a little bit further, and you'll find a road to the right which runs parallel to the train line. Keep walking on this sandy path, about a hundred metres from the main road. After one hour of walking you will reach the village of Gevgelija [in Macedonia].' Barring a couple of midsummer changes to the way people crossed the Macedonian border, this turned out to be an extraordinarily accurate set of directions. At a time when traditional travel guides seem increasingly irrelevant, I'd stumbled across a *Baedeker* for the refugee era.

There was one passage I found particularly telling. In the preamble to the guide, the author offers some advice to the undecided traveller – and some clues to why so many people suddenly tried to reach Europe in 2015. 'You'll be asking yourself: should I do it alone, or seek a smuggler?' the author writes. 'Everyone's asking himself this same question. The most important thing to know is that not every way is secure, and not everyone who dealt with a smuggler reached their intended destination. Study the reasons and then trust in god . . . I advise you to do more by yourself.' These are wise words – and ones that on the whole seem to have been heeded. In 2015 Syrians realised they didn't have to get to Libya to reach Europe, and didn't have to rely more than fleetingly on the services of a smuggler. They could just go it alone, and go now – thanks, in large part, to Facebook pages like this one.

There were nevertheless several other factors. The first was the cost. The longer the Syrian war lasts, the larger the group of people with the money to get to Europe. Two years ago, most people who wanted to leave hadn't saved up enough. Two years on, more of them finally have the funds – borrowed from friends, or saved from their salaries. They also don't have to pay as much. To cross the Aegean, you need just $1000 – less than half the cost of a Syrian's seat on a boat from Libya. This allows more people to make the trips – and to take more relatives with them. In previous years, many Syrian fathers went to Europe alone, in order to save money, and in the hope that they could then apply to be re-unified with their families once they won asylum in Europe. Now a higher number of fathers can afford to travel with their families in the first place. And they see more incentive in doing so: word has spread that the family reunification procedure takes over a year. Some fathers would rather expose their children to the comparatively few dangers of the Aegean than abandon them for such a long period of time.

But why Europe? Why couldn't they stay in the Middle East? The answer is that many of them had already tried it. Around 4 million had tried to settle in the Middle East. The biggest proportion were in Turkey – nearly 2 million. As I've already noted, nearly 1.2 million were in Lebanon, meaning that a staggering 20 per cent of Lebanese residents were Syrian refugees. Six hundred thousand reached Jordan – a tenth of the total population. And around 140,000 registered in Egypt, with perhaps double that total thought to be living under the radar. Faced with such an extraordinarily high influx, the refugees' new hosts couldn't cope, and left their guests almost entirely reliant on hand-outs from the UN. To make matters worse, even these hand-outs quickly began to diminish. In the winter of 2014 the UN began to cut its food subsidies for many Syrian families seeking refuge in the Middle East, after a funding shortfall of 40 per cent. Refugees had even less reason to wait out the war in the region. And even if the UN was still running its subsidies system at full throttle, it's arguable that it wouldn't have made much difference. In the four Middle Eastern countries that are bearing the brunt of the crisis, most Syrians are either by law or in practice denied the right to work,* and restricted from accessing public hospitals and schools. Most countries in the region now ban Syrians from entry. So, in the long term, few Syrians

* Turkey eventually let Syrians apply for work permits in January 2016 – but by then the horse had already bolted.

have the chance of building a new life in the Middle East – and as a result many will now consider leaving, regardless of whether or not the UN has money for hand-outs.

It's a state of affairs that makes a mockery of the UK's strategy for dealing with the refugee crisis. The British prime minister, David Cameron, often implies that the UK shouldn't have to welcome significant numbers of Syrian refugees because Britain is one of the few countries to donate its fair share to Syrian refugee camps in Jordan and Lebanon.[2] This is disingenuous. First, only a fifth of refugees in those countries actually live in the camps.[3] Second, the aid does so little to improve the long-term prospects of those who've made it inside, and as a result it's of limited use. What aid offers refugees is a short-term fix. But, by this point in the war, they're after a long-term future. So even if you think it's generous of Britain to donate this money (and I don't; I think it's a figleaf that allows British politicians to avoid doing something more effective), it's hard to pretend that it's a successful strategy. If Syrians saw the aid as the answer to their problems, they wouldn't have begun gathering in such high numbers on the shores of Turkey in the summer of 2015.

'Want a life jacket?' I'm strolling down one of the main drags in Izmir, a port halfway down Turkey's western shoreline, and every third or fourth shop assistant has a deal to offer me. 'Original Yamaha,' shouts a salesman. 'Come in and try one.' As is common on the migrant trail, he has mistaken me and my backpack for a refugee.

Izmir is Turkey's smuggling capital, and no one is really bothering to hide it. On this road, street vendors sell party balloons for refugees – not to celebrate with, but to act as a watertight case during the sea crossing. (You stuff your phone inside them, and then tie shut the opening.) In some of the boat shops you can't turn without bumping into another pile of rubber inflatables. On one of the days I visit, there are sixteen stacked in beige-brown boxes on the floor of one shop, all numbered with the same inscrutable code, SK-800PLY, and all newly delivered from China. And if the shopkeeper's maths is right, all of them will be discarded on a Greek beach within a couple of days. For this is one of the places where you can buy the boats that take refugees to Europe – and where they are sold at a rate of nearly a dozen a day.

Perhaps a third of the shops on the street are now selling life jackets to refugees, at least as a sideline. A kebab shop has a dozen for sale, including little ones for children, and there are even a couple in a store that specialises in police uniforms. But it's the clothes shops that are really cashing in. Some have relegated their jeans and shirts to the basement, and are now pushing life jackets as their main product. In the shop windows, the mannequins now model garish orange life vests, instead of suits and dresses. Inside, the salesmen fuss over prospective customers as if they're about to buy their first tuxedo. They measure and adjust the life jackets as if they're suits for a wedding, not protection for your sea cross-ing. I almost find it funny – until I look at the mannequins in the children's section, which are also dressed in Yamahas, and the business seems more macabre. Later I discover that some of the cheaper life jackets are filled with foam, which absorbs water rather than keeping you afloat. Suddenly it seems a very dark business indeed.

The largest proportion of boats for Greece leave from the area that surrounds Izmir and land on Chios, Samos or Lesvos. Others start from Bodrum, a smaller resort town to the south, best known in Europe for its hotels and beaches. From there the smugglers drop you to the Greek islands of Kos, Leros and Kalymnos (the choice is left to the smuggler rather than the passenger).

Izmir is no stranger to humanitarian catastrophes. Back in 1922, when the city was known as Smyrna, it was the site of one of the worst events of the Greco-Turkish war, a conflict that ended with the mass exodus of Greeks from Asia. Hundreds of thousands of Greek residents were forced from the Greek-majority city, or died in it when Turkish soldiers set fire to the historic centre, creating an inferno that couldn't be extinguished for a week. Thousands of refugees fled to the city's harbour, and were left stranded on the quay, hemmed in by the sea in front of them and the Turks behind them. American and British boats waited in the harbour, but were initially unable to intervene, supposedly for fear of causing a stampede.

Over eighty years later, it is easier for a refugee to leave the city – far easier. The warren of streets that surrounds Basmane Square is full of brokers sidling up to scared Syrians, easily identifiable by their backpacks and apprehension, and offering them trips to Greece. Once a deal is struck, they're hustled into shabby hotels that the smugglers often block-book for this purpose. Late at night, the passengers gather nearby, where the smugglers arrange for trucks and buses to drive them for a few hours through the darkness to the relevant shore. Sometimes this is a hellish trip that sees people squashed like cattle inside what in fact used to be cattle trucks. Sometimes the process is far less arduous: they just take public transport.

To highlight the ease with which the process works, one smuggler, twiddling a toothpick between his teeth, takes me for a stroll, and points out a bland white building that stands opposite one of the main gathering points. That's the city's police headquarters, he grins, eager to highlight how Turkey does little to stop its Syrian guests from leaving. A government spokesman later denies this, pointing out that police have arrested over 80,000 migrants in 2015. But the blatant nature of what goes on in the smugglers' quarter in Izmir – which is squeezed between the police directorate to the west, and another police station a few hundred metres to the east – suggests the Turkish government has not been as proactive as it could have been in stopping it.

Different smugglers described different working practices, but each network operates in broadly the same way. There are the brokers, like Abu Khalil, whose job it is to find the forty or fifty passengers to fill each boat, and keep them entertained in the hotels until it's time to go. Then there are the drivers who bring them to the shore, and the five workmen who deliver the rubber boats and engines, and assemble them at the departure points. If the network smuggles mainly Syrian passengers, then the network will likely be staffed by Syrians, usually working for a Syrian boss. But that man will also need Turkish partners – the landowners who control the beaches that the boats leave from. Typically, these landowners will work with several networks, taking a significant cut of the latter's profits, since their complicity is so crucial to the smugglers' success.

'You can't just leave from any place, so I would say the Turkish guy is the major player in the process,' argues one smuggler. 'Without him, the trips would not take place.'

The scale and tragedy of the trade are best summarised to me by a chance encounter in Izmir, one afternoon in the summer of 2015. Abdulsalam, my Syrian colleague and translator, strolls beside me as we wander down a busy street not far from Basmane Square. We've just turned down umpteen offers to buy a life jacket, when Abdulsalam spots someone he thinks he knows. Is that Mohamad? A guy he used to play football with in northern Syria before the war started? From the other side of the wide pavement, squinting through a crowd of strangers, Mohamad is wondering the same thing. They both grin, approach each other, and embrace happily. They haven't seen each other since Syria – and yet here they are, meeting once again in a crowded street in Turkey. They look as though they're from slightly different generations. Abdulsalam seems older and tired. Fresh-faced Mohamad could still be a teenager, his short hair gelled into spikes. But in fact they're roughly the same age – in their mid-twenties – and were once close friends. They try to recap the last few years in a few seconds, there and then on the pavement. Abdulsalam explains what he's been up to – working with aid organisations, and also people like me. Mohamad says he used to be an electrician.

And what about now? He seems well dressed.

'Oh, you know,' says Mohamad. 'I'm working here.'

In Izmir?

Mohamad looks sheepish. 'Yeah. I'm working *here*.'

There is a pause, and then an admission.

'I'm a smuggler.'

It's both a sobering and a telling moment. Here are two young friends, former teammates, forced apart by a war. The first of them is now paid to interview smugglers. The other is one himself. What are the chances of that? Not high – but not too low either. With no legal employment available to most Syrians, smuggling is one of the few trades that provides a Syrian in Turkey with a steady income. It's certainly the only reason both men have come here to Izmir today. Otherwise they'd probably both be in Europe themselves.

I've spoken to several smugglers in Izmir, but none has been too lucid on the economics and mechanics of their trade. But Mohamad has some time on his hands, so we sit down in a cafe next to one of the life-jacket shops that formerly sold clothes, and talk about the business over a ball-shaped chocolate cake called a çikotop.

Mohamad is living well. He's getting married next month – an expensive undertaking that most young Syrians can't afford in this environment. And that's all thanks to his family's smuggling business.

Mohamad set out his accounts like this: in peak season, a boat of forty passengers paying $1,200 brings in a turnover of $48,000. The brokers take up to $300 of each payment – which leaves at least $36,000 for the rest of the group. The costs of boats and outboard engines fluctuate, but at the peak of the year the most expensive boat costs $8,500, and the engines $4000. The mechanics and the driver collectively need another $4000, while hotel rooms for the refugees collectively cost around $500 a night. The beach owners are paid in different ways, but they often charge a 15 per cent levy on every passenger's fee – meaning they pocket around $6000 per boat. At the end of all this, the lead smuggler is left with at least $13,000. If he undercuts his brokers, and also squeezes on board another ten passengers, he could end up doubling his profit. And so many often do – cramming in fifty passengers rather than the promised forty, and sending them out without enough fuel. Migrants who get cold feet on the beach sometimes report they're forced on board at gunpoint. Of course, Mohamad's firm would never do anything like that.

'Anyone who wants to go will go,' he says. 'Some people try seven or eight times until they make it. We can't stop it. The people risking the journey from Damascus, they're the ones who are making this happen.' And with that, it's time to go. Mohamad insists on paying for my cake, and presents it to me in a little plastic doggie bag.

Refugees tend to receive a much lower standard of customer service. The car journey from Izmir to the coast is sometimes worse than the sea crossing. Passengers can find themselves shoved into the backs of vans that stink of animals, and are sometimes left to stand in an airless vehicle, squashed against their companions, for the duration of the long drive to the departure point. Groggily they emerge in the hours before dawn, and are often made to walk the lengthy final stretch of the journey to the boats. That's if they get there in the first place. Police do stop and arrest some refugees, while others get ambushed by bandits. One smuggler admitted that his gang used to attack its own customers, until they realised it was bad for business. If they do manage to get to the beach, refugees often find they'll be travelling with ten or fifteen more than their brokers promised. But it's too late to say anything. One passenger will be selected to drive the boat (the smugglers tend not to do it themselves until the winter months, when navigation requires more skill). And then they'll be packed into the inflatable, and pushed out to sea. If they're lucky, they'll land on a Greek beach within a couple of hours. If they're not, they'll be intercepted by Turkish coastguards, who seem to do just enough guarding of their coasts to ward off accusations of total negligence. Increasingly, refugee boats are also being hijacked by masked gunmen, who rob the passengers, disable their engines and leave them to drift. Who these men are is not clear. Some people think they're members of the smuggling gangs, keen to squeeze their clients for all they've got. Some activists believe they're Greek nationals, trying to deter people from coming. Some of their boats seem to emerge from the Greek coastline, but no one knows for sure. The Greek government, naturally, denies responsibility.

Sometimes it's the sea itself that gets people. Throughout 2015, well over 500 people drowned trying to cross the Aegean,[4] most notably Alan Kurdi, the Kurdish toddler who washed up face down on a Turkish beach. Compared to the Libyan crossing, the trip across the Aegean is not as traumatic. But it is still a highly dangerous journey in such flimsy boats, and with so many people squeezed into them. All it takes is slightly choppier waters, or a tear to the inflatable, and the boat can capsize or begin to fill with water quite quickly. The fuel also often runs out too soon. Nasima, an airline receptionist from Kabul, who I meet soon after her arrival on Lesvos, says her boat nearly sank earlier that day. The engine stopped, and then the boat began to fill with water. She and her companions threw all their belongings into the sea, to try to make the vessel more buoyant. The women emptied their handbags, and began to use them as buckets, scooping water out of the sinking boat. Nasima had a number for the Greek coastguard, and because she was still within range of Turkish phone masts, they picked up. But they couldn't understand her. So instead she called her family. 'I started to cry,' she remembers. 'I said: I think I'm going to die.' And then a Greek fisherman arrived to rescue them, and a few hours later she's safe and dry behind McRostie's restaurant on the quay at Molyvos. We shake hands. It is, Nasima says, the first time she's touched the hand of a male stranger.

The wall guarding the old stadium in Kos Town, the capital of the island of Kos, is quite hard to climb over. I discover this in the small hours of a warm summer's night as I try to get into the locked stadium from the street outside. There is a tree next to the wall, but the bottom of its trunk is wide and branchless. I place my feet on the wall, and the weight of my torso on the trunk, and try to inch myself upwards in bursts. I'm left with a grazed back and a bark-stained shirt, but I'm no closer to entering the stadium. Eventually I spot a bicycle leaning against the wall, further along the street. Its frame gives me the leg-up I need, and a few seconds later I'm hauling myself over the top and into the stadium. The bike's bent wheels suggest I'm not the first to try this trick.

If anything embodies the tensions on the Greek islands in 2015, and the incompetent European response to them, it's the scene I witness after I ease myself into the stadium's shallow, unsheltered stands. There on the stadium's sandy pitch sit a few hundred Syrians. They've been locked there in the heat of the Greek summer for more than a day, and most of them haven't had access to water or toilets. 'Water,' a Syrian banker had gasped at me a few minutes earlier, just after he was finally allowed to leave, and just before I decided to try to enter. 'All I want is water.' A few bottles had been handed to some of the crowd about twelve hours earlier, he said, glugging on an Evian I had in my bag. 'And even then it was only the people at the front.'

It's a few weeks after my trip to Lesvos, and the situation on the islands is even worse. The Greek government has spent the last few months simultaneously begging the EU to ease up on its austerity measures, and contemplating whether to leave the EU entirely. It has no time or energy to devote to the secondary crisis in its islands, which worsens by the day. The number arriving in places such as Kos and Lesvos is now four times higher than the entire 2014 total, causing a huge logjam. When the flow was slower, refugees would be given temporary documentation within a couple of days – paperwork that would then allow them to change money, buy a ferry ticket to the mainland, and then work their way towards the Macedonian border. Now that several thousand refugees are arriving every day, even this basic system isn't working. Each island has just half-a-dozen officials to process the refugees, meaning that they're sometimes forced to wait for over a week till they can leave the island. This is bad enough on Lesvos, where the island's mayor has at least created some temporary camps for refugees to stay in. They're awful places – dirty, overcrowded, and lacking regular deliveries of food and water. But at least they exist. On Kos, the mayor pretends there's no state facility for people to stay in while they wait for their papers. Instead, the richest migrants pay for hotel rooms. The poorer majority sleep on the streets and beaches, and several hundred take cover in an abandoned hotel called the Captain Elias.

Life, it should be stressed, goes on. The migrants, many of them carrying their life savings, bring their own economic benefits. According to the mayor, tourism doesn't particularly suffer, despite the scare stories. At an open-air cinema next to the stadium, filmgoers incongruously watch Pierce Brosnan's latest offering – and the soundtrack can be heard over the wall. But the mayor, a certain Georgos Kiritsis, still wants to clear the streets – and that's why one day he tells all the Syrians on the island to report to its dilapidated old stadium. Inside, the island's officials promise, they'll finally be given their laissez-passer – and once that's done, they'll be able to leave the island on the next ferry. It is in theory an admirable initiative. In practice, it turns out to be a disaster. 'They said: come, come, come – we will give you papers,' Youssef the banker explains. 'And then they locked us in there like a prison.' Younger men can still haul themselves in and out over the aforementioned wall, using the now-warped bike frame as a ladder. But most can't, and in the midday heat aid workers from MSF say Syrians are fainting at a rate of one every fifteen minutes. Clashes unsurprisingly ensue, and the Syrians are beaten back with shields and truncheons, and sprayed with fire extinguishers. It is a disgraceful scene – people fleeing a war, treated as if they are still in a war zone.

By the time I climb over the wall, the situation is calmer. Hundreds are still locked inside, but the crowd is thinning out, as people are gradually given the documents they were promised. A few hours later, all the Syrians on the island have finally been given their papers, and I leave the stadium with the last of them at about 4 a.m. The catastrophe that had seemed so likely twelve hours earlier, after Mayor Kiritsis ordered everyone inside, has mercifully been avoided.

Still, what on earth had he been thinking? Seeking an answer, I call his office several times on the afternoon that the fiasco unfolds. Naturally, he is always unavailable. So the following day, after I emerge from the stadium with the last few Syrians, I visit his office in person. His secretaries say he is still too busy to meet, so I reassure them that I'm happy to wait until a gap in his schedule opens, and park myself outside the only door to his office. An hour later he is forced to emerge – and bustles straight past, promising to return within half an hour. Another hour passes, and his secretary, presumably in desperation, tells me I can find him at a restaurant near the stadium. I present myself at the restaurant in question and ask the manager where Kiritsis is sitting. 'The mayor?' replies the manager. 'He hasn't been here today.'

Realising I've been hoodwinked, I trudge back towards the stadium with a couple of colleagues. Thinking about lunch, we look into another restaurant – and spot Mayor Kiritsis reclining at a table with two friends, tucking into a large open sandwich. Gotcha. We park ourselves at his table, and the mayor gives in, agreeing to answer a few questions. Or rather, he agrees to dodge them. What was he thinking, I ask, locking 2000 Syrians into a stadium, and leaving them there without water in the heat for a day? Kiritsis plays dumb. Locked in, he replies, inside the stadium? No one had been trapped inside for more than two hours, Kiritsis claims.

'There is no need for them to be stuck in there for more than that,' he deadpans. 'There is a constant flow of people.'

He's good at ducking and diving. Earlier in the summer, he'd agreed with a reporter's suggestion that refugees shouldn't even be given water to drink. Today, he's all warmth and smiles. We have to welcome refugees, he says, because they're going to keep coming. He'd love to do more, but central government just won't help him.

The head of Greece's asylum system, Panagiotis Nikas, can agree only up to a point. True, he tells me later, the financial crisis has left him with just fifty people in his department, instead of a hundred and fifty. But what help he can offer has been consistently rejected by Kiritsis. 'On the island of Kos we don't have the cooperation of the mayor at all,' says Nikas by telephone from Athens. 'He thought that if he doesn't facilitate our operation, the people would go away. But now he sees that if no one cooperates, the situation gets worse.'

Amid the finger-pointing and evasion, it isn't always clear who is in the wrong, and who isn't. There's a reason for that: no one wants to take responsibility. As a result, the Kos stadium fiasco is a worthy symbol of all that is wrong with

Europe's reaction to the refugee crisis. It's not just the mayor who isn't pulling his weight, or his colleagues in the federal government – it's the rest of the continent too. Instead of trying to help the Greeks deal with what clearly requires a pan-European response, the rest of the EU has left them to it, in the hope that the crisis will disappear if they pretend it doesn't exist. MSF has been here for a while. The UN refugee agency and the International Rescue Committee are beginning to help out. But, in the main, the response is being co-ordinated by volunteers and under-resourced local officials. And through incompetence if not malice, the latter's actions are unsurprisingly often negligent, occasionally dangerous – and increasingly divisive.

By prioritising Syrians, and accelerating their transit through the islands, the Greeks bestow a lesser status on migrants of other nationalities, many of whom have just as reasonable a claim to asylum. This causes resentment and fights among the different ethnic groups. It also creates an incentive for non-Syrians to pretend to be from Syria.

No one really knows how widespread this kind of fraud is. Inevitably, though, it casts doubt over the precision of UN data, which is the main source of information about the origins of refugees. If the UN gets its statistics from the Greek police, and if the Greek police themselves rely on people's identification documents (and sometimes just on people's word), then how can we be sure that so many of the refugees are from Syria? On most Greek islands, people's passports are scanned for authenticity after they arrive, while those without documents are given linguistic tests to check they speak the Syrian dialect. But the system isn't perfect, and the lead-up to the Paris bombings in November 2015 highlights the relative ease with which someone can enter Europe with bogus documents. Anomalies clearly do occur, though the extent to which this is happening can't be known until all the many claims are processed more carefully by the countries where the refugees end up. This will take many months or even years – and, until then, the data from the likes of the UN and IOM are the best we've got.

In a dusty field that straddles the Greek–Macedonian border, quite where Greece ends and Macedonia begins is not entirely clear. Several Macedonian soldiers are nevertheless very sure where the line lies. 'Get back,' one shouts through the darkness, herding hundreds of refugees a couple of metres further south from where they stood a moment ago. 'Get back to the Greek border.'

The crowds shuffle briefly backwards, and the soldiers seem satisfied. 'Please,' a Syrian mother calls back, a toddler in her arms. 'We are a family. Where should we go now?' It is a filthy spot, filled with the detritus of past travellers. Surrounded by farmland, the only lighting comes from a nearby train track, and the only bedding is the sand the woman stands on.

'You must sleep here,' comes the Macedonian's reply.

It's now early July, and I've come to the cusp of Macedonia to witness the first major change to the refugees' route through the Balkans in 2015. After reaching the Greek islands, people are registered, fingerprinted, and then allowed

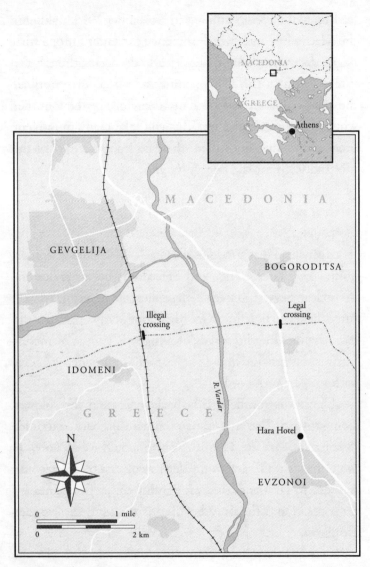

Greek-Macedonian Border

to make for the Greek mainland. From there, migrants head for Macedonia and, for the first few months of the year, they could do so by walking uninhibited through the field that I'm standing in. It was just as the Syrian *Baedeker* had promised on Facebook: '. . . walk a little bit further, and you'll find a road to the right which runs parallel to the train line. Keep walking on this sandy path, about 100 metres from the main road. After one hour of walking you will reach the village of Gevgelija.' In Gevgelija, the first village inside Macedonia, they weren't allowed to board public transport. So people either jumped into freight trains, paid over the odds for a taxi driver, or simply walked all the way to Serbia.

By June, the clandestine nature of the process was starting to cause problems for the Macedonian government. Gangs were kidnapping refugees as they walked through some of the country's northern villages, and the ensuing press coverage was an embarrassment for Skopje. So, in late June, Macedonia's parliament voted to give refugees three-day visas – which would allow them to pass through the country legally, and give them the right to take the train all the way to the Serbian border. This caused an unexpected problem: a huge bottleneck in Gevgelija, where thousands of refugees now queued to get their papers from the village's understaffed police station. To clear the backlog, the Macedonians then decided to block their southern border for a few days, and outsource the logjam to Greece. It's the first sign that the Balkan countries won't stand idly by as one of the biggest exoduses in European history crosses their territory. At one point, 2000 were stuck there on the border, with soldiers firing in the air to keep them back. After the queues cleared in Gevgelija, a dribble of refugees was allowed through. But progress is slow, and every night the informal crossing now shuts again – leading to the drama I witness this evening.

Despite the gentle croaks of nearby frogs, and the familiar clicking of the crickets, the mood is tense. Every so often the crowds edge forward, trying to inch the invisible border a few steps further north, and a soldier meets them with a raised truncheon and a bark. 'Go back,' he shouts. 'If we don't have silence, we'll have a problem.'

One of the Macedonians seemingly sees the border in just as fluid terms as the migrants, and goes to drink from a tap on the Greek side. 'Sabr,' he says to a lawyer from Aleppo, using the Arabic word for patience. 'You Muslims know what that means, right?'

As the night draws on, the crowd does grow more patient. After all, for someone like the lawyer, an amiable man in a Stetson, this is hardly his worst run-in with an army. He was arrested four times by Assad's men, and his scarred, dis-coloured arms are the result of one of Assad's bombs. The prospect of a long wait at the Macedonian border, even after a forty-mile walk to get there, is by contrast met with a shrug. Everyone's like this, once it's clear they've got to stay for the night. What's a night outside in comparison with the horrors they're fleeing from? 'Someone without their own country', says one Syrian, as he gets ready to sleep at the border, 'hasn't got anything to lose.'

The Greeks aren't supposed to let people get this far north. The papers the refugees receive on the islands stipulate that they shouldn't go within a certain range of the country's northern border. This is policed up to a point. When I get on a train from Thessaloniki to the border with Macedonia, my passport is checked – repeatedly. So is my brother's. Tom lives in London and I live in Cairo, so we've decided to meet in Greece for a rare few days together. With our dark hair and backpacks, the police obviously think we could be refugees.

As the train heads north to Macedonia, we see the route the real refugees are forced to take. The train leaves Thessaloniki, Greece's second city, and follows the path of the Vardar river. Watching from the window, every few minutes we can see a group of refugees on the riverbanks, hiking the sixty miles to Idomeni, the village where they'll leave the country. Eventually they'll join the railway track themselves, and walk next to it until they reach Gevgelija. One group rests at the bend of the river, and waves at my train. Leaning out of the window, I wave back. Then a branch of foliage hits me in the face.

Before they leave Greece entirely, many refugees take stock at a strange place called the Hara hotel. Locals say it was about to go bust late in the summer of 2014 – until the outriders of the exodus started stopping there and spending some of their life savings. There's nothing very special about it, a modern one-storey building with terracotta tiles on the roof. Now the Hara has nevertheless become the warped equivalent of a monastery on one of the medieval pilgrim paths across Europe – a crucial way station for the footsore traveller. Tellingly, the Hara's twenty Google Maps reviews all date from the start of the refugee crisis, and all but one is in Arabic. 'A nice and pretty hotel,' says one. 'Very dirty place,' says another.

No one's too sure how this place became such an icon on the migrant trail. It first caught my attention back in April, when I came across several mentions of it in refugee forums on Facebook. Others will have heard about it the same way. Then there's its location. The big banner in Hara's car park reads: 'WELCOME TO GREECE'. Yet for the refugees walking past, it's the last building they'll see before leaving the country. Standing in the car park next to the petrol pumps, you can see into Macedonia, and the fields you'll have to cross to get there. A bit further to the south, the Astro hotel doesn't have the same strategic location.

Tom and I arrive late at night, so all we see are the red lights of a few Macedonian casinos, twinkling in the distance. That seems to be the main economy over the border in Gevgelija: gambling. It's past midnight, but the Hara never seems to sleep. Each night we stay here, there are people bustling around at all hours. Some are refugees setting off in the darkness, perhaps in the belief that it's safer to walk when you can't be seen. Others arrive here during the small hours, in taxis driven from Thessaloniki. The car park is a constant carousel of cars, coming and going at all times. Once the passengers get out, they often sit on the hotel stoop, charging their phones, planning for the road ahead, and exchanging stories about the journey here. One group of Syrians sip on a round of Cokes, and lament how they got in a smuggler's taxi back in Thessaloniki. After they left town the driver stopped the car and forced them at knifepoint to hand over their prized Syrian passports. Arabs with less convincing reasons to claim asylum in Europe will pay several thousand euros for fake or stolen Syrian documents. Amid the Hara's changing crowd, a noisy refugee activist called Vasilis is one of the few permanent fixtures. He roves around the local area, advising refugees in need. Vasilis remembers when the first crowds of Syrians came this way in late August 2014: 'And I thought, what the fuck!' He has the longish brown hair and piercing eyes of a Gallagher brother, circa 1999, and holds forth with the same bullish cockiness as the Oasis frontmen. Smugglers are sons of bitches. Syrians are just bitches, but in a nice way. Vasilis himself is a recovering journalist – but not like other journalists, who are bitches in a bad way. Greece's northern neighbour, meanwhile, 'isn't Macedonia, it's Mafiadonia!'

We enter the building itself to find a crumpled man called Simos sitting behind the cash desk. A drawing of a younger Simos is pinned to the drawing board behind him, revealing that he's both the owner of the establishment, and that he's seen better days. The youthful Simos had a chiselled jaw, a black flop of hair, and piercing eyes. Today's incarnation sports a chin that blurs into his neck, greying skin, and a dull gaze. The recent rejuvenation of his business has not enlivened the man himself. Nor, unfortunately, does the prospect of two more customers. Spotting our backpacks, Simos sighs. 'Syrians? Thirty euros.' We produce our British passports, and he sighs harder. He's given us a lower price than he needed to, and gets his own back by refusing to produce a receipt. Or any clean linen.

The next morning, when I announce myself as a journalist, his skin turns to a still paler shade of grey. 'Simos is not here,' says Simos, after I suggest a quick interview. 'Simos is in Thessaloniki.'

Just five minutes?

'I think you are leaving today?' Simos replies hopefully.

Two minutes?

'You are leaving today,' he says with more certainty.

As it happens, I say, I'm hoping to stay for another night.

'Forty euros then.'

'Wasn't it thirty last night?'

'It was forty.'

'Thirty?'

'Forty.'

Round two to Simos, and he disappears into his office. A frosty barwoman resumes the conversation, not to defuse the situation, but to maintain Simos's cold welcome. He doesn't want to talk to you, she explains – he doesn't want to talk to anyone. 'You think he wants this? Thousands of people outside every day? No one wants this.' I'm surprised – isn't he making a fortune from all this? Aside from a full house every night, Simos gets a healthy second income from selling vast amounts of processed food to passing refugees. The reception is piled high with canned meat, tinned fish, biscuits, crisps, bread and water. 'Big profit', as Vasilis the activist would later summarise. But the barwoman is having none of it, keen to foster the impression of Simos as the worst businessman of all time. 'Profit?' she says. 'You can't make a profit here. Yes, he takes more money, but he also has to pay more staff. He's just the wrong person at the wrong place at the wrong time.' I'm almost convinced, until I remember the missing receipts.

Out in the car park, dozens of refugees are starting to gather in front of the Hara. Some have stayed overnight within its walls; others have slept in the car park. Still more are beginning to arrive on foot, and the rest appear from the backs of taxis. They'll all leave today for Macedonia, but first they want to join forces with other families. Everyone's heard what happens to those who walk through the forests alone. Or at least they've heard the rumours on Facebook – of muggers and bandits ambushing lone stragglers and stealing their phones and passports. Over time these stories take on the shape of legend. Vasilis loves to recount to anyone in earshot the presence of houses full of smuggler armies on just the other side of the border, hundreds of bandits to a building. 'Daesh isn't in Syria – it's there,' he says, using the Arab name for Isis. 'Almost every day we have a hundred Syrians getting beaten inside the Macedonian border.' True or not, no one wants to run the risk – so they gather in large numbers for safety.

Two of the newcomers are Fattemah and Nasser, a couple from Yarmouk, the Damascus suburb wrecked by fighting in 2012. The face of their one-year-old son Hammouda is pockmarked with days-old mosquito bites, and Nasser carries him in a homemade baby-backpack fashioned from the remains of a child's life jacket. It's a legacy of their trip across the Aegean nine days earlier. Nasser had originally bought a proper baby-carrier back in Turkey, but he soon had to leave it in the sea. Halfway to the island of Samos, their boat ran out of fuel. The passengers began to paddle, and the longer the journey took, the more the waves washed into the boat. Still a few hundred metres from Samos, the boat was in danger of sinking, so Nasser and his companions threw everything but their most essential possessions into the sea. By the time the boat was within reach of the shore, everyone was sitting in several inches of water, and Nasser was holding Hammouda high above his head.

Today Hammouda is in better spirits, climbing over his parents and pawing them enthusiastically. I give him my pen and notebook to play with, and he squiggles on its pages with fervour. Nasser is pleased at his artistic vision – he is himself a sculptor, decorator and interior designer. Fattemah, a teacher, is less impressed with the red-ink stains now spreading across Hammouda's hands and shirt. The pen and paper are returned. Hammouda resumes his clambering.

In the car park, adults are also starting to move. Long lines of refugees are now descending into the fields behind the Hara, just as the Facebook groups advised. The news about the border blockage still hasn't filtered through, so everyone's still reliant on weeks- or even months-old information. It takes young, mobile risk-takers to trailblaze a new route. Now that the flow is increasingly formed by families, the average migrant is happier to trust in group-think.

For now, Nasser and Fattemah want to wait. They and the other families who arrived with them have other friends who are trying to catch up. These stragglers took a taxi from Thessaloniki earlier in the day, but they keep getting turned back by police. So their outriders have to wait a few more hours. There's little left to do but talk, so the couple reveal a little more of their backstory. They've been on the move, it turns out, for almost as long as they've been married. They had wanted to hold their wedding on 12 December 2012 – they liked the symmetry of 12–12–12. But so did many other couples in Yarmouk, so in the end they had to settle for 10–12–12 instead. It was a blessing in disguise. Two days later, on their preferred wedding date, Assad's MiGs began strafing the area. Yarmouk was soon wrecked, its buildings ruined and its residents queuing for food as far as the eye could see. As Nasser puts it, the area was turned 'from a beautiful place to a line of ants'. The couple escaped in a rush to another area of Damascus, but on arrival Nasser realised he'd left behind his ID, and several hard drives containing all his designs. He shows us some pictures of his work that he's saved on his phone. It's an odd, exciting mix of Escheresque murals, sculptures and, best of all, a water wheel. Desperate to save all this, he snuck back into Yarmouk, now the site of a fierce battle. Retrieving his stuff proved simple enough. But, on his way back, he found himself in the middle of a gunfight. His path to safety ultimately lay on the other side of a wide road overlooked by a trigger-happy sniper. Friends of his tried to cross it – and were shot dead before reaching the other side. Hoping to avoid a similar fate, Nasser kept shouting for five hours that he was a civilian not a soldier, and therefore needed safe access. But he couldn't be sure that he'd been heard or believed, so he stayed put. Eventually another family cowering beside him decided to risk it. They sprinted across and made it to safety, so Nasser followed in their wake. One pace, two paces, three paces – nothing. No guns, just silence. Four paces, five paces. He got halfway across the road – still nothing. Then suddenly his bag snaps, and all the things he's come to fetch fall to the ground. Disaster. Should he pick them up, and risk making himself a bigger target? Or save himself, but waste the journey? On impulse, he stoops to the ground, and gathers his things. And that's when the sniper shoots. Nasser feels the shimmer of the bullet as it passes him. The sniper had missed. Nasser had survived.

Back in the car park at the Hara, the crowds are thinning out. It's past the middle of the afternoon, and most people have now headed towards Macedonia. If they don't leave now, the couple's group might have to stay the night at the border. But their absent friends still haven't arrived, so they're forced to wait another hour – and, to pass the time, Nasser and Fattemah return again to their memories of their flight from Yarmouk.

Hammouda was born into a miserable situation, around a year after their escape. His parents were moving between friends' houses. Their own home was destroyed, and Nasser's father and sister were dead. In war-torn Damascus, where houses were being destroyed not built, there was no work for interior designers. Nasser ended up carrying cement to keep his family alive, doing jobs that previously he'd have contracted other people to do. Life was unbearable enough when people started disappearing from their latest neighbourhood. The regime or its proxies would turn up in a van and round a few people up – and take them to the front lines to fight. At that point, Nasser's mother said they should try to flee the country. And so they did – for the third time in two generations. Nasser's parents had fled Palestine in 1948. He'd been born in Kuwait, but when Iraq invaded in 1991, the family fled once more to Syria. And now Nasser was on the move again. 'We're fleeing from everywhere,' he says.

Just as Hashem al-Souki found, the sheer act of leaving Syria was exhausting and financially depleting. Fattemah and Nasser headed north towards Turkey, which required going through a litany of regime checkpoints. At each, the soldiers always wanted bribes – sometimes as much as 1000 Syrian pounds. At the last one, Nasser had only 450 left, and the soldiers were satisfied. Others who had less were beaten till their teeth fell out. The Isis checkpoints weren't any better: if the jihadists found any women who were travelling alone, they arrested them, perhaps to keep them as slaves. Travelling as a family, Nasser, Fattemah and Hammouda made it through – and reached Turkey in November 2014.

Turkey shoulders a bigger burden of Syrian refugees than any other country – but it doesn't recognise the rights of refugees from the Middle East. They are given year-long leaves to remain, but they mostly don't have the right to work.* Nasser found illegal work as a labourer, shifting lumps of marble for well below the minimum wage. He tried to show his bosses that he could do something more lucrative for them. After hours, he would carve small blocks of marble into sculptures of ducks and cormorants. The manager told him to stick to the manual labour. Seven months later, he and Fattemah realised they had little choice but to try their luck in Europe. First came the sea, then a sixteen-hour walk to find shelter in Samos. Then a week's wait for papers. And now, two days later, a few miles shy of the Macedonian border. Each place they reach is strange and new to them. Indeed the whole continent is bizarre, and wandering through it for the first time feels a bit like doing a driving test without your glasses. 'The journey is a mystery,' says Nasser. 'But you have no choice. You have to go. You have to save your family.'

* Turkey finally allowed Syrians to apply for work permits in January 2016, by which time it may have been too little too late.

Their friends never arrive. They're held up once more in Thessaloniki, so at 6 p.m. Nasser's and Fattemah's group of Syrians gathers in the car park to leave without them. There are about fifty of them, slinging their rucksacks over their shoulders. One man is stooped under three of them. Many carry their things in bulging plastic bags, and some like Nasser have babies in their arms. One family is pushing a baby's buggy.

A few of them exchange nods, and then they're off. They round the fence of the Hara, and drop down into the fields below. Most of them are stooped under the weight of their baggage, but they rumble along at a pace that belies the burden on their shoulders. Nasser has Hammouda tied to his front, a bag on his back, and a grimace on his face. Fattemah frowns too, clutching her back with one hand, and a blue bag full of Hammouda's nappies with the other. The weather is also moody, the walkers marching under a canopy of dramatic skies. Golden sunshine brightens the edges of the grey cumulus clouds, streaming from behind the blue silhouettes of mountains on the other side of the valley. But few here have time to enjoy the view, straining with their bags, worried about the road ahead. Fleeing your home isn't just physically draining, says Nasser, who knows better than most. It's emotionally exhausting too, and no one does it unless they absolutely have to. 'My father went out of Palestine, we had to leave another time from Kuwait, and now we've left Syria,' Nasser says. 'Every time you travel from one place to another you have to make new friends, find new houses, new memories. Everything changes. You have to be so strong. Because you're starting everything again from scratch.'

Right now the immediate concern is a steep, deep ditch that blocks the group's path, half a kilometre from the Hara. The children and elderly slip and slide as they inch their way up its sandy bank. The biggest problem is the buggy. Should they take it? Is it worth the hassle? Probably not. The baby is hoisted out, and its buggy is left to stand alone on the far side of the ditch.

Onwards walks the group. Where to, no one's completely sure. They know they need to get eventually to the field that's written about on Facebook. But first there's the River Vardar to cross. A road leads over it. Is this the way? Some people, gazing into their GPS maps, think there's a better path to the south. Others point out that there's no way of crossing the water there, and the water is quite deep. Suddenly a car interrupts the discussion, shooting down the road and over the river, sirens blaring. 'Shorta!' someone shouts. 'Police!' There's a surge away from the road and the bridge, until wiser heads prevail. If the police had wanted to arrest them, they would have stopped there and then. People begin to nod, and they head back towards the road, and hurry across the bridge. It's a tall structure, more of a causeway really, so, on the other side, there's no immediate way of returning to the perceived safety of the farmland below. The road will eventually descend to ground level but, in their anxiety, the refugees don't want to wait that long. To the side of the road, a sharp scarp leads down to the fields. It's the definition of a slippery slope, unsafe for adults with children. Or so I think, until mothers with babies strapped to their backs, and arms weighed down with bin-liners full of belongings, rush past me, vault the chicane, and shimmy down the escarpment. Anxious people fleeing wars have a different threshold for safety.

We plough on, still two miles south of the border. To our right, a slim bit of woodland separates us from the river. To our left is a field of sunflowers, and beyond it a field of sweetcorn. Far to the west stands the line of blue cut-out mountains. A gentle splurge of white clouds rises behind them, like a wave breaking in hyper-slow motion on the side of a quay. A separate block of clouds hangs directly above us, and a few specks of rain fleck our cheeks. It is a bewitching scene in which the surreal landscape seems to chime with the bizarre nature of what we're about to do. To add to the odd-ness, the woodland to our right suddenly hollows out to reveal a handful of old Greek men, sitting in a clearing out-side an incongruous burger van. No one says anything, but they stare at us like mourners watching a passing funeral procession. It feels simultaneously like a moment of both empathy and confusion. Of commonality but also division.

The surprise encounter sends a pulse through the refugees, as if suddenly reminded again that they can encounter strangers at any time – not all of whom mean well. For this reason, it's sometimes hard to get people to trust me on the trail. How do they know I won't misrepresent them? How do they even know I'm a journalist? My conversation-starters in Arabic help to build a rapport, but some people naturally don't want to take the risk of talking. Women are often warier than men, which is why this book doesn't contain so many female voices.

A few hundred metres on, everyone starts poking around in the woods, trying to find sticks and staffs to ward off attackers. Fattemah picks up one so small it's almost useless, and she and Nasser laugh at the farce of it all. They smile at each other, she throws the stick away, and squeezes Nasser's hand instead. Someone else's child toddles next to him, and reaches up to grip Hammouda's hand too. In truth, Fattemah isn't feeling so happy. MSF and the Red Cross reckon that 20 per cent of the women walking this route are expecting babies.[5] Fattemah is one of them, she reveals as we walk through the fields. She's four months pregnant, and carrying the weight of her unborn son has given her excruciating pain in her stomach and lower back. Walking is hard for her. She hasn't been able to eat or drink enough. She's finding it hard to control her bladder. After walking for sixteen hours on Samos, she collapsed – and the doctors who subsequently treated her said she had almost lost her baby. Back in Turkey, she'd wondered if she should have come at all, and she cries when she tries to explain her reasoning. It was a Hobson's choice, she says. Either she braved the journey, and risked losing her unborn child, or she stayed put, forcing both the baby and Hammouda to grow up either in a war zone or in poverty. 'I didn't ever expect that I would have the [unborn] baby,' Fattemah later says of her choice. 'I thought maybe I will lose one baby but save another one: Hammouda. I thought: I can provide a good life for Hammouda, so it's worth it.'

Walking towards Macedonia, Fattemah's wondering whether she was right. Her unborn baby hasn't moved in a week, so she wonders if the exertions of the journey have caused a miscarriage. She's sent a message to her mum to ask what she thinks. For the moment, she fears the baby is dead.

The group marches on, past another oddly placed burger van. Whether these are always parked here, catering for the Greek farm workers, or whether they've moved here to catch the migrant footfall, I never find out. Someone plucks a sunflower from its stalk, and replaces it with a bottle. A rainbow appears, and finally a few people stop to marvel at the scenery. The dark grey of the sky is now set against the dark green of the fields, and it makes for a pretty picture. It's a last memory of Greece – we are now within a few hundred metres of the border. Hammouda marks the occasion by practising his oration. 'Da, do, da, do,' he says as his father beams.

At last, the group decide to trust in their own instincts and momentum. They'd originally set out to reach the border at the exact same spot where all the Macedonian soldiers have gathered. That's where Facebook said to cross it, so that's where they'd wanted to go too. It didn't make much sense to me, given the situation there. Then again, I had information they didn't have – and weren't very interested in hearing about. They trusted the advice of their friends on social media better than a foreign journalist. But, in the end, they reach the border at the wrong place anyway. Looking on their GPS maps, they realise they're a mile east of where the soldiers were standing. So the self-assumed leaders of the group just shrug, and cross the border there and then.

It's an odd experience, stepping across a border like this. On the ground, there is nothing to denote the boundary. On the Greek side, there is a field of sweetcorn and, on the Macedonian side, a vineyard. In the middle, there's no marker that reveals you're moving between two countries rather than two farms. On the GPS, there's little fanfare either – just a slim black line, and a blue dot that lets you know where you are in relation to it. For the phoneless grandmother behind me, it takes a while for her to infer from her companions' conversations that she's finally left Greece. 'Hamdila salama,' a fat man drily informs the woman, striding alongside her in a vest and breeches. 'Welcome home.'

In moments like these, you realise the absurdity of dividing the earth into fairly arbitrary parcels of turf. It's a facile point to make, but sometimes even the facile feels profound when you're wandering through Europe with people whose future depends on repeatedly flouting these invisible divisions, and whose own homeland is currently in the process of being divvied up into a new set of arbitrary parcels.

The Syrians themselves have more immediate things on their minds. It's a relief to be inside Macedonia, and people celebrate by plucking a few blackberries from the brambles in the vineyard. Some of them try the grapes on the vines, and spit them out immediately: the grapes aren't ripe. But Fattemah keeps chewing. Her pregnancy is making her nauseous, and the bitterness of the grapes helps her overcome the worst of it.

But their initial delight at reaching a new country, and my relief at avoiding the logjam a mile to the west, is soon dashed. A few minutes later, the whoop of a siren heralds the arrival of an army jeep, careering down a farm track towards the Syrians. They've been spotted. The jeep stops in front of them, and five armed soldiers get out. They're gentle, but firm. They explain that the only way legally to cross the border in an illegal way is at the legal illegal crossing point where Tom and I had been yesterday. Slowly and sombrely, but grateful to be treated with a modicum of civility, the Syrians head westwards to join those already waiting there. They arrive twenty minutes later to find hundreds sitting on the ground, all queuing to cross the border. 'You see this?' says Nasser. 'This is what Syrians have become.'

They slump to the floor. Fattemah begins to massage Nasser's back. Hammouda plays peekaboo with Tom. They've made it to Macedonia. Now it's just Serbia and Hungary to come.

Yama Nayab, an Afghan surgeon, may sit in a Serbian thicket 3,500 miles from Kabul, but he still wants to evoke the customs of home. 'Please at least take this,' Yama says to me, holding out a cup of dirty water drawn from a nearby well. 'In Afghanistan, it would be our duty to offer you food as our guest.'

The irony of Yama's ingrained hospitality could not be starker. Stabbed four times in the chest by the Taliban earlier in 2015, he recovered and fled the country with his wife and two toddlers. Since then, they have walked and bussed through Pakistan, Iran, Turkey and Bulgaria to the overgrown grounds of this disused brick factory a few miles shy of Serbia's northern border. To get to northern Europe, most people walk north through Macedonia to Serbia. Yama is one of a minority who comes instead via Bulgaria – and he joins the main route here in the northern Serbian countryside.

Hungarian-Serbian Border

'Wherever I find a safe place,' he says, 'a country that accepts me and gives me a chance, I will start my life there.'

Serbia, with its barely functional asylum system, is not an option. So one logical place to look would be the land that lies just beyond the border: Hungary, or at least the European Union to which it belongs. Instead, Yama – the model host – has just discovered that Hungary will not welcome him as a guest. In the days before our meeting, Hungary's self-described 'illiberal' government began drawing up plans to stop people like Yama – by building some kind of barrier along its 110-mile border with Serbia. Twenty-five years after the fall of the Iron Curtain that cut the country off from Western Europe, Hungary wants to create something similar.

In one sense, it's easy to understand why: with thousands now arriving in the Balkans every week from Turkey, the country almost all of them will eventually funnel through is Hungary. Once refugees cross Hungary's southern border, they're inside the EU's Schengen zone, which means that in theory they should be able to get anywhere within western and northern Europe without encountering another passport check. In 2010, fewer than 2,400 were recorded crossing into Hungary like this. In just the first half of 2015, that figure has been matched fifty times over.

'This is a necessary step,' the Hungarian government's spokesman, Zoltán Kovács, tells me when I call for a chat about the fence. 'We need to stop the flood.' 'Need' and 'necessary' are seductive words, though. Very few of those reaching Hungary actually want to stay there. If Hungary gave up the farce of arresting and interning captured migrants for a fortnight, they would be in and out of the country within forty-eight hours. When I point this out to Kovács, he says Hungary nevertheless has a duty to prevent migrants from reaching the rest of the European Union. A reasonable argument on the face of things – but in reality, it's a little bit disingenuous. If Hungary does build its fence, and if it works, the flow of refugees will merely shift west to Croatia and Slovenia. It's a good thing that Hungary's neighbours didn't show such fair-weather friendship back in 1956, when hundreds of thousands of Hungarians fled their country to escape the fighting between Soviet troops and Hungarian rebels.

Then again, Hungary's move in truth has little to do with showing solidarity with other Europeans. It has a lot to do with internal politics. The main opposition to prime minister Viktor Orbán's hardline government is a party called Jobbik, which lies even further to the right. To ward off Jobbik's challenge, Orbán wants to prove that he can be every bit as reactionary as his rivals. First he erected a series of billboards, nominally aimed at immigrants (but written in Hungarian), telling them they couldn't take the jobs of locals. Later Orbán argues that migrants endanger the very foundations of Christian Europe. He also circulates a questionnaire about 'migrants and terrorists' that seems less an honest attempt to canvass opinion on the two distinct groups of people, and more a heavy-handed stab at conflating the pair in the eyes of his electorate. 'Do you agree', reads one leading question, 'that mistaken immigration policies contribute to the spread of terrorism?' The fence is a continuation of this dog-whistle politics, aimed at those inside the country as much as those outside it. And the sad irony is this: the people the fence will nominally deter are often far more at risk from terrorists than the people the fence will nominally protect.

Yama Nayab, sitting a few miles south of where the fence will reportedly run, is a case in point. A surgeon with the Afghan army, he was approached by a Taliban fighter as he returned home one day near the start of this year. 'Why are you working for the government?' the man said to him. 'Here in Afghanistan the Americans and the pagans made a government – and you are working for that government.'

Then the man got out a knife. 'And then he did this,' says Yama, pulling up his shirt to reveal four pink scars circling his heart.

I meet Yama in the undergrowth behind an old brick factory in northern Serbia, just outside the town of Subotica. It's called Ciglana, and it's one of the main hideaways for refugees hoping to make it to Hungary, a place where they can rest and take stock before the big push. The casual visitor will find it hard to find them. The refugees hide in a vast stretch of overgrown sweetcorn fields that nestle between a sewage works and a rubbish tip, where the crops have long knotted with nettles, bushes and grass flowers. Migrants call the space 'the jungle', and it is not hard to see why. It's very easy to get lost. Weaving through the tall and thick foliage, to a soundtrack of crackling crickets, you hear the voices of different clusters of refugees, and step across the detritus of migrants past. But, eerily, you rarely see them and finding them happens almost by chance. It's a bewitching, sometimes alarming experience. You'll be working your way through a thicket, with nothing in eyeshot but greenery.

Then suddenly a small hollow will open up in the undergrowth to reveal a huddle of a dozen Afghans – often waiting till nightfall before making for Hungary.

Tibor Varga first remembers people coming here in 2011, when there was just a trickle of migrants heading through the Balkans. The place had been lifeless for three years, after the brick factory closed and the smoke stopped spouting from its tall chimney. Then, one winter, Tibor started spotting strangers heading into its grounds. Tibor's the local priest, and his van is one of the things I suddenly find myself face to face with, after wandering aimlessly through the jungle's paths. Tibor and his van are frequent visitors to this wasteland. Clad in a tracksuit and a baseball cap, he comes here every day to hand out food to the most vulnerable. As far as I can make out, he's the only person providing any kind of regular humanitarian relief.

The way he describes his motivations is intriguing to me. Tibor seems driven by both his kindness and a delight in swimming against the current. As a Christian, his generosity is rooted in his religion – but there is also an element of realpolitik to what he does. 'I'm totally convinced that when you help the needy, you're helping god with something,' he says, leaning on his van. 'If you ask a bank for a loan, you have to pay it back. And if you give a loan to god, he will pay back with much more interest. That's the economy of what I'm doing.' When describing how he hands out food, he switches from the language of a bean-counter to that of a prophet. 'If there is a multitude, I adopt some biblical way of dealing with it. I tell them to sit down, like when Jesus made the miracle of the five thousand, and he told everyone to sit down.'

Tibor's flock is usually Afghans. In peak season Afghans form 16 per cent of those arriving by boat to Europe, the second-largest group of boat arrivals, and their proportion of the total rises as summer turns into winter. And while Syrians are given priority at most stages of the journey through Europe, the plight of Afghans is becoming as critical as that of their travelling companions. According to the Afghan government, 80 per cent of the country is not safe.[6] That's because extremist groups including the Taliban and Islamic State's local affiliate continue to wage an insurgency in many provinces, and have begun to retake territory they were previously forced from. Civilians are at risk from frequent bomb attacks from all sides – an obvious example being the destruction of MSF's hospital in Kunduz by US airstrikes. They're also in danger on an individual basis: many Afghans are fleeing because they, like Yama, have received specific threats from extremists. Some are targeted because they work in jobs perceived by the Taliban to be too Western, and others because they refuse to fight with the group. One young man in the jungle shows me the scar tissue that snakes down his lower leg. A Taliban fighter had shot him there as punishment for refusing to leave school to train with the jihadists. Another, a former kick-boxer, says he fled after a teammate was assassinated for pursuing what the Taliban feels is too foreign a pastime. Some Afghans I meet first tried to find sanctuary in Pakistan or Iran – but in recent months both countries have begun to turf out Afghan refugees, increasing the pressure on Europe. Iran has even sent Afghans to fight for Assad in Syria.

Hiding in the bushes, the Afghans I meet are scared and tense, worried that they'll soon be caught and fingerprinted, or returned home. But they're also already relieved. Here they are, clean shaven, and dressed in Western brands and with Western haircuts that some of them paid for in Belgrade. They say they were never allowed to wear anything similar in their villages in Afghanistan. One remembers the sheer joy of being handed T-shirts and jeans by their smugglers, as they left home for the first time. 'We never wore these clothes before!' he smiles, tugging on his Calvin Klein knock-off.

It's a hint of the unique nature of the Afghans' journey. Their route is longer and more circuitous than most other groups on this trail. Some cross the mountains into Pakistan, and then head onwards to Iran. Most head directly to Iran itself – a dangerous, exhausting two-day hike that sees some migrants shot dead by border guards. Neither Iran nor Pakistan makes it easy for them to stay, so then they walk into Turkey – in another epic hike that is just as long and fraught as the one across the Iranian–Afghan border. Once inside Turkey, they then take the boat to the Greek islands – or take the land route into Bulgaria and then Serbia.

The choice depends on their smugglers. For a fee of around €10,000 each, the Afghans I meet in the jungle have contracted a smuggling network to organise every step of their journey to Europe. At each new stage of the odyssey to Europe, they call this man, who then sends them a set of new directions. 'Sometimes they give me GPS, sometimes they give me a map, sometimes they send me a car,' says Yama. To ensure that he's not scammed, Yama's family pays the money in instalments that are released only once he's successfully completed each leg of the journey.

It's a vast sum of money that Yama would rather not have paid. But each time Europe tries to protect its supposedly Christian nature with decidedly unChristian tactics, the smugglers are the biggest winners. Tibor Varga has an interesting take on this irony, as I leave the jungle later in the afternoon. Europe, he says, is frightened that an influx of foreigners will erode European values. But what values will there be to uphold if we abandon our duty to protect those less fortunate than ourselves? What incentive do we give to refugees to maintain the fabric of our society if that fabric is so ragged in the first place?

'If Europe is not able to show a better way of life to them, then they will think that their morality is better than ours,' says Tibor. With his tubby paunch and avuncular expression, he seems gentle and measured enough. But in the wilds of the jungle, under these darkening skies, Tibor's words have the righteous thunder of an Old Testament prophet. 'They need to face some higher standards of morality,' he says. 'If not, they will set their own.'

Crouched in the darkness, 500 metres from the Hungarian border, fifteen Syrian refugees whisper about how they should cross into the EU. A few miles back, they switched off their phones. Then they picked up sticks to protect themselves from local gangsters. Now they're organising into pairs: going two by two means they might not trigger the heat sensors that they believe line the border. And it is at this moment that Mohamed Hussein, a twenty-three-year-old pharmacist, absent-mindedly decides to light a cigarette.

'Put it out!' comes the collective hiss, betraying a rising sense of fear. Several in this group have previously been jailed for a fortnight by the Hungarian police after crossing the border, before being returned to Serbia. Now they're trying again. 'The border between Greece and Macedonia was very easy,' whispers Selim, a sales manager from Aleppo. 'But this is the most difficult bit, the Hungarian border.'

There's still no fence here, so if they can cross this invisible line undetected, they will be back inside both the European Union and the Schengen zone for the first time since Greece. In theory, they'll then be able to get to Germany or even Sweden without being stopped at another border. In practice, many of them may be arrested and given the option of claiming asylum in Hungary. Those who'd rather avoid settling in one of Europe's most xenophobic countries will get two weeks in jail, and then they'll be deposited again on the Serbian side of the border. Selim is one of several men I've met who've tried this process three times this summer.

The cycle starts ten miles to the south in Kanjiža, a town of ethnic Hungarians that, in another kind of border tyranny, nevertheless lies in Serbia. The town was previously best known for its giant mayflies, millions of which hatch and mature en masse during a single week in early summer. Dormant for 364 days of the year, the yellow insects rise from the waters of the Tisza river, which runs past the town of Kanjiža, at the end of June. Then they mate. And then, a few hours later, they die – leaving their eggs to sink to the bottom of the river for another year. It is a mesmerising spectacle known locally as 'the blooming', and it draws a fair number of tourists. The Tisza mayflies are extinct in most of Europe, and one of the few places they still visit is Kanjiža.

Now the town is a thoroughfare for a different kind of visitor. After entering Serbia from Macedonia and Bulgaria my new Syrian friends – Selim, Mohamed and their fellow travellers – were given a three-day transit visa that gives them the right to cross the country. (Serbia isn't a member of the EU, so it has no obligation to make refugees claim asylum there.) They made for Belgrade bus station, and from there they rode to the main square in little Kanjiža.

No refugee stays here long. Every Kanjiža afternoon sees a constant rotation of Syrians arriving and departing through the town square. Watching from a window opposite the bus stop, a young hotel receptionist is amazed. 'We're such a small town,' she says. 'We've never seen anything like it.'

As they do on the Macedonian border, everyone gathers together for protection. They form groups of twenty or thirty to ward off any potential bandits, and then march out of the town like platoons of legionaries, two abreast, fifteen lines deep. Sitting on park benches, or in the two restaurants on the square, Syrians share rumours about the dangers of the journey ahead. If they're not worried about the Hungarian border guards, then they're afraid of the bandits they'll meet en route. 'Did you know', one man asks, his eyes widening, 'that they have tasers?'

I find it easy to get sucked into this kind of myth-making – not least because there's an element of truth to it. The previous night, the town's police had asked a trio of Syrian Kurds if they'd take part in a police line-up that was taking place in a few minutes. The Kurds hadn't wanted to, unsurprisingly scared that it was all some kind of trick. So Sima Diab, a photo-journalist and colleague, and I came with them to make sure that nothing untoward happened. All five of us waited for a while at the station, before a policeman came to hustle us into a room with a two-way mirror.

'You, you, and you – come with me,' said the Serb to the three Kurds. 'And you too.'

I wasn't sure who the fourth person was meant to be. Then I realised he was looking at me.

'Me?' I said.

'Yes, you. We need a fourth person in the line-up.'

And so that was how I came to take part in the identifica-tion of a Roma teenager. I was number one in the line-up, and the teenager was number two. What had he been arrested for, I asked. The accused said nothing. But the police had an answer: he'd mugged a Syrian refugee. I've no idea if that was true, but it made me start to buy into all the rumours of the bandits hiding in the woods of northern Serbia.

It's therefore with a whiff of trepidation that Sima and I join the fifteen Syrians assembling outside the Ujaz hotel, late the following afternoon. It's a scene that seems both literary – as if these are the participants of *The Canterbury Tales* gathering in Southwark ahead of their pilgrimage – and entirely ordinary – fifteen blokes off to watch the football. It doesn't yet feel like they're planning to cross the hallowed borders of the European Union. They're not in any great rush. They mill around, joke, charge their phones, and wait for the stragglers to arrive. Only Mahmoud, a pale man with a moustache, seems tense. He has one item of luggage – a box of Persil washing powder – and he grips it with surprising fervour.

At forty-five, Assad's the oldest. He looks like the actor John Goodman – chubby, bearded, and with a comic grimace – but he's a lot quieter. He also looks like a tourist, wearing a bumbag and posing for a photo in front of the hotel. Most of them look a bit like tourists, in fact. The majority are in shorts and T-shirts – as if they're off for a stroll round town rather than into the next country. It's not that they're poor, it's just that you can't take much with you when you're fleeing a war. In fact, those coming to Europe are usually drawn from Syria's merchant classes. People with the savings to pay for a boat across the Aegean, and to reach Turkey in the first place.

Assad, for instance, used to own three coffee shops until the war put paid to his business. Nehyad, a slowcoach who's one of the last to leave the hotel, owned a mobile-phone shop. Wajeeh sold cameras, used to work at the Four Seasons, speaks Russian, and is working on his Japanese. Selim is the spit of Sean Penn – and was a sales manager at a crisp factory in Aleppo, before his home near the ancient citadel was hit by a rocket. Some of them know each other from their comfortable lives in Syria. Selim's here with his nephew, Zacariah. Others join them along the route – people like Ahmed, dressed in a smart leather jacket, jeans and a black satchel, as if he's a graphic designer off on his commute to work. Then there's Nizam, a twenty-four-year-old computer scientist, and his friend Mohamed Hussein, a pharmacist covered in tattoos and radiating energy. He arrived on Lesvos three weeks ago, where he was met off the boat by a motley crew that included the Kempsons and a TV reporter to whom he apologised profusely for his presence. 'We are so sorry to come to your countries, but we have to,' Mohamed had told ITV's Emma Murphy. 'There is no way else.'

'Ready to rock 'n' roll?' It's been an hour of procrastination, and Wajeeh's finally keen to get on the road. He's already tried the route once (and failed), while Selim's done it twice (and failed), so they emerge as the group's natural leaders. In the land of the blind, the men who've been arrested and deported most times by the Hungarian police are king. We amble off, past the town park, and up into the main square of Kanjiža, where other groups of Syrians are also preparing to leave. At around the same time, a wedding procession emerges from a nearby church. The line of suited Serbians makes its way up the western side of the square, in an amusing juxtaposition with the lines of Syrians forming on the eastern side. In contrast with the Syrians, some of whom are striding off with a smile on their face, the Serbians' pace is sombre and slow. A few Syrians gamely clap and cheer the newlyweds. The bride and groom give them the side-eye. They look miserable.

For the members of our group, used to the hustle and bustle of Syrian cities, the low-key vibe of the eastern European countryside is a source of bemusement. 'It's so quiet,' Wajeeh whispers, in mock concern. 'Don't raise your voice. They will wake up!'

The group's own spirits are high. At the back of their minds are the stories of the bandits and the police, but for now everyone tries to forget about all that. 'Let's go,' Mohamed says to his new companions. 'I just want to walk.'

And so we do, heading eastwards out of Kanjiža and towards the Tisza river. We process past the little pizzeria with no name. Past the town's one bar. Past the Art Garni, the four-star hotel that's too expensive for the Syrians. A placard that says in German: 'ZIMMER FREI'. A man watering his front garden. A sign to Horgoš, a place I'll grow to know better in the next chapter.

All the while, Mohamed talks and talks, seemingly unencumbered by much emotional baggage, or indeed anything physical; his only earthly possession is a pair of Beats headphones. 'I love progressive rock!' is one of his opening gambits, and it's no understatement. 'I learned to live from that music and its ideals,' says Mohamed in total sincerity. 'I feel like I was born in the eighties, even though I don't believe in reincarnation.' The conversation pinballs into a discussion about atheism. 'I wish I wasn't called Mohamed,' says Mohamed. 'I love England, I love its thinkers. Darwin. Richard Dawkins – he's great.' He then relates the pair's writings to the journey ahead. 'It's not the strongest, nor the smartest, but the one who's most adapted to nature who will survive. That's the first law of evolution, and the first law here.'

We're now striding past the very last houses of the town. A couple on an evening stroll heads in the opposite direction. A farmer in a green tractor slowly overtakes us, waving his encouragement. Now it's just a few miles of fields and woods until Hungary, and thoughts begin to turn to the thieves and border guards who might lie in wait. Mohamed, needless to say, is the odd one out. 'I'm not scared at all,' he says. 'We're escaping from Isis, not the robbers.' But others are experiencing a paradoxical mixture of fearlessness and paranoia, anxiety about what's to come, but the simultaneous con-fidence that it's hardly worse than what's come before. Nizam, Mohamed's friend from home, is running through possible scenarios in his head: making a run for it; getting caught; having to try again. But he also remembers what he's running from in the first place: the rocket that killed his father. Compulsory conscription. The advance of Isis.

At this point, the Tisza river forks away from the road, and so too do the men. Just west of the water there's a narrow wood, and just west of the wood there's a dyke to deter the Tisza during the flood season. We hurry into the gap between the woods and the dyke. The Tisza will run until Hungary, so we'll aim to follow its flow all the way to the border. Walk-ing beside Mohamed, so close to the river, I'm reminded of another young man who encountered the Tisza, some eighty-two years ago. The man was Patrick Leigh Fermor, who later described crossing the Tisza on his horse Malek in the book *Between the Woods and the Water*. It was the second in Leigh Fermor's trilogy about his journey from Holland to Istanbul in the early 1930s, a trilogy that has since become one of the best-loved works of travel literature. Readers warm to its hero, an eighteen-year-old ingénu, as he walks across a Europe in flux, and discovers a continent about which he previously knew little. One night he stays in a farmer's barn, the next in a count's castle. It's a wonderful story that has inspired a few reconstructions by people trying to trace his route and in the process recapture the raw sense of liberation and exploration that Leigh Fermor's work conveys (Nick Hunt's charming *Walking the Woods and the Water* is the most recent). For me, none of them ever reaches the heights

Leigh Fermor set. In the age of mass travel, of interrailing, of TripAdvisor, and of Schengen, you can't really get close to what Leigh Fermor did. And I say that as someone who's lived as vicariously as anyone through Leigh Fermor's wanderlust; I wrote an undergraduate dissertation about his account of his travels.

One reason his work is so popular, and so imitated, is perhaps that his readers – deep down – know all this. They know that his experiences can't be recreated; that Europe will never again be the site of the same mystery, adventure and uncertainty as it was in 1933. In some quarters, this realisation has contributed to the fear that travel is now dead; the subsequent reappraisal of what it is to travel; and the conclusion that it is only by rediscovering an enthusiasm for the everyday, and the close to home, that we will be able to overcome the loss of the epic travel experience.

When I first read Leigh Fermor's books, I remember being simultaneously elated at the adventures he described and saddened that it was no longer possible to recreate them. Walking with Mohamed, however, I realise that all this angst comes from a place of extreme privilege. With their EU passports and credit cards, Leigh Fermor fans may struggle to find adventure in the fields of eastern Europe. But for this group of Syrians, hurrying along in the shadow of a dyke, ears pricked for cops and robbers, it's a continent that still presents frequent danger – and considerable mystery. They navigate Europe not with a *Rough Guide* or *Lonely Planet* – or a book by Patrick Leigh Fermor – but with scraps of advice and hearsay gleaned from Facebook groups and WhatsApp. To them, Europe is a confusing blur, filled with places and even countries they've never heard of. Their conception of it is dependent on fleeting bursts of WiFi connection and 3G coverage, in the same way that a miner's understanding of his coalface is limited to what his headtorch shines on. In the process, the refugees' journey constitutes a reimagining of Europe's geographic space – one where the continent is no longer conceptualised as a neat map of fifty individual countries with separate jurisdictions, but a dark tunnel of largely indistinguishable Balkan states that surfaces eventually in Germany or Scandinavia.

Walking in the opposite direction to Leigh Fermor's meanderings towards Istanbul, these refugees are not his successors. Their travels are prompted by desperation rather than dilettantism, and are infinitely more dangerous than anything he experienced in a trip that became increasingly luxurious as time went on. But the experience of a young Syrian in the Balkans today nevertheless offers some kind of contemporary comparison to what a young Leigh Fermor weathered in 1933: the experience of wandering, with no get-out clause, through a wild and unknown continent – an experience that many had thought was no longer possible. There may even eventually be other parallels, as Europe's contemporary discourse – increasingly defined by radicalism at both ends of the spectrum, the dwindling of solidarity between European states, and the scapegoating of refugees and persecuted minorities – starts to mirror that of the 1930s. Only time will tell whether the political polarisation that was beginning to splinter the European continent as Leigh Fermor walked across it in 1933 will again rear its head in the years that follow the great Syrian migration.

'Shabab!' whispers Selim, whose mind is on more immediate matters. 'Phones off.' We are now a mile down the dyke, and the men's fears of what lies in wait for them are starting to increase. There's a rumour that the Hungarian police will be able to detect them if their mobiles are on, and Selim doesn't want to leave anything to chance. At the same time, everyone's now worried they're entering bandit country, so people hurry into the woods to gather some sticks. 'Something to hit them with,' says Wajeeh, emerging with a gnarled bit of wood. Suddenly everything seems less *Canterbury Tales* or Patrick Leigh Fermor, and more like something from Cormac McCarthy's *The Road*. There are still a few villagers walking their dogs up on the dyke above the Syrians, and a couple of them are friendly enough. But in the frazzled minds of the refugees, these could still be the scouts of the thieves.

Real or imagined, their fears are infectious. Sima decides to return to Kanjiža while it's still light and safe. It's a quarter to eight, the sun is setting, and she doesn't want to risk the possibility of getting mugged in the darkness. The rest of us stumble on, flinching at every sudden sound. Wajeeh points out a clearing where he says the Serbian police lay in wait on a previous attempt, and took €10 from each walker. After a few minutes, someone sees something that brings to life everyone's worst nightmare. One of the men at the front of the column points into the woods, and growls. 'There's people in there,' he says. 'Who are they?' Everyone turns his head to the right. The faces of strangers can be seen in the trees.

The Syrians raise their sticks. The bandits start walking towards them. They're saying something . . . in Arabic. Are they Arabic bandits? Then Wajeeh realises their mistake. 'Are you Syrians?' he calls into the woods. 'Yes, we're Syrians,' comes the reply. Everyone exhales, laughs at their paranoia, and nods respectfully as the other group of refugees emerges from the trees, each carrying a staff. They use the interlude as a cigarette break, and Assad pops into the bushes for a piss. 'He's always doing that,' says Wajeeh with affectionate derision.

The sun sets, and with the darkness comes another wave of uncertainty. Are they still on the right path? someone asks. Of course, says another; there's no other path to take. But shouldn't we check it on the GPS? No – the Hungarians might pick up the signal. 'Let's go on a bit further,' says Selim, the Sean Penn lookalike, and we press on.

The moon comes out, and then the midges. The group comes to another halt, as they debate whether to walk inside or outside the woodland. Assad has another piss. Wajeeh enters the woods, to see if there is indeed a path inside it, but re-emerges a few minutes later, shaking his head. 'Webs of spiders,' he smiles. I look at his shirt. He is indeed covered in cobwebs.

Onwards into the night. People pick at the leaves of the trees lining the path. The path itself is now grooved with deep tyre tracks that make it harder to walk – but this group seems to be making better progress than those who set out earlier in the day. Every few minutes now, we pass huddle after huddle of Syrians who've sat down at the edge of the woods to catch their breath. It's an eerie sight, thirty people sitting silently in the darkness, their faces only half lit by the moonlight. Sometimes they rise in unison, without a word.

Sometimes they just sit there like ghosts. Every so often you can hear a baby cry.

Mohamed's thoughts turn to Hungary's recently announced plans to build a barrier on the fence, an idea that makes him snort. 'We are Syrians,' he says. 'We can solve anything. We made the first [written] language, so we can break the wall. If they use electricity, we will take gloves and cut it.'

Mohamed's perseverance is a case in point. On his left wrist he has a tattoo that honours Pink Floyd – 'Syd Barrett, he is a god to me!' – and on his right wrist, an image of a ship. It's to remind him of the boat he tried to take from Turkey to Italy last December: a 72-metre cargo ship, very different from the spindly inflatable he took this year. It sank on New Year's Day – 'Everybody was celebrating,' he laughs, 'and the boat was sinking' – and he was left in the water near Cyprus. But he wasn't deterred: with nothing to lose, he kept trying until he made it to Europe – a lesson that the Hungarians would do well to heed. 'They are not going to solve migration like this,' he says. 'They need to solve the real problem and get rid of Bashar al-Assad and Isis.'

But right now these particular Syrians face a more pressing concern. On the dyke above the river, still a couple of miles from the border, they can make out two mysterious cars. Are those the local thieves they've talked so much about – or the police? Or a group of smugglers? 'Man, I'm so stressed,' says Nizam. 'Keep your voices down,' Selim interrupts. 'And hide in the woods.'

Everyone rustles into the trees. They crouch down and wait. Someone farts. Everyone squints at the cars on the dyke. One is a white saloon, the other a white hatchback. 'They could be police,' someone whispers. 'They could be smugglers. They could be thieves.' The possibility that they might be villagers living on the other side of the dyke does not cross anyone's mind. The paranoia rises. In the gloaming, people can't see each other's faces. Who's that? Who's this? No one's sure they haven't been infiltrated by outsiders. 'In the end,' says a suddenly deflated Mohamed, 'this isn't a picnic.' Then the cars' lights flick on, and everyone takes a deep breath. Then the cars drive away, and everyone breathes out. Again, they creep from the woods, and again they press on.

Nehyad twists his knee. Someone drops his euros, and someone else hands them back. Perhaps to calm his nerves, or perhaps because he hasn't got any, Mohamed chats away, nineteen to the dozen. He thinks of England (the land where the sun doesn't set). He remembers coming out as an atheist in Syria (he was proud). He explains the chemical effects of ecstasy (the dopamine drains from your brain). He imagines how he'll celebrate, if and when he gets asylum (buy a ticket to Tomorrowland, a music festival).

Mohamed's still in this kind of exuberant mood when the group halts, 500 metres shy of the border. They've all heard another urban myth that there are heat sensors on the border, which in reality is just marked by a striped pole and a sign. But group-think is a powerful thing, and they decide that passing the sign in pairs is less likely to trigger the sensors than if they go as a group. But Mohamed, high on the thought of Tomorrowland, isn't really listening – and it is at this moment that he lights his cigarette, to the consternation of his companions.

Nothing happens, of course. The Hungarian police do not emerge suddenly from the ether. Mohamed simply puts out the cigarette, and the men return to whispering among themselves, geeing each other up. 'If we stick together, we can do this,' Mohamed tells Nizam, his travelling companion since Turkey. Then the group rises, and walks towards where Hungary's wall will shortly stand.

'This wall, we will not accept it,' says Mohamed, and bounds over the border.

8

To Sweden?

Hashem's last push towards Scandinavia

Monday, 27 April 2015, 11.50 a.m.

Northern Europe

Has he blown it? The train has come to a halt inside the German border, and with his sudden outburst about the view, Hashem wonders if he's just given the game away. What if the police get on, and someone rats on him? What if one of the passengers is a policeman?

An old woman arrives, and asks someone to change his seat. Then a balding man with a straggly beard. So far, so normal. But what about the border guards? Are they on the platform? From this angle, peeking from behind the *Süddeutsche Zeitung*, Hashem can't see.

A minute passes, then another. After an age, the train moves off. The woman making the announcements on the tannoy switches to German first, French second. A sigh of relief: Hashem's in Germany. The country has yet to become the destination of choice for Syrians (which it does in late summer when the German government makes it easier for Syrians to come here) but it is more welcoming than most EU countries. Hashem puts down the *Süddeutsche Zeitung*. Just two borders to go.

Saarbrücken gives way to Mannheim, and Mannheim eventually cedes to Frankfurt, where Hashem gets out. Finally he can smoke again. He leaves the station and lights one, two, three cigarettes. Across the road, Syria's state airline has an office. Or, rather, did have one. It's shuttered shut now.

Hashem goes back inside, and waits on the platform for the train to Hamburg. A huge hoarding for the *Frankfurter Allgemeine* looms overhead. His heart is pounding. The next few hours will decide the rest of his life. He needs another smoke, and discovers a small designated smoking area marked out on the platform with white paint. To a newcomer, it's bizarre. If I cross this line, he thinks, it's not allowed? But if I stay this side, it is? So what's that woman doing smoking over there?

Three and a half hours later, Hashem's in Hamburg, another beautiful city that he'll catch only a glimpse of. With another hour to kill, he strolls in the streets surrounding the station, and marvels at its two Gothic clock towers. He likes the order of things, how everyone waits at the traffic lights until it's their turn. Now that Sweden seems within reach, Hashem's appetite begins to return, and he buys a small slice of pizza for a couple of euros. He thinks about staying the night here: there are sometimes border checks in Denmark, and you're more conspicuous if you travel at night. In the end, it's all academic. He has no one to stay with, and without a visa he can't take a bed in a hostel.

So very soon he's back at the self-service machine, thumbing at its unresponsive screen for his tickets to Copenhagen. He's getting better at this now. First there'll be a train to Flensburg, the last town in Germany. Then another to Fredericia. Finally a third will sweep him from Jutland, the Danish mainland, to Copenhagen, which lies on the island of Zealand, just south of Sweden.

The train to Flensburg is the least comfortable of the five he's used so far. He sits in the bike compartment, and has to shuffle along when a cyclist asks for more space to lock up her fold-up. The countryside is pancake flat, perfect for the white windmills the train passes every other mile. Wind energy, Hashem thinks: a good concept. The conductor, a big tattooed man, stamps his ticket, no questions asked.

The sun is setting as he arrives in Flensburg. The 20:56 to Fredericia is waiting just across the platform, and the Danish border lies just a mile or so beyond it. Hashem gets on board and finds the seat furthest from the door. The language on the tannoy changes from staccato German to blurred Danish.

Hashem hides behind his latest bit of camouflage: the pink cover of Danish Rail's on-train magazine, *Ud & Se*. And then Hashem waits. It shouldn't be long till he knows his fate: in five minutes he'll be in Padborg, the first station inside Denmark, and the penultimate border. What will await him there?

Something bad, he thinks at first. There, standing on the platform at Padborg, are two Danes wearing what look like uniforms. Hashem sinks into his seat and prepares for the worst. The two uniforms board his carriage. But then the train eases off again. If they were going to check his passport, wouldn't they need to get off afterwards? He waits some more. He abandons the pink train magazine, and pretends to be asleep. One of the uniformed men approaches. The clink of his keys grows nearer and nearer, until finally he stops beside Hashem's table. Hashem peeks at him, through the crack in his eyelids. It's just the ticket inspector, replacing his colleague.

At 10.31 p.m., the train draws into Fredericia. It's the furthest north Hashem's ever been, and his shivers show it.

It's cold. He waits in the pristine Danish waiting room, Poul Henningsen lampshades hanging from the ceiling. He gets a copy of the *Politiken* newspaper, his latest bit of camouflage. He can't smoke in the waiting room, so he goes in and out, in and out, bouncing between his dual fixes of nicotine and warmth. At just past 11 p.m., the dance ends: the train to Copenhagen arrives, and soon he's ploughing east to the capital.

Two and a half hours later, in the small hours of Tuesday morning, Hashem sets foot on the platform in the Danish capital. Thirteen days after leaving Egypt, six after arriving in Italy, he is just one half-hour train ride from the holy grail. But first he needs to buy a ticket.

That proves hard. The first booth he tries requires a credit card. Syrian refugees don't carry many of those. The second, which takes cash, reveals a bigger problem: he's now outside the eurozone, and he hasn't any Danish krona. And at 1.30 a.m., there aren't many bureaux de change to help him out.

So Hashem limps around the airy red-bricked concourse, trying to find any shop that will first take some euros, and then give him change in krona. McDonald's is the only option, but even as he enters it someone else is being told that no, McDonald's will not take euros. Try the 7-Eleven down the road. Hashem leaves the station for the empty streets outside, and eventually finds the 7-Eleven. It's on a crossroads lit like a Hopper painting. Will they take euros? Through the medium of hand signals and broken English, the man behind the counter says yes – but only €10 notes. But that's not enough. The ticket to Sweden costs the equivalent of €18 or €19, so Hashem needs to pay with a €20 note, and get the largest amount of change he can. The shop assistant gives in. All right then.

Hashem lurches around for the cheapest thing in the shop. Eventually he finds the smallest pack of gum, and gets the change in krona.

He limps back towards the station's Gothic walls. The clock above the entrance reads 1.54 a.m., so he has eighteen minutes till the next train to southern Sweden. He puts the krona in the slot. It's just enough for a ticket, so finally he can cross the Øresund. The screech that accompanies the printing of a one-way train ticket has never sounded so good. He takes the escalator down to the platform level. Hashem has one more train journey to go. One more border to cross.

It could not come soon enough. Hashem is exhausted – physically, mentally and emotionally. The past three years have been punctured by constant trauma, and frequent humiliation. The past two weeks have seen him risk arrest, death and starvation to cross a sea and a continent. He is thirsty, hungry, smelly, sleep-deprived, and now a bag of nerves. And every step he walks, he feels a pang from his infected foot.

His journey is one of epic heroism – a kind of latterday Homeric odyssey. But, right now, he just feels miserable and nauseous. His knees wobble from the cold, and from the fear. He clicks his teeth, and paces around the platform until finally two white lights appear in the tunnel in the distance. His ride to Sweden is here. One more train journey to go, one more border to cross.

The train glides east, stopping first at Ørestad, then Taarnby, two areas in east Copenhagen. If the sun were up,

Hashem would be able to see Ørestad's eccentric new housing estate, whose balconies jut haphazardly outwards like the quills of a giant porcupine. But it's dark, and in any case Hashem has only one place on his mind: Sweden. Getting there without being arrested is the difference between finding a short-term sanctuary and securing a long-term future.

It's late, but people still hop on and off. Hashem darts his eyes at each of them: for all he knows, anyone could be border police. The train reaches Copenhagen airport, the last before Sweden. Now just the straits of Øresund and the bridge that spans them lie between Hashem and the promised land. He presses his hands together, rolling his palms over each other, again and again.

A man sitting two rows away wakes up with a start, and looks in shock at where he's ended up: a few stops further than he wanted. Hashem barely registers it. He's thinking of what lies ahead.

The train enters the bridge. Outside, it's pitch black, so he might as well still be in a tunnel. Only the lights of the distant Swedish shoreline reveal that Hashem is about to cross the fifth and final border of his fortnight-long ordeal. Across the world, this bridge has become famous as the inspiration for *The Bridge*, a police procedural about a body found spreadeagled on the line that marks the boundary between Denmark and Sweden. Hashem hopes nothing as dramatic will happen tonight.

The lights of Sweden draw closer and closer, until at last his window draws level with them. He's crossed into Sweden. The train slows, passing lamp-post after lamp-post until it eases into Hyllie, the first station on Swedish soil. The change is almost imperceptible: only the lettering on the signage (the Danish ø has turned into a Swedish ö) indicates he's in a new country.

Will there be one final surprise? Hashem looks from the window for a policeman to appear on the empty platform, and foil him at the last. But no one gets on. Not one passenger. The doors clunk shut, and onwards they roll.

Has Hashem done it? He can't quite believe it, and he needs to double-check before he celebrates. 'Are we', he whispers, too scared to say the words out loud, 'in Sweden?'

He gets the all-clear, and a grin breaks out across his face for the first time in days. He gives a thumbs up, first tentatively and then emphatically. He scratches his right ear, letting the realisation sink in. It's 2.41 a.m., 22 April 2015, and he has reached the place he hopes to call home for the rest of his life. Hashem shuts his eyes and raises his eyebrows. And then lets out a long lungful of breath.

In Malmö, the first major city in Sweden, he calls Hayam, far away in Egypt. 'Hello,' he says. 'I've arrived.'

9

A Gate Clangs Shut

The explosion of the Balkan route,
Europe's moral crisis, and the closure
of the Hungarian border

Hungary, Austria, Serbia, Croatia; September 2015

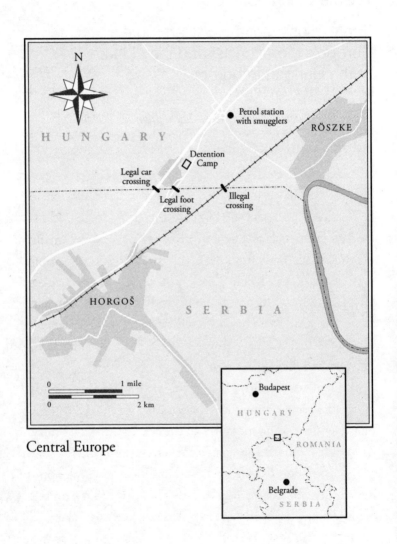

Central Europe

Hurtling through the darkness, a mile north of Hungary's border with Serbia, Hans Breuer duels with his satellite navigation system. In pristine German, the sat-nav insists he head west, along the most direct route to his home in Austria. But on this evening in early September, Hans has other ideas – swerving into a dirt track that the GPS doesn't recognise.

Amid gentle chides from the sat-nav, the sixty-one-year-old switches off his headlights, so that no one will see where he's gone. Then he bumps and veers through a warren of unmarked farm trails and shepherd paths that lead eventually westwards, but away from the main roads. After twenty minutes, he brakes to a halt in a dark field, and turns to a blanket on the back seat. 'OK,' says Hans to the blanket, 'you can come out now.' From under the fabric, three heads emerge – a Syrian Kurd, Galbari al-Hussein, and her two children, Hussein and Shahed.

Suddenly exuberant, Hans beams with pleasure. 'Friends of my mother', he announces dramatically, 'escaped the Nazis by pretending to be members of the SS. Hearing this story all my life is what has prepared me for this situation!'

It's a situation that even Hans himself couldn't have predicted three months earlier. Usually Hans isn't found on the Serbo-Hungarian border. In fact, he's not really found in the modern world at all. He calls himself Austria's last wandering shepherd, and occasionally Austria's last wandering Jew.

When he's not herding his flock of sheep across publicly owned Austrian countryside, or playing Yiddish songs with his band, he lives in a pair of unheated wooden wagons on the edge of a forest in the south-east of the country. It's the kind of place where the lights dim when he fires up the kettle – and there's no running water. He and his second wife, twenty-six-year-old Mingo, scrub the dishes with lemon juice rather than soap, and their two toddlers play with acorns instead of Lego. The toilet is a shed in the garden filled with back issues of the *Jewish Socialist*, as well as the latest edition of *The Land* – an ephemeral magazine about land rights that gives Hans both great joy and great frustration. 'It has taken me half a year to read it,' he solemnly confides after I return from the shed one evening. Not because of any bowel issues, he clarifies, but because of his patchy English.

The driving principle of the mag, as I discover in the shed while skimming page two, is that 'the roots of justice, freedom, social security and democracy lie not so much in access to money, or to the ballot box, as in access to land and its resources'. It's a battle cry that hints at why a singing shepherd might be found helping three refugees to escape the grasp of the Hungarian border patrol, some 300 miles from his flock, his family and his garden shed. But to understand properly what brings Hans here, on this evening in early September, we first need to recap on what's happened in the Balkans in the few months since we left Mohamed Hussein as he vaulted into Hungary in June.

The number of refugees walking through the Balkans has exploded. Back in June, around 1000 people were landing every day on the Greek islands, which was itself unprecedented.

Now in mid-September, the average is 5000, and later in the year, it will rise to as high as 9000.[1] And at every ensuing stage of the Balkan route, be it in Macedonia, Serbia or Hungary, a similar number are now in transit at any one time. The footfall is astonishing, and its consequences tragic. The chaos on Kos or Lesvos was bad in June and July, but it's now become exponentially worse, with tens of thousands of migrants waiting in filthy and often sodden conditions for their papers. The western route that Hashem al-Souki took in April is now almost forgotten, even though near record numbers are also still landing in Italy. That's how big the Balkan crisis has become.

The media has responded in kind. In the first half of 2015, the refugee crisis wasn't exactly being ignored – but it wasn't in the news every day either. Now it's the international story of the year. When I reported on the Macedonian border closure back in July, my own newspaper had found it such a sideshow that it didn't put the story in the paper, and apart from my online report there was no other coverage in any outlet. When the border closes briefly again in August, every news crew in Europe is on it, as if the closure is unprecedented. Meanwhile, on Lesvos, the Kempson family deservedly become minor celebrities. Channel 4 profiles them, calling them the angels of the Aegean, while the *Sun* and the *Independent* run 'exclusive' interviews.

That it's the midsummer silly season probably helps; an absence of other news stories draws attention to worthier things. But the main reason for the spike in coverage is the sudden and collective realisation of just how close the crisis is, and just how human its victims are. Two events bring these points home more than any other. The first is in late August, when seventy-one refugees are discovered dead in the back of a smuggler's truck parked at the side of a road in Austria, with putrid juices dripping from the door. The second comes a week later, when the body of a Kurdish toddler, Alan Kurdi, is photographed face down on a beach in Turkey, having drowned with his brother and mother in a failed attempt to reach Kos. Suddenly Europe cares. Alan's corpse is on the front pages of dozens if not hundreds of European newspapers the next day, including that of the *Sun*, whose columnist Katie Hopkins had only a few months before described migrants as cockroaches. 'Show me bodies floating in the water,' Hopkins had written in April. 'I still don't care.' Fast-forward to September, and her editors evidently now disagree. In October, they'll be back to their migrant-baiting worst – but for a few weeks in the middle, they're forced to change their minds by the brilliance of one Turkish photojournalist. As a specialist who's failed for months to prompt this kind of shift with my own coverage, it is a humbling reminder of my own insignificance.

Amid this outcry, people begin to question the language they're using to describe the situation. All year, the media have classed the people arriving by boat as migrants. It should be a perfectly neutral word; it's been used for years to refer to any person moving between countries, for whatever reason. But as the summer goes on, the word – like other initially neutral descriptors before it, such as asylum seeker and immigrant – is increasingly used by some outlets in a more negative sense. In certain quarters, 'migrant' comes implicitly to mean someone who's travelling for economic reasons, rather than for as yet undetermined ones. And so, as public sympathy for migrants rises in August, there's a drive by the UN refugee agency[2] and by news groups such as al-Jazeera[3] to use less pejorative language to describe these people on the move. As an alternative default, they suggest the word refugee. Overnight, the migration crisis is therefore redefined in liberal circles as a refugee crisis, and anyone who queries the change is seen as unsympathetic to the plight of its protagonists. Personally, I can see the logic in the tweak: the crisis is one overwhelmingly propelled by people who would qualify for protection under the 1951 Refugee Convention. In the short term, it makes sense to use language that highlights their right to protection, since it might remind politicians of their duty to provide it. For this reason, throughout this book I've fallen into the habit of referring to people who are likely to be defined as refugees as exactly that – refugees – particularly when writing about the Balkan route. Where I'm in danger of repeating the word too often, I'll use migrant as an alternative, but mostly for stylistic reasons. In the medium-to-long term, though, I think this is a slightly unhelpful development, and I'd prefer to see the word 'migrant' reclaimed and returned to its proper, neutral usage. Firstly, it's more accurate. When you're describing a large group of people whom you don't know, it makes sense to define them by what they're doing (which you can be reasonably sure of) rather than why they're doing it (which you can't). Migrant is the most efficient way of achieving this: in its purest sense it simply means someone on the move – and casts no aspersions, positive or negative, on why they set out in the first place. Secondly, many of those who push for the use of 'refugee' do so by defining refugees in opposition to migrants. Refugees, they say, deserve rights, whereas migrants don't. Refugees had good reason to leave home; migrants did not. This is a problematic differentiation. In attempting to separate the two groups, we imply that it is easy to distinguish between them. In reality, as I've attempted to explain in earlier chapters, it is increasingly hard to do so. There is often overlap, and many people's experiences might fit the definitions of both categories. By wrongly exaggerating and simplifying the difference between them, we therefore risk delegitimising them all. And, finally, even if it were possible to make a clean linguistic division between the two, I'm not sure it would be useful. The point of delineating between different kinds of migration is to draw a line between who has the right to move and who doesn't – and in turn to identify which people should be prevented from moving in the first place. But, in reality, history proves that prevention may not be possible, and so too does the current crisis. People have always moved. The story of humanity is essentially the story of human movement. In the near future, people will move even more, particularly if, as some predict, climate change sparks mass migration on an unprecedented scale. The sooner we recognise the inevitability of this movement, the sooner we can try to manage it.

In the aftermath of the Kurdis' deaths, the governments of the EU are under pressure to do exactly that. For months, European leaders have refused to share more than a token number of the refugees landing in Greece and Italy (let alone the far greater numbers still in the far smaller countries of the Middle East). Their callous expectation is that the countries bearing the brunt of the crisis (Germany, Greece, Italy and Sweden) should be left to deal with the problem themselves. It's a troubling abandonment of one of the binding principles of the European Union: solidarity between member states. Scared of a continent-wide swing towards the far right, and unwilling to admit the inevitability of the situation, most of Europe's politicians are prepared to forgo any last dregs of statesmanship in order to stave off their nationalist rivals. In response, Germany's chancellor, Angela Merkel, says the fallout from the situation is an even bigger threat to Europe than the eurozone crisis, while a UN spokesman tells me that the unity of the continent is at risk.

To an extent, the deaths in Austria, and of the Kurdis, help inch the debate onwards. But not by much, and not with any grace: after a series of bad-tempered meetings, the countries of the EU finally agree in September to share 120,000 of the refugees who'll land in Italy and Greece over the next two years, and to resettle 40,000 of those still languishing in Lebanon, Jordan and Turkey. Britain opts out of the agreement, but promises to admit 4000 refugees every year for the next five years. Wonks in Brussels hail all this as a huge step forward, given Europe's previous intransigence. In reality, it is a pathetic failure. More people are now landing in a single day on the island of Lesvos than Cameron will welcome to Britain in the next twelve months. More will land in Greece in a single month in 2015 than the rest of the EU will share between them over the next two years. Ten times as many are currently sitting in Lebanon. As hundreds of thousands continue to arrive, drown, or shiver in the rain throughout the Balkans in the winter of 2015, Europe's response constitutes an abdication of decency.

The integrity of a few countries shines through, most obviously Sweden and Germany. Overwhelmed by the influx, both countries eventually step back from their commitments – but for most of the year they welcome above and beyond their fair share of refugees. Sweden pays a particularly high price, as its asylum system comes close to collapse, and a far-right opposition party shoots up the opinion polls. Germany fares slightly better – in an ageing German society, an influx of fairly educated, working-age immigrants has its advantages. But it still requires considerable political courage for the German chancellor, Angela Merkel, to sell such a policy to a wary electorate. And Merkel is certainly courageous, promising to welcome any Syrian, regardless of whether they've already been fingerprinted in Greece, Hungary or any other EU country. Yet, in its kindness, Germany inadvertently adds to the problem, prompting a new surge in arrivals on the Greek islands. When I'd previously asked Syrians where they wanted to end up, I drew a range of answers: Holland, perhaps, or Sweden, Austria or the UK. Now almost everyone says they just want to reach Germany.

The pragmatism of the lower Balkan countries is also increasingly apparent. Having previously tried to block the path of refugees, or slow them down, Macedonia, Serbia and Greece have now bowed to the inevitable and created a de facto humanitarian corridor to Hungary. When I first visited the Hara hotel in northern Greece, in the early weeks of the summer, refugees had had to make their way there on foot or in illegal taxis from Thessaloniki. On my second visit there in September, I find that Greece is now allowing private coach companies to drive refugees all the way from Athens to the hotel – albeit for horrendously marked-up prices. (Even Simos is friendlier, though he doesn't recognise me, and is alarmed to find I know his name.)

At the border itself, Macedonia is doing something similar. Instead of blocking the way with a line of policemen and troops, sparking terror and pandemonium, there is now a numbered ticketing system. I arrive at the same time as a family of haberdashers from Aleppo, and they are soon able to join group number 106, a line of fifty fellow Syrians waiting patiently to cross the border. Group 105 is already over the other side. Once in Macedonia, the haberdashers will swiftly receive transit papers at a camp that was built recently for this specific purpose. Before long, they'll amble over to a new, makeshift train station assembled in recent weeks solely for refugee use. By the evening a special train will have taken them straight to the Serbian border. An equivalent scheme exists there too. Instead of trying to prevent or ignore the flow of refugees, officials have now recognised its inevitability, and are instead trying to organise it. A route that used to involve long stretches of walking can now be completed almost exclusively in coaches and trains, organised by Balkan governments. A route that was previously suitable only for the young and able is now increasingly accessible to families with children. It is an encouraging reaction to the reality of the situation, and one that the countries of the EU would do well to follow.

For now, even the Hungarians have stopped trying to stop the unstoppable. Their famous fence is built – but at this moment in early September it's just a few rolls of barbed wire. As a result, it's useless. Refugees realise they can cross it fairly easily by smothering its spikes with a sleeping bag or coat. I cross it myself in twenty-seven seconds, simply by treading on its coils with my boots. I'm sure others have done it in half as much – every few metres you can find the torn clothes of migrants who've successfully breached the fence in recent weeks. 'Oh, they come from everywhere,' admits a Hungarian border guard. 'Here, there, and over there,' she adds, pointing to a nearby spot where the fence lies particularly low, not far from where I'd walked with Mohamed Hussein.

The upshot of all this is that Hungary, for the time being, has given up the ghost. By 15 September, they'll have built a taller, better fence. That's the day they'll also roll out a new law that criminalises irregular border crossings (for now, it's just a civil offence). Until then though, despite their rhetoric, they're quietly letting refugees walk straight into Hungary. Realising that it's better to filter refugees through one particular point, rather than have them cross the border surreptitiously at hundreds of different ones, the Hungarians have created a gap in the fence a few miles north of Kanjiža. There's a disused railway line that crosses the border there, and migrants are allowed to use it to cross unobstructed from the Serbian village of Horgoš into the Hungarian village of Röszke.

I spend half a week on this old railroad at the gates to the EU. Gone are the clandestine night-time trips that I'd experienced with Mohamed Hussein. Now thousands walk along it every day, in broad daylight, and police do not attempt to stop them. There are pregnant women, and women carrying babies. There are families of seven, with toddlers picking their way along the wooden sleepers. In fact, one of the most striking differences between the scene now and that from earlier in the summer is the increase in the number of children, women and invalids. There are people in wheelchairs. There are men limping on sticks. And there is a boy wheezing on his crutches. It is a wave of humanity that, despite its best intentions, not even the xenophobic Hungarian government can repel. As they cross along the railway line at Röszke, the waiting policemen simply smile. 'Is this Hungary?' asks one Syrian. 'Yes, it is,' says an officer, and waves him on. Rather than trying to prevent the flow, Hungary is simply trying to manage it.

Nevertheless, once they're on Hungarian soil, the refugees are not being treated in anything like a humane way. They're being allowed to pass through the country towards Austria and then Germany, which has promised to welcome them with open arms. But only after being registered – and in the process robbed of their dignity. After entering Hungary along the railway at Röszke, most of the refugees are then herded into an empty field, and forced to wait there in the cold for several days until space opens up in the registration camps nearby. Once they get to the camps, life is hardly better. As they wait to be registered and fingerprinted, the refugees are kept in cages, and fed like animals. In one leaked video, guards can be seen throwing food at crowds of caged Syrians and Afghans, as if they're monkeys in a zoo. As ever, it's the smugglers who ultimately benefit, as refugees look for ways of escaping the border guards; avoiding the humiliation inside the camps; and getting to Budapest, the Hungarian capital, under their own steam. I watch as the boy on crutches – fourteen-year-old Hassan – heaves himself into a petrol station that lies a few minutes from where refugees are locked in cages. As expected, over by the cashier's office, five podgy bald men sit around a wooden picnic table. These are the men that Hassan and his three friends have come for.

They approach the table. 'Budapest? Four persons?' asks Hassan's brother. 'How much?'

The smuggler with the most hair responds. 'Twelve hundred euros,' he says, his mouth full of salami bap. 'For the whole car.'

Would 900 work? No, but he'll settle for 1000 – and a deal is struck. The four Syrians hurry into the car, a black hatchback, and their injured brother sits in the front seat. Then a fifth and youngest sibling sprints in from the road, crowding the back seat with four passengers.

'Money,' says the smuggler, still holding his bap. 'Now.' They hand over their cash, and the Toyota races out of the car park. And then in through the other exit walks another Syrian family. Around the corner, another family is waiting. The smugglers are dangerous and untrustworthy, as the deaths of the seventy-one in Austria show. But if you want to get out of southern Hungary without being humiliated in the camps, these criminals are nevertheless the only alternative.

The only alternative, that is, until the emergence of people like Hans Breuer. As news spreads of how refugees are being treated on arrival in Hungary, dozens of ordinary Austrians and Hungarians are descending on the area near the Röszke railroad. Their aim is to secretly rescue refugee families who've managed to evade the Hungarian border guards – and then drive them from southern Hungary to eastern Austria, where they can continue their journey as normal. The volunteers want to give refugees the chance of circumventing the Hungarian camps, without having to place their lives in the hands of smugglers. And Hans Breuer is one of them.

Which is why, on 13 September 2015, I find myself driving with Hans from his hut in Austria to the Röszke railroad. And why, once we've arrived in the area, he starts talking to a bush. 'My friend,' he says to the foliage. 'My friend, are you still there?'

Hans hasn't gone mad. The area around the border is an archipelago of fields patrolled by policemen. To get to the volunteers and their cars, or to reach the petrol stations and their smugglers, refugees have to hide in the undergrowth. Hence this conversation with the bush: Hans has told a Syrian artist to meet him here, so that they can discuss the details of his escape in semi-privacy. 'Hello?' says Hans, peering into the leaves of the bush. 'My friend?' But his friend isn't there.

Hans is suddenly rattled. On the drive down, he'd been full of bravado. He'd picked up a Hungarian hitch-hiker called László, and proudly told him what he was on his way to do. László didn't speak great English, but once he understood what Hans was saying, he grew alarmed for Hans's safety. So he called a friend of his, and asked him to explain to Hans in English that he risks years in jail if he is caught. Listening to László's friend on the phone, Hans rolled his eyes. 'Tell him I thank him a lot, and it's nice that there are Hungarians who are not assholes,' Hans said irritably. 'But I know all this shit!'

A few hours later, Hans is less complacent. What if the Syrian had been arrested on his way to the bush? What if that passing police car is searching for us? 'Don't talk so loudly,' he whispers after I started chatting to some Syrians in Arabic. 'We don't know who is an infiltrator.'

Chastened by the episode with the bush, Hans decides he can't just pick up random Syrians from the countryside. Instead, he calls some activists who are working in the fields where refugees are herded after they cross the border, and where they're held until there's space for them in the camps. The activists there have a good relationship with both the refugees in the fields, and the police guarding the fields' perimeter. The cops think the activists just want to hand out food, rather than organise secret rescue missions – so they allow them to wander around the area, talking to refugees.

One of the activists picks up, so Hans pops the question: does she have any families who need to be transported to Austria? Indeed she does: a Kurdish woman and her two kids – so we drive over to the field where they're all waiting. We get lost several times, but eventually we get there as the sun has almost set. Hans has some crates of water in the back of his car, so he parks up and begins to unload them, as if he's just delivering supplies. He doesn't want it to seem like he's here to rescue any refugees. Several activists arrive and help him move the water, turning the whole process into a distraction. Two policemen are momentarily interested, but then toddle off once they've worked out what they think is going on. At that point, the three Kurds are hurried into the back of the car. The blanket that we met earlier in the chapter is thrown over them. There is some fumbling beneath its fabric – and then silence. Hans starts the car, and begins a three-point turn. The two policemen renew their interest in what's going on, and start walking back towards us. A Hungarian activist seizes the initiative and begins to extravagantly help Hans with his manoeuvres. She gesticulates wildly and issues loud instructions – anything to distract from the three Kurds huddling under the blanket in the back. It works. When the cops reach us, they too point and wave – somewhat redundantly, and very ironically – and we're able to ease off without further problems. The light has gone, and a few minutes later, so too have the police in our wing mirror.

Thus begins the battle with the sat-nav, as Hans leaves the main road network in favour of the back ways of the Hungarian countryside. The last thing he wants is to run into a police checkpoint, and there won't be any of those in the muddy single-track paths that wind between the farms. After several wiggles through several fields, Hans is confident we're safe for now. He stops the car. 'OK,' says Hans to the blanket. 'You can come out now.'

Adrenalin pumping, Hans is triumphant, as though he's just pipped his rivals at the end of a long-distance race. But he's doing all this for far more than mere excitement. For Hans, this fight is personal. His father, a Jewish dissident, fled Austria for Britain shortly before the Second World War, and his eyes redden when he compares the two eras. 'It makes me cry again and again if I think of my father, of his situation, and of other immigrants – and I put it together with these people,' Hans says. 'Friends of my parents, Jewish people, tried to emigrate to Switzerland [before the Second World War], but the Swiss put them back to the Nazis at the frontier. There is too much similarity between these two situations – one seventy years ago, and one now.'

Nowhere is this synergy more obvious than in Hans's car, where the son of a survivor of the first refugee crisis has rescued some survivors of the second one. These parallels increase even further once Hans starts singing. On an earlier journey with a carload of Syrian Palestinians, he'd sung Yiddish folk songs and they'd joined in with the chorus.[4] This night, he tries a recent composition – another Yiddish tune set to lyrics about the plight of refugees. 'All my shoes got torn to pieces at the Hungaaaaarian border,' sings Hans, to the tune of a Jewish wedding song.[5] 'Macedonians shot at us with tear gas to make oooooorder. They forced us to give fingerprints – and took away our phoooones. We have to sleep just on the ground – can feel it in my bo-ooones.'

He breaks off. 'Look,' he smiles. 'It's a work in progress, OK?'

It's a rich experience, riding with Hans. He's a man who bridges some of the different eras of European history, and is quick to connect the dots between them. Hans doesn't just spot the overlap between Europe's treatment of Jewish refugees and that of Syrians today. Hans also remembers when it was the Hungarians jumping the border fences, rather than erecting them. Aged only two at the time, he doesn't have first-hand memories of this himself. But when he was a child, his parents told him stories of how the Hungarians streamed into Austria in 1956, after the October uprising against the Soviets – and how they were welcomed. 'Back then people had such solidarity, even though they had nothing,' he says. 'This was the tradition of the post-war – the people who brought refugees out across the border were heroes.'

Hans also draws connections between the rise of fascism in 1930s Europe and the rise of something similar, if smaller, today. His parents fought against Austria's fascists back in the pre-war years, and he's prepared to follow in their footsteps if right-wing extremists continue to make inroads into European society today – not least in Hungary. He taps his steering wheel, and nods at the lane stretching out in front of us. 'This is preparation for the fascism that is rising in Europe,' Hans warns. 'I do it to set up resistance structures for the Hungarians that don't want to spend ten years in jail. When this is finished, and I have to bring out a man who is wanted by Orbán, I will have to know how to use the muddy roads. I'm training for that.'

On the back seat, Galbari al-Hussein and her two children have more pressing concerns. They don't know who these two slightly odd strangers are. They escaped Isis country just eight days ago, and took a gamble by getting in this car. They're less keen on singing, and more on getting to Germany. 'We are frightened, we are frightened by everything,' says Galbari, sitting in the darkness. 'Please can we just keep driving.'

Shaken from his reverie, Hans starts the car again. 'Come on, Hans,' Hans says to himself. 'Stay focused. You have not won yet.' We plough on, jolting down the bumpy tracks, with farmhouses looming occasionally out of the gloom. In the back, Galbari is still not very certain about what's going on. 'We are scared,' she says, in faltering English. 'Where are we going?' I start replying in faltering Arabic, and Hans feels cut out of the loop. 'What are you saying?' he asks. I tell him I'm trying to explain who we are and where we're going.

Hans shakes his head. Experience tells him this isn't a good idea: he thinks it's best to keep things vague until we're in Austria, lest we raise their hopes prematurely.

It's hard to explain this logic to Galbari. She's in a car with two strange men, and she needs to know what's happening. To calm her down, I give her my phone so she can call her family. Wrong move. She immediately tells them she'll be in Vienna in a few hours, and says she can meet them tonight. When I relay this to Hans, he starts to panic – there's no way we can get to Vienna tonight. The discreet rural route he's planned will get them to southern Austria, not to northerly Vienna. His wife can drive them first thing tomorrow to the capital, but he'll be too tired to get them there himself tonight. 'I'm sixty-one years old,' he says. 'I need to sleep!'

Galbari doesn't get why Hans won't take her to where she wants. Hans doesn't get why she can't grasp the stupidity of driving along main roads where police are watching for cars like this one. While we argue, we re-emerge for a period on a main road, and Hans flinches as we pass a police car. It's a tense few minutes, and I'm caught in the middle, translating between a man who doesn't completely understand my English, and a woman who doesn't completely understand my Arabic. Eventually Hans stops the car once we're back in the countryside, and we clear the air with a new set of introductions and explanations.

'My name is Hans,' says Hans, 'and I am a shepherd, a singer, and a Jew.'

From the back comes a warm and immediate response.

'Jews, Muslims, Christians – it's not important,' says Galbari. 'We are all humans.'

Tempers calmed, Hans starts the engine once more. The Husseins fall asleep in the back. Hans drives on through the night, relying on his forty years as a shepherd to guide him. It's given him a rich knowledge of how farmland is parcelled up, and how paths weave within it. In this part of Hungary, Breuer knows that land was for centuries held in common ownership, meaning that the fields host a rich network of byways that can take the modern driver a long way towards Austria without having to use a main road. On land that was always privately owned, Hans says, the paths tend to lead to nowhere – they just connect individual landowners with their own individual plots. Whereas the common land we're driving through once needed to be accessible to many different people from many different places. So its roads lead on and on. 'It's a wonderful landscape,' Hans says with admiration. 'All the roads are connected!'

His enthusiasm for the commons is nevertheless about more than just the practical help it gives him in situations like this. He loves the philosophy behind this configuration of land, the idea that the countryside is to be shared between villagers, and enjoyed by everyone. Among other things, it's what drove him to become a wandering shepherd, herding sheep across land he doesn't own. Hans is the link to a Europe whose heroes are not kings and soldiers, but forgotten rebels like Michael Gaismair, who took over part of what is now called Austria in the sixteenth century, and tried to create a proto-socialist republic. Four hundred years ahead of his time, Gaismair believed in the concepts of not just common land but of free hospitals and schools. 'Can you imagine Obamacare,' asks Hans, tearing up, 'but in 1525?'

His belief in the commons is also another reason why helping refugees is such a personal fight for Hans. Just as he believes that anyone should be allowed to work the land, so too should anyone be allowed to cross it. 'For me, when I'm doing my shepherd job, the most healthy thing and the most nature-like thing is to migrate,' says Hans. 'Humans used to migrate; they did not stay in the same place in winter. They would move.' Hans wishes they still would – and that's why he's driving this car, well past midnight, through the back-ways of south-west Hungary.

It's at about 1 a.m. when Hans begins to flag. He's been on the road for sixteen hours now, and the driving and the jolting are taking their toll. 'I don't fall asleep,' he reassures me. 'But sometimes I hallucinate. My hands still do the job, but I don't remember where we were the last ten minutes.' On the back seat, Galbari has the opposite problem. All of sudden, she wakes, sits bolt upright – and screams. Then when she realises she's in safe company, she falls instantly back to sleep. Hans nods compassionately. 'My own mother, she did not sleep easily,' Hans remembers. 'She was tortured by the Gestapo, and she screamed every night.'

We fall into silence. The Syrians keep on sleeping. Hans weaves this way and that through the fields. And so it is that six hours after hustling the Syrians inside his car, Breuer approaches the Austrian border, unseen and unstopped by anyone. He finds a tiny road that straddles the dividing line between Austria and Hungary, the kind of track known only to a local. Then he swings the car over the border, along a lane unknown by GPS. We've made it.

'The shepherd', Breuer says, as the Syrians snooze in the back, 'is at home.'

It's the last journey of its kind that Hans will make. Not because of his own reluctance, but because soon there won't be anyone to rescue. Two days later Hungary finally manages to close its southern border with Serbia, after months of failed attempts. Their piddling first fence had failed to deter anyone, so the government has had both soldiers and convicts working day and night to construct a bigger and better fence. This enhanced version is finally finished on the 14th. As a result, the Hungarians promise to shut the border – at long last – as soon as the clock strikes twelve on the 15th.

I turn up to the Serbian side late on the evening of the 14th. I'm fresh from my trip with Hans that began just the other side of the fence, and I'm keen to witness what feels like a moment. This has been the gateway to the bulk of the European Union for several hundred thousand people over the past few months. Where will they go now?

By the time I arrive, the railroad has already been blocked with the carriage – and subtlety – of a freight train. For the last few hours of the 14th, refugees are therefore being funnelled through the formal border crossing, half a mile to the west. Many of them haven't been told that the border will soon close, so there are still hundreds trying their luck, late into the night. As midnight approaches, there is still a queue in front of Hungary's iron gates, stretching back into Serbia for a couple of dozen metres.

Midnight comes and goes. For a few fleeting minutes, there is some humanity in the darkness. The Hungarians seem to soften, continuing to admit some of the remaining stragglers, even after the deadline. At ten minutes past midnight, there are still families running, limping, waddling and panting up the road that leads to the border gate. More than 200,000 people have successfully crossed this line so far this year, so no one wants to be the first to be locked out of Fortress Europe.[6]

'I'm hoping, hoping, hoping,' says a Syrian engineer as he steams up the final stretch. 'We need to pass through this border. We lost everything in Syria – homes, friends and family.'

Behind him are mums with babies on their backs, and dads with babies strapped to their fronts. There are grans from Iraq, and granddads from Afghanistan. There are kids fleeing the remains of Aleppo, and Palestinians running from Yarmouk, a generation after their parents first fled from Israel to that now desolate Damascus suburb. There is a Moroccan, all the way from Fez to find a job. There is, as usual, a man in a wheelchair. And an Iraqi on crutches – a tubby twenty-two-year-old from Baghdad, one of the very last few to heave his way across the border.

I ask him how he feels to be hobbling over the border in the nick of time. 'Mabsut,' he wheezes, in between gasps of air. 'Happy.'

And then the gates clang shut. At around twenty past twelve on 15 September, Hungary finally blocks the main route used by refugees to reach the safety of the European Union, leaving around a hundred people stranded. Later in the night, Hungarian police erect a flimsy second fence behind the main barrier of the crossing, just in case anyone hasn't got the idea.

And perhaps they haven't. With nowhere else to go, the rejected, dejected refugees simply slump on the tarmac. Pressed up against the gate, one of the first families to be turned away from Hungary struggles to compute what's going on. The dad, a printer called Radwan, has brought two babies and three older children all the way from Yarmouk, the second time in as many generations that his family has had to flee their home. First they left Palestine. Then Syria. Now even Europe has shut its doors to them.

'We're Palestinian Syrians, where else are we supposed to go now?' asks Radwan. 'We're coming from destruction and killing. I shouldn't have to take five children all the way here for us to be shut out here.'

Exhausted, shocked, and unsure of what to do next, Radwan and his wife Mayada collapse against their rucksacks. He cradles his three-year-old son, who hasn't spoken since leaving Syria two weeks ago. She rocks their youngest to sleep. They spend the rest of the night huddled on the tarmac. And so do around a hundred others, all locked out of the European Union.

What happens next, I wonder. When one route to the EU closes, how long before people find another?

In the end, it takes longer than I thought it would – for now, people stay put. There's now no handy Facebook guide to tell everyone where to go. The next day, thousands of refugees just turn up here at the Hungarian border, for lack of anywhere else to head. Tensions boil over as crowds of tired, disorientated and frightened Syrians begin flinging bottles over the fence into Hungary. Then follows a bizarre episode in which the Hungarian riot police, protected by several layers of fences, fire teargas and water cannon to control a riot occurring on the territory of another sovereign nation. At least seven children are hurt in the melee.

Finally, after two days of deadlock, people start considering alternatives. There's another route that all the journalists are talking about – through a country that lies to Serbia's west. It's called Croatia.

Limping along in flip-flops, a burly businessman from Iraq is one of the first refugees to test the new route. Serbia has a 200-mile border with Croatia, but the northern part of it is marked by the River Danube, whose width makes it hard to cross. So Ahmed Riad and his two friends are crossing via the flat farmland that spans the southern bit of the border. There are fields of landmines in the area, relics of the Balkan wars in the 1990s. Riad has seen far worse in Iraq – so here he is, striding down the dusty farm track that leads between Šid, the last town in Serbia, and Tovarnik, the first little village in Croatia.

He's been to Croatia before – as a tourist in 1982. He doesn't remember much, he says, just the blue buildings of a university. Now, thirty-three years later, he's returning as a refugee, and his first sight is a thin blue line of police, standing in the fields just over the Croatian side of the border. 'The police are waiting for us?' Riad asks his friends. 'Will they send us back?'

Croatia

And without knowing the answer, he walks across the latest frontier of the European migration crisis, and into Croatia. 'It's terrible,' he says to me, in his last words before leaving Serbia. 'They must accept us, they must help us.'

As it happens, the Croatians are happy to oblige. Perhaps it's because they themselves have recent memories of war and flight. Up the road in Vukovar, Serbian troops besieged Croatian freedom fighters in the early 1990s, and later massacred over 200 of them in a farm in the nearby countryside. Locals here know what it's like to flee an atrocity, and so when people like Riad turn up at their border, their response is more humane than that of the Hungarians.

That's fortunate – within a day of Riad's crossing, thousands are now marching in his wake across the pancake-flat fields. When Riad walked this way, there were just a few tyre prints marking the dusty track that connects the fields of Serbia with the fields of Croatia. A day later, every inch of it is scored with footprints. From little kids' feet to big size twelves – what had been a placid surface just twenty-four hours earlier is now being ploughed in plumes of dust by an exodus of refugees. As ever, many are invalids. One of them particularly moves me – Mokhtar, a twenty-three-year-old Syrian who can barely walk as he hobbles into the European Union. Shortly afterwards he tugs up his shirt to reveal the cause of his limp. There between his shoulder blades is the scar from when a Syrian soldier stabbed him in the spine with a bayonet during protests in Homs in 2011. Mokhtar was left paralysed for six months, and four years on he can only stagger.

How does a major migration route shift direction so suddenly? In this case, Facebook has little to do with it: there are limits to the speed at which the hive mind works. Information can be shared only as long as people have the internet. As they hop between countries, most refugees get online only fleetingly, so the news of Hungary's border closure takes a while to reach people.

The Serbian government can take some of the credit for the new route. After Hungary remains unmoved by requests to reopen its border, Serbia simply starts bussing people to Croatia. It's a decision that most of the first few busloads don't properly understand. One passenger asks if they're going to need to cross another sea. 'What's the name of this country?' a second man asks me. 'Cro . . . Cro–atia?'

The Serbian government might itself have been prompted into action by the initiative of a few trailblazing refugees. While most people stayed put at the Hungarian border, unaware of the possibility of a Croatian exit, a few of them upped sticks immediately – even before Serbia made its move. They are mostly single men like Riad the Iraqi, and youngsters like the three Ahmed siblings, who I meet as they stride briskly towards the Croatian border, desperate to make up for lost time. Up at the Hungarian fence, the trio had quickly looked at a map of Serbia, and worked out the last town before the Croatian border. Then they'd taken a taxi there, got out, and immediately began marching through the fields that led to the border. As they approach the border, the eldest sibling, a newly qualified doctor, admits they had no idea of what to expect. 'We just heard about this route,' he says, slightly short of breath. 'We thought we should check it out immediately, see if it is a route or not.'

These are the people who forge new ways through Europe – the unattached men and the twenty-somethings who have nothing to lose. They're the fastest-movers, and the most daring (or foolhardy) decision-makers, since they have no family to weigh them down, or cloud their decision-making. If you're not trying to carry several children across a continent, you can move more quickly and take more risks. But, for parents, every calculation you make along the route is infinitely harder. 'It's much slower when you have children,' a father called Nooreddine tells me. 'Your children have luggage, not just you. And you have to look after them. They need more rests and toilet breaks.' Tellingly, Nooreddine's family left home in Syria a fortnight earlier, a full week before the group of students he crosses the Croatian border with. Now both groups are at the same place in the trail, and the family is about to get overtaken again. 'The crowds we walk with change all the time because we go so slowly,' explains Nooreddine.

Families like Nooreddine's are about to encounter another problem, over the border in Croatia: the possibility of being separated from each other. The Croatians may be more welcoming than the Hungarians, but they are ill prepared to deal with such a huge influx of people in such a rural, remote area. In the coming months, well over 400,000 will pass through here[7] – far more than ever went through Hungary. For the first few days, the Croatian government has little idea of how to move them on from the villages that lie just inside their eastern border. Initially, refugees are stuck in little rural train stations, waiting for specially commissioned trains that arrive only once a day. Nooreddine is one of thousands waiting in

Tovarnik station when I arrive, all desperate to leave. And they won't all be able to. The trains have space for only 1000, even with people crammed into the aisles – and yet there must already be 1,500 people on the platform. They won't all get on.

So when the next train finally arrives, well past midnight, absolute pandemonium ensues. The Croatian police, clad in helmets and carrying truncheons, form a human wall in front of the carriages, trying to create some sort of order. They're restrained, refusing to raise their batons. Sensing weakness, the crowds of Syrians, Iraqis and Afghans surge forward, squeezing through gaps in the police lines. The biggest men make it on board first, and attempt to yank their relatives after them. There are raised fists, and a few shoves – understandably, given the situation. If you lose your family here, you might all end up in different European countries. Or you might never see each other again. Separated from their families, dozens of people have simply vanished.[8] Meanwhile, teenagers routinely aren't allowed to board with their parents and younger siblings – because they look too old to be travelling with their families. Further along the platform, my colleague Sima Diab witnesses one such heartbreak. She watches as police allow one family on board, but block the path of their oldest son. They don't believe he's their relative. Once inside, his father pokes his head through the window of the train, and scans the heaving crowd for his boy. He breaks open the back of his phone, wraps the sim card in paper and throws it to the young man. 'Call us,' he shouts. Cradling their younger daughter, his wife is in tears. As Sima recalls later, 'The train station and the bus scenes are the most difficult. Families torn apart temporarily, sometimes brought back together, children screaming and crying. Fear fear fear.'

Once the carriages fill up, the commotion subsides into a weary silence. But the tension doesn't end. The train simply stands there on the tracks all night. Earlier, it had been the train that never came; now it's the train that never leaves. From its windows, refugees gaze wide-eyed onto the platform, too exhausted to ask when the train will finally depart, but too tense to fall asleep. On the platform itself, still more people arrive throughout the night, having just walked here from Serbia. They curl up on the concrete, and some of them begin to snore. Miles from the nearest hotel, I join them. A few metres away, a baby snoozes inside a small suitcase. It's the warmest place its parents could find.

The following day, there's a similarly chaotic scene on the other side of the country, where those lucky enough to get a train out of Tovarnik are now trying to leave Croatia via its northern borders. Some of them try to leave for Hungary again. (Ironically, after forcing migrants westwards into Croatia, the Hungarians now discover that people can still breach their territory through the unfenced Hungarian–Croatian border.) Others head for Slovenia, and I later meet a couple of hundred who've been stopped on a little bridge that marks the boundary between Slovenian territory and Croatian. Slovenia will later relent, but for now they're trying to stop the flow. And as ever, this response is illogical. For the umpteenth time in my travels around Europe, a Syrian reminds me that there is little point in trying to stop his desperate countrymen – or the increasingly diverse range of other nationalities following in their wake.

Europe has the right to make life hard for people crossing its borders, concedes the young software developer as he waits on the bridge. But, in the end, he says, nobody wins if Europe doesn't try to streamline the process. 'Be careful what you wish for,' he says as he waves at the increasingly restless crowd of refugees behind him. 'Look how people are behaving. They can't be controlled.' Instead of continuing with a chaotic process of unmanaged migration, he reckons Europe should accept the inevitable and give people visas to fly to the continent in a more organised fashion. At least you'll then be able to control who enters Europe. 'Why make us do all this trip?' he asks. 'Just organise it, give people visas so they can come on the plane. If you don't, people will keep coming.'

Two months later, when two of the nine Paris bombers are suspected to have arrived in Europe with a boat of refugees, the words of this man come rushing back to me. Never has the creation of an organised system of mass resettlement seemed, to me at least, like a more urgent and necessary response.

This is not everyone's reaction, to say the least. In the aftermath of the Paris attacks, there are many calls to do the opposite: to pull up the drawbridge, and turn our backs on refugees. In America, thirty-one governors say they will now refuse to house Syrians in their states for security reasons. In

Europe, an opinion poll suggests that 88 per cent of Czechs believe that refugees pose as big a threat to Europe as Isis.[9] Citing similar fears, Poland's new conservative government takes only a few hours to renege on their centrist predecessors' promise to share some of Greece's and Italy's refugee burden. In Slovakia, the anti-migrant prime minister, Robert Fico, noted triumphantly, 'Hopefully, some people will open their eyes now.'[10]

It is, however, the likes of Fico who need to wake from their fantasies. Europe's isolationists may not feel the ethical need to protect people who've fled from Paris-style attacks that occur every day, rather than once a decade. It's nevertheless time for them to recognise the practical problems with the security solution they seek.

Put simply, it is impossible to completely seal Europe's borders. For years, our politicians have tried – but each time people kept coming, or came by another route. After increasing numbers of migrants tried to breach Spain's enclaves in northern Africa in the 1990s, the Spanish built a fence to block their path. It didn't work. So they built a second, which didn't work either. Then, several years later, came a third – and only then did the fortifications begin to deter people in the way the builders had initially hoped. Even after that, access to Europe was simply achieved via other routes – first through Libya, and now Turkey. The lesson wasn't learned. In 2011, Greece built a fence along its Turkish land border, and in 2014 Bulgaria followed suit. Both were a waste of time. Thousands still walked through Bulgaria in 2015, while many more dodged the Greek fence by sailing to the Greek islands. After a false start, Hungary's fence ultimately worked – for

Hungary. But it was no solution for Europe, with nearly half a million people simply re-routing through Croatia.

Other deterrents also failed. Europe suspended rescue operations – but people still came in record numbers. Next they went after the Libyan smugglers – but the mission was a failure. Then in November 2015 the EU paid Turkey to police its borders better – but thousands still left Turkish shores every day. Short of attacking the migrants (and some vigilantes have already tried) there was little more Europe could do to stop the flow with conventional border enforcement.

The only thing left to try was the destruction of a seminal treaty that is at the heart of Europe's post-war identity: the 1951 UN Refugee Convention. In spring 2016, Europe increased its hand-outs to Turkey from €3 billion to €6 billion, in exchange for Turkey agreeing to readmit all asylum-seekers landing in Greece. The countries of the Balkans simultaneously closed the humanitarian corridor that had stretched between Greece and Germany over the winter. Around 50,000 were then trapped in Greece, the losers in the world's most macabre game of musical chairs.

Again, this did not stop the flow entirely. Despite the threats of deportation, and despite the increased difficulty of moving through eastern Europe, more than 25,000 people still made their way secretly through the Balkans in the months that followed the creation of the EU–Turkey deal, as it came to be known.[11] When I visited the Greek–Macedonian border one final time in September 2016, I found the discarded belongings of migrants who had crept through the undergrowth over the summer. There were sleeping bags, sardine packets – and distressingly, even a toddler's shoe. The

EU's claims of having shut the Balkans route were manifestly false. Clandestine migration continued.

However, the EU–Turkey deal did drastically reduce the number of people coursing through the Balkans in the semi-regularised fashion that we saw in the second half of 2015. By mid-summer 2016, just a few hundred people landed on the Greek islands every week, rather than the tens of thousands of the previous year.

The isolationists rejoiced. Their celebrations nevertheless came at great moral cost. Tens of thousands of needy refugees were abandoned in squalid limbo in Greece. Depending on their individual backgrounds, they were meant to be either relocated to other European countries, or deported back to Turkey. In reality, both plans had barely been set in motion by the end of 2016. Greece's EU allies failed to relocate more than a few thousand refugees, leaving the majority stuck in freezing conditions throughout the Greek winter. And bureaucratic wrangling meant that very few had been deported back to Turkey.

But to even contemplate the deportation of so many people, Europe had severely compromised the humanitarian principles that underpinned the continent's enlightened post-war settlement. In order to deport people back to Turkey, the EU had to pretend that Turkey was a place that respected refugee rights. While Turkey has generously welcomed many more Syrians than the rest of the world combined, Syrians in Turkey are not afforded basic privileges. Despite recent legislative changes, most refugees can't work legally – and so instead earn pitiful wages on the black market. Many Syrian parents therefore enrol their children not in schools but in sweatshops in order to ensure the whole family doesn't starve. Worse still, numerous witnesses report that Turkey has forced hundreds of Syrians back to Syria, and now shoots refugees trying to get back in (Turkey denies both claims).

By accepting the principle of deporting refugees from Greece to Turkey, Europe has therefore ridden roughshod over the 1951 Refugee Convention – a charter created in the aftermath of the Second World War, partly to ensure that the continent did not repeat the mistakes of the Holocaust. Just as we did in the 1930s, Europe is once again sending thousands of people back to places where they risk considerable danger and hardship. We risk unravelling the progress we have made as a continent since 1945. The very identity of post-war Europe is at stake.

What's more, in practical terms, this moral lapse isn't exactly working. The numbers are down, but not finished. People are still walking through Bulgaria. Smugglers are still advertising trips from Turkey all the way to Italy. The flow between Libya and Italy hit a new record in 2016. We may have ended the biblical flows of autumn 2015, but things are still remarkably similar to how they were in the spring of that year.

There are two obvious conclusions. First: whether we like it or not, people will – to some extent – keep coming. Second: given this fact, Europe's current approach to migration benefits no one. Not the refugees, who'll keep on drowning at sea and suffocating in the back of smugglers' vans. And not the Europeans, who in their refusal to admit the inevitability of the situation are making things far more chaotic than they need to be.

Daniel Trilling, an astute chronicler and analyst of European migration, has even argued in the *London Review of Books* that this is in fact not a European refugee crisis, but a European borders crisis.[12] Trilling's point is that the flow of refugees to Europe is in fact fairly moderate, particularly in comparison with Middle Eastern countries. It is therefore not the arrival of the refugees that has caused a crisis, but Europe's heartless and brainless border management. Personally, I see it as an asylum crisis, the chaos at the borders being just a symptom of the continent's various and dysfunctional asylum systems. But our conclusion is the same: this is predominantly a problem with Europe, not with the people trying to breach its borders.

So what's the solution? There isn't one. Or, at least, there isn't a solution that would see an end to the flow of refugees to Europe. The refugee crisis is not a possibility that can still be avoided, but a certainty that can only be mitigated. We may not want people to come, but even with the destruction of the 1951 Refugee Convention, we are not able to entirely stop them.

Accepting this reality is the key to managing it. In the course of researching this book, I've asked hundreds of refugees why they're risking death to reach Europe. The most common answer is this: because there is no other option. Many cannot return home, or start new lives in other countries in the Middle East or north Africa. So they have nothing to lose by trying for Europe. This means that they will continue to cross the sea in leaking boats – and to block roads, cause tailbacks at borders, and prompt delays on the Channel Tunnel – until there is a safe, legal and realistic means of being relocated to Europe.

For many in Europe, the implications of this will be hard to swallow. The reality is nevertheless clear: the only sane, logical, and long-term response to the crisis is to create a legal mechanism for vast numbers of refugees to reach Europe in safety. This is very far from a perfect scenario. It is nevertheless the least-worst one. At the current rate, whether we want them or not, hundreds of thousands of refugees might still arrive on European shores within the next two or three years. How much chaos this movement will cause depends on how orderly we make that process of resettlement. If the process continues to work as it does at present (which is not at all), the kind of social meltdown feared by the continent's reactionaries will become far more likely. Even in times when the rate of immigration has been far slower, multiculturalism has faced significant challenges – from the Bradford riots to the Danish cartoons crisis. It's naive to pretend that absorbing so many people so quickly won't spark something similar. But it is only through the mass resettlement of a significant number of refugees that we can begin to mitigate the fallout. It's only at this point that we'll be able to manage where migrants go, and when they come.

Clearly, this cannot be the only strategy. The wealthy Gulf countries – who, like the West, have stoked the fires of the Syrian war – should also share their part of the refugee burden. So too should the rest of the Western world – not least the USA. The countries with the largest Syrian refugee populations – Turkey, Lebanon and Jordan – should be encouraged to give all Syrians the right to work, with no strings attached. Most importantly, the Syrian war needs to end.

But counting on these alternatives is quixotic. Europe has spent the past five years hoping that the conflict will stop before Europeans have to do anything about its fallout. To continue with the same failed strategy would fit Einstein's definition of madness. The war is of course the main cause of the crisis, but we should have learned by now that there are no easy ways of ending such a complex conflict. As I update this latest edition of the book in January 2017, the world's major powers claim to have orchestrated yet another ceasefire and another round of negotiations. Even if this process succeeds, it's naive to expect it to create a Syria to which many refugees would quickly return. A post-conflict Syria will likely be full of recriminations, cantonisation, and further rounds of displacement. The last time Europe faced such a biblical movement of people, in the aftermath of the Second World War, their migrations didn't really get going until after the fighting ended. Syria may be no different.

It is equally short-sighted to expect Turkey, Lebanon and Jordan to save Europe when Europe offers them little in return. This has been the strategy for the past five years – to use the Middle East as a holding pen for Syrians. The strategy has failed. After five years in limbo, with no right to join the local labour market, Syrians no longer have any reason to remain on that side of the Mediterranean. Throwing money at refugee camps, as many European leaders advocate, may help some people in the short term, but it is no long-term solution if Turkey and its neighbours do not simultaneously offer refugees the right to work.

To improve the status quo, Europe needs to encourage refugees to place more faith in the formal processes of resettlement; and simultaneously persuade the countries of the Middle East to give refugees access to the labour market – a right that despite recent cosmetic changes, Middle Eastern governments are still refusing to provide. One means of making both goals more likely is the resettlement of substantially more refugees within Europe's borders. Swiftly relocating large numbers of Syrian, Afghan, Iraqi and Eritrean refugees within a viable time frame is – ironically – a proven way of persuading those still on the waiting list to stay put in the transit countries of the Middle East and north Africa. Similarly, once those transit countries have been relieved of some of their refugees, it will be easier to convince them to make life better for the ones they're left with.

How many would need to be resettled? In order to have an impact, the total has to be in the region of several hundred thousand. Anything much lower just won't make a difference. In 2015 the EU promised to relocate 40,000 Syrians and Eritreans awaiting asylum in the Middle East, while the UK separately pledged to receive just 4000 a year until 2020. These were both tiny, token numbers – collectively just 1 per cent of the roughly 5 million Syrian refugees who have already left home. As a result, these meagre pledges did nothing to discourage the tide of people crossing the sea through illegal means, since in statistical terms people knew they were still highly unlikely to be resettled through the formal channels. The conclusion is obvious: we need to promise to welcome a far bigger number in the long term in order to persuade them to stay put in the short term. We can't stop the refugees; we can only hope to manage their arrival in a more organised manner. Mass resettlement is the obvious means of achieving that.

Such a scheme won't stop the boats entirely, and it won't satisfy isolationists such as Slovakia's Robert Fico. It nevertheless offers a more realistic chance of making Europe more secure than the unworkable strategy they propose. If we're genuinely worried about the refugee crisis leading to more Paris-style attacks, then we should be moving away from the current failed approach, and towards a system that would enable Europe to screen more refugees before they arrive; work out who they are and where they're from; and decide where they should go, and when they should arrive. In the process European governments would have a better chance of weeding out potential bombers. Turkey, relieved of some of its 2.7 million Syrian refugees, would have greater motivation to give Syrians the blanket right to work. And the refugees themselves would not need to drown in the Mediterranean.

Such a massive resettlement programme also has a precedent. The UN's refugee agency (and the UN's Refugee Convention itself) was created to deal with exactly this kind of international catastrophe – the fallout from the Second World War, when between 12 and 14 million Europeans were displaced.[13] Migration experts also like to point to the aftermath of the Vietnam war, when Western countries eventually resettled 1.3 million refugees[14] from the surrounding region of Indochina.[15] If such a project was achieved once, it can be achieved again. If Lebanon with its tiny population of 4.5 million can manage, then the world's richest continent (population 500 million) can too.

'We should do for the Syrians what we did thirty years ago for the Indochinese,' François Crépeau, the UN's special rapporteur on the human rights of migrants, said as early as April

2015.[16] 'And that's a comprehensive plan of action where all global north countries – and that includes Europe, Canada, the US, Australia and New Zealand and probably other countries – offer a great number of Syrians an option so that they would line up in Istanbul, Amman and Beirut for a meaningful chance to resettle, instead of paying thousands of euros only to die with their children in the Mediterranean.'

Such a utopian system will nevertheless function only if refugees can be persuaded to stay in the countries they're allocated. The reason the migration crisis slowly spread throughout 2015 from the islands of Greece to the sports halls of Germany, via Austria's motorways and Hungary's train stations, is because some European countries treat refugees more humanely than others. As a result, refugees aim for the places that will give them the most stability. Germany is more appealing than most other EU countries, for instance, because unlike its neighbours it offers asylum to Syrians whether or not they've previously been fingerprinted in Greece. Sweden is an attractive destination because, among other things, it is perceived to be faster at reuniting refugees with their families.

As a result, a mass resettlement programme would work properly only if the asylum system in each EU country operated to the same high standards as its neighbours'. To ensure that, we would need to implement a common European asylum policy. Just as the European Convention on Human Rights essentially standardises legislation in every European country, under a common asylum policy each country would need to give refugees the same level of benefits, and grant them the same length of residency. If each member of the EU can agree to treat its asylum seekers in the same way as every other member, there will be no incentive for those asylum seekers to seek a better a deal elsewhere in the continent.

Could such a system ever see the light of day? It's always been a highly unlikely scenario, and in the time since the first edition of this book was published – in which we've witnessed the Brexit vote, the election of Donald Trump, and calls from far-right leaders like Viktor Orban for a counter-cultural revolution in the EU – it has become unlikelier still. Most of our leaders are too afraid of losing political capital at home. But if they genuinely want to soften the impact of the refugee crisis, then these are the kinds of pragmatic policies that they will need to consider. If they don't – and if the Syrian war drags on, and life becomes ever more unsustainable for refugees in places such as Lebanon – then the mess will continue.

The choice is not between the current crisis and blissful isolation. The choice is between the current crisis and an orderly, managed system of mass migration. You can have one or the other. There is no easy middle ground.

10

Status Pending

Hashem's anxious wait for asylum

Friday, 23 October 2015, 12 noon

Sweden

Throughout his ordeal, Hashem rarely cries. Today, sitting in the little public library in Skinnskatteberg, he really wants to. It's been six months since he arrived in Sweden, six months of purgatory – and he's still waiting to find out if he's been granted asylum. Spring turned to summer, and now winter is almost here. With every passing day, he wonders more and more whether the decision that was supposed to be a formality will instead never come. Today, his fears appear to be confirmed.

The day starts as usual. Hashem checks his account on the website of the Swedish migration agency, Migrationsverket. As usual, no decision has been made. He goes downstairs to have breakfast at the reception centre where he's been billeted. 'Centre' is perhaps too formal a word: it's a converted hostel – a pair of two-storey buildings filled with dormitories. There's a communal dining hall on the ground floor of one of the blocks. It's here that Hashem eats three meals a day, alongside the seventy other asylum seekers living on the site.

Later in the morning, Hashem decides to head for the village library to borrow a Swedish grammar book. He turns right out of the centre, heads down the slope, crosses the footbridge that leads over the railway line, turns left, and then veers right past the village bank. On his left is one supermarket, on his right another. And a bit beyond the latter, past a grid of detached houses, is the Skinnskatteberg library.

Hashem comes here a few times a week, for want of something better to do. In broken English, he talks to the librarian, who he thinks is called Lily, but he can't quite remember. He looks at the two children's books that are in both Swedish and Arabic; one's about geography, and the second involves some ghosts, and is titled *Bort alla Spöken!*

Today, Hashem takes advantage of the library's internet and starts scrolling through Facebook. There are the familiar posts about what's going on in Syria. And then there's the one that makes him want to cry. Sweden's political parties, someone's written, have collectively agreed to end permanent residency for Syrians, with the exception of those who've come as a family. And for the men who haven't, the post claims, there are to be restrictions on their right to family reunification.

Hashem's head starts to spin. If this is true, everything he's prayed for over the past six months has come to nothing. He is safe. But his family, alone and afraid on the other side of the Mediterranean, are not. And now they never may be.

Hashem hurries out of the library and back to the centre, to find out what everyone else is saying. If anything, they're even more despondent than he is. Wasim, a Syrian who's been here for a year, is shouting and punching the walls. A friend messages him on WhatsApp to explain that the decision won't be put into place until the new year, and that he still has a couple of months to get permanent residency. But, for Hashem, it's little consolation. The number of new asylum seekers in the Swedish system has slowed decision-making almost to a halt, and Hashem's case might not be resolved for another six months. It was the wrong decision to go alone. He knows he can't afford to send his family to Turkey and then Greece, but maybe he could borrow the money to send at least one of the boys. But that would risk them drowning – precisely the thing he'd wanted to avoid by going to Sweden without them.

'Unfortunately,' he despairs in a message he sends me that day, 'my dreams have crashed.'

Six months earlier things had seemed so much brighter. On 29 April, the day Hashem arrives in Sweden, we shiver on the platform in Malmö station, waiting for the first train that will take him northwards to his brother-in-law, Ehsan. The sun is just beginning to rise, and so are Hashem's spirits. 'When I was in Egypt,' he says to me on the platform, 'I said that if I sank I would just be losing one person. But if I succeeded I'd be offering the chance of success to three people – my kids, Osama, Mohamed and Milad. Well, thank god, I secured a beautiful future for them.'

We hug goodbye. I've shadowed him since Italy, so it's been a bonding few days. To watch this dignified man limp across an unknown continent – exhausted, frightened, and yet ultimately determined to provide his family with a safer future – has been a lesson to me in love, resilience and devotion.

Hashem boards this final train, seconds before it departs. As it pulls out of the station, Hashem is still searching for his seat, just as he still searches for his place in the world. As the train disappears into a glistening new dawn, I muse to myself that in both respects he's at least in the right carriage.

Five hours later, after a last set of changes, and even a broken-down train, Hashem arrives in Avesta, a town north-west of Stockholm. Ehsan is at a Swedish class, so Fatima is there to take him back to the couple's house. He eats, washes and tends to his infected foot. Before long, he falls fast asleep; it's been a fortnight since he slept in a proper bed. He's woken up a few hours later by Ehsan, and the pair embrace for the first time in two years. A wave of relief sweeps over Hashem: he's with family now, and they know what he has to do to claim asylum. Over dinner they tell him what to expect when he applies for asylum, and the next day Ehsan puts him on the train to Gävle, the nearest town with an office for Migrationsverket.

Hashem gets out at Gävle, walks the short distance to the agency's office, and enters. Ehsan has already told him that he'll be warmly received, but Hashem is still nervous. 'Hello,' he says to the security guard in his faltering English. 'I'm Syrian, I'm refugee.' The security guard smiles. 'Welcome,' he says, and takes Hashem to a receptionist. She writes down his details, gives him a key, and shows him to a bedroom upstairs in the centre. Inside, there's a mattress, a pillow, bed linen, a towel, a toothbrush and shampoo – everything he needs to live in comfort for a few days. For perhaps the first time in his life, he feels as if a government is treating him as a human. The second to last time he'd visited a government office in Syria, they'd taken him to a jail cell. In Egypt, he'd been insulted by government officials, and even briefly kidnapped by someone purporting to be one. Here, in Sweden, they are letting him live in dignity.

Hashem spends the weekend in Gävle, and on the Monday he's given a preliminary interview with an asylum caseworker.

He'll have a fuller conversation later in the year, so for now they just want to establish the basic facts of his case. What he says seems to pass muster, and the next day he's told to board a bus that'll take him to his permanent lodgings.

The bus cruises serenely through the Swedish countryside, past fields and lakes, and through tall forests. Hashem marvels at the calmness of it all, the lack of traffic, the greenery. It's different from anything he's experienced before – and so is the village the bus reaches, a couple of hours later.

This is Skinnskatteberg, a tiny, remote place of just 4000 residents, ninety miles south-west of Gävle, and a hundred north-west of Stockholm. It's not somewhere you would usually want to billet seventy frightened foreigners. But such is the flow of refugees to Sweden that the authorities are struggling to find places to house the newest arrivals. This makeshift centre in Skinnskatteberg is the best they could find for Hashem and his cohort. Hashem's first reaction is that it's quite pleasant. There is a little lawn outside with some chairs. Behind the building is a pretty wood. It's on a gentle slope, so if you go outside and stroll a few paces, there's a pleasing view of the village and the spire of its huge white church.

Upstairs, however, a shock is waiting. He's shown to his room, and to his horror he finds he's to share with four other people. It's not that he minds – after all, a fortnight earlier, he'd had to share a deck with 500 others. The problem is that since being tortured in Assad's prisons, he's suffered from some of the symptoms of post-traumatic stress disorder (PTSD). And they're symptoms that make it difficult to share a room with other people. Panicking, he tries to explain the situation to the Migrationsverket staff. He needs his own room, and a doctor, he says in Arabic. But, without an interpreter, they don't understand him, and he's too embarrassed to explain further. Soon they leave, and they won't be back for another week. Migrationsverket officials are so stretched that they can visit the centre only on a Tuesday, between 1 p.m. and 2 p.m. For the rest of the time, the residents are on their own.

Still, at least he has somewhere to live. At least he's in Sweden. And at least the village is pleasant. He's impressed by the church. He discovers a lake at the southern end of the town, and enjoys strolling around it. He is happily astonished at the absence of police or soldiers on the streets, and at the fact he never hears any fighter jets overhead. He could not be further from Syria – or Egypt for that matter.

Tuesday comes round again, and with it the chance to tell the migration agency about his problem. The allotted hour arrives, and Hashem turns up at the dining room to make his case. Again, he's shocked to find that there aren't any interpreters. Again, he tries to explain his situation. But again, no one understands him. Embarrassed and humiliated, he heads back to his room. The same thing happens the next week – and the week after. It's a miserable situation. Hashem needs a doctor and some privacy, but he can't even tell anyone. Eventually, I call the Migrationsverket on his behalf. They say that while they don't always come with interpreters, he can nevertheless ask to speak to an interpreter by telephone. And it's up to him, not me, to make the request himself.

There are doctors Hashem can see independently of the Migrationsverket. But they're in Västerås, an hour away by bus. And that return bus ride costs 100 krona – a seventh of the roughly £50 that the Swedish government allocates him per month, in addition to giving him food and lodging. He can't really afford it, but makes it there anyway. At last he's able to see a doctor for a session. He feels relieved – comforted that someone, at last, understands him, however fleeting their encounter may be. A room nevertheless still eludes him.

On the fourth week, he shows the visiting officials a message written in English, requesting his own room. Finally, they agree to his request and, for a few happy days, Hashem has both medical support and privacy. Unfortunately, it's not for long. Hashem returns from a walk a week later to find that a fellow Syrian asylum seeker has moved into the bedroom with him, seizing the previously vacant upper bunk. Hashem is so upset he spends the night sitting in the dining hall, too frightened to sleep. To add to Hashem's woes, an Eritrean man at the centre then takes a dislike to him after Hashem makes the mistake of saying hello to one of the Eritrean's female compatriots. The man spots the interaction, decides to confront Hashem about it – and ends up punching him. Whenever the Eritrean subsequently encounters Hashem in the corridor, he insults him. Hashem is left frightened to leave his room, but uncomfortable staying inside it. He's escaped from the hell of Syria and Egypt. Unfortunately, Sweden so far offers him only purgatory.

Back in Egypt, Hayam, Osama, Mohamed and Milad are also living in limbo. They've now lost their primary sources of income: due to a funding crisis, the UN has cut their food vouchers, while Hashem can no longer put money on the table. There's no work in Skinnskatteberg and, besides, he can't yet speak Swedish. Hayam finds work as an Arabic teacher at a school for Syrian children in 10 Ramadan, but it pays only 400 Egyptian pounds a month. This is barely more than £30, and comes to less than half the rent she needs to pay. Savings and donations from friends help get her over the line every month, but they are struggling to pay for food. When the Eid el-Fitr festival comes around in midsummer, her neighbours, along with the rest of the Muslim world, are preparing for their biggest meal of the year. Hayam calls a friend in floods of tears because she can't afford to do the same.

The hardest part, though, isn't the poverty, but the sense of social exclusion. As Syrians, life is bad enough in Egypt. The xenophobia has dropped since its peak in 2013, but they still feel like social outcasts. Without Hashem they've also lost their protection. In a patriarchal society where harassment is rife, it's difficult for Hayam to go about her business in an ordinary way. Everyone knows she's alone now. She has to shut herself inside to avoid unwanted attention – leaving home only to work and to shop. She lets the boys out to play, until Osama is threatened by a boy with a knife. Now she's worried about letting any of them out at all. Soon, home begins to feel like a prison. When Milad, the youngest, starts playing with a ball one day, her downstairs neighbour angrily demands the family stop making any noise whatsoever. 'I don't want to hear anything at all,' he says, leaning on their doorframe.

She asks her landlord to intervene, but he tells her that if she doesn't like it, she can simply leave. Then he starts charging her extra for electricity, and Hayam begins to feel uncertain around him too. It's a feeling of utter isolation. She's been through this before: in 2012, when Hashem was kidnapped by Assad's intelligence services, and she didn't hear from him for six months. This time, at least Hashem is on the other end of a Viber call, or a WhatsApp message. But, unlike in Syria, here in Egypt she has no family and very few friends to look out for her. And she must endure all this in silence. She can't show any weakness in front of her children, nor can she let Hashem realise the extent of her loneliness. She knows he is finding life hard enough as it is. Ironically, thousands of miles away, Hashem is of the same mindset. He can't let Hayam know how alone he feels himself. At the very moment when they need each other most, the pair of them can't let each other in.

Hashem's misery lifts when Migrationsverket moves him again to his own room. Then he makes peace with his Eritrean adversary, and his immediate life begins to brighten once more. Now his only problems are the boredom and the loneliness. He has his asylum interview in late August, and until then he is just counting down the days. There's a rock by the lake that he walks to every day, and where he establishes a new daily ritual. He sits on the rock for several minutes, gazes out across the water and then calls Hayam on Viber. Sometimes he goes to the library to break up the mono-ony. He devours news of any kind – about Syria, about Sweden, even about Britain. He discovers a person called Jeremy Corbyn, the new leader of the British opposition. Later he follows the debate about bombing Isis, and feels ambivalent about it. Assad is the source of Syria's problems, and Hashem still doesn't understand why the West puts up with him. But if Assad can't be targeted, then there are worse things than attacking Isis. After all, it's the jihadists of Isis who provide Assad with his last traces of international legitimacy.

At the centre, Hashem avoids getting too close to fellow asylum seekers, now wary of getting on the wrong side of anyone. Over time he nevertheless builds a rapport with a few of them, and discovers that Syrians aren't the only people fleeing terrible trauma. He learns more about Eritrea, and Iraq, and he's reminded once again that all the asylum seekers are in this together. Well, almost all of them – there are two or three people from north Africa and Lebanon who seem to be here on false pretences. They're working the system: in the six months that it'll take for the government to rumble them, they'll take the benefits, and work on the black market. Once they're caught, they'll go to another European country and find illegal work there. It doesn't particularly matter to them if they eventually get found out; they're just here to earn a bit of money in the short term.

But Hashem isn't. He's here to get asylum, and so the waiting feels like an ordeal. Time goes so slowly – until one day some of the local villagers begin Swedish classes in the church hall. It isn't a government project – it's just something that half-a-dozen pensioners have decided to do by themselves. Grey-haired Gustav is the jovial man in charge, while Eva and Kerstin are the two women who teach Hashem's class. It consists of three Eritreans, an Afghan and Hashem – so it's hard to find a common language to communicate in. Kerstin and Eva have also never taught Swedish before, so the classes have a rambling quality. On the day I visit, they struggle to explain the difference between *vilke, vilka, vilken* and *vilket* – four different connotations of 'which' – and Hashem struggles in turn to understand. But the lessons are about so much more than just the language. 'It's about the connection!' says Hashem after the class ends. He gets to make friends with real Swedes, and those Swedes, some of whom are a bit lonely themselves, get something out of it too.

In particular, Hashem warms to Kerstin, a frail widow who lives alone in a wooden cottage out in the woods. She gets him to fix her computer, and a bond is formed, leading to Hashem regularly stopping by for tea after class. Her house is unlike any he's previously been to. In one room Kerstin has a giant weaver's loom. In another there's a table built from parts first carved in 1623, a lampshade made from the wheel of a cart, and green wallpaper full of clover leaves. It's an unusual home – but one of the first in Sweden in which Hashem has felt properly welcomed by a born-and-bred Swede.

The eve of his interview finally arrives. Hashem's not nervous – he's excited. 'It's my day of destiny,' he says to himself. He showers and shaves. He sets his alarm for 6 a.m., and asks Ehsan and Hayam to call him to make sure he's up in time. There's no need, in the end. He's up, alert, and early for the 6.45 a.m. bus ride to Västerås. When the bus moves off, he uses the journey to arrange his thoughts, anxious to give the best possible account of himself in the interview. He goes over in his head what happened when he left Syria, and why – and wonders what kinds of questions he'll be asked.

Hashem finds out, soon enough. Getting out at Västerås, he walks through the all but empty streets to a nearby office block. He takes a lift to the seventh floor, and waits outside the Migrationsverket office until it opens. At 9 a.m. on the dot, Bouzang, his caseworker, approaches him and invites him into her office for the interview. Hashem glances at her colleagues, sitting quietly at their desks, and with a pang of nostalgia he's reminded of his own offices in Syria.

Bouzang asks him a series of methodical questions over the course of the next two hours. Where is he from in Syria? What kind of an area is it? What is the situation there? How did the war affect him? Why was he put in prison? Had he ever expressed a political affiliation? Why did he leave? The questions are firm but respectful, and to Hashem the process seems fair. His interrogator has a gentle manner, and Hashem feels relieved. 'You look like my sister,' he blurts out at one point, and she smiles.

The next day, back in Skinnskatteberg, Hashem starts a new routine. He begins to log on to the Migrationsverket website every morning, to see if there's been a decision in his case. He knows it'll take a few weeks or so, but he figures it can't hurt to check. But, after a month or so, it does start to hurt. Each time he logs on, the website shows no change in his case. He checks and checks and checks. Still nothing. And as September turns into October, he starts to worry. Is there something wrong? Did his interviewer not believe him? The general political climate doesn't help. As autumn wears on, more refugees than ever are flooding into Europe – and thanks to its progressive policies, Sweden continues to bear a disproportionate burden of the crisis. Of the roughly

800,000 people to have arrived in Europe by this point in 2015, at least one in seven has ended up in Sweden, even though the country accounts for just one in fifty EU citizens.

More than 120,000 people have arrived here,[1] and Migrationsverket expects the total to reach at least 170,000 by the end of the year. Around 10,000 people are now arriving every week, compared with 4000 during the summer. The spike is now mainly caused by Afghans, whose arrival rate surges above that of Syrians in the final few weeks of the year. But, whatever their nationality, the effect is the same. A few years ago, caseworkers hoped to reach a decision on every asylum application within two or three months; now some speculate each one might take two years.

Politicians get tetchy. The far-right Sweden Democrats, some of whose first members had links with neo-nazism,[2] win more and more supporters in the polls. The main opposition party, the Conservatives, proposes to end permanent residency for Syrians. Then the centre-left government, headed by the Social Democrats, also loses its nerve, promising that the policy of permanent residency will end within a few months. Access to family reunion will also be restricted. Hashem begins to panic. Will his decision arrive in time? With all the pressure that the asylum system is under, presumably not.

In fact, the pressure is so great that Migrationsverket calls on the Swedish army to help manage the situation. The department also begins to work with the country's civil contingencies agency (MSB), a government agency usually involved in the aftermath of natural disasters or in overseas humanitarian catastrophes. By early November 2015, they cannot find enough housing for refugees, some of whom are consequently forced to sleep on the floor of five reception centres. Despite some centres quadrupling their manpower in recent months, many agency officials begin to work double shifts and at the weekends. The preliminary interview that Hashem had when he first arrived in Sweden is quietly phased out. There just isn't enough time.

I visit Sweden during this period, and migration officials talk in apocalyptic language. 'We don't have any more space,' the agency's top spokesman tells me. 'Right now we're just looking for people to have a roof over their heads.' As someone familiar with other parts of the European migration trail, the scenes in Sweden to me seem contained and organised compared to the chaos in places such as Lesvos – where refugees are now walking and sometimes sleeping in the rain, with little institutional support. But, in Sweden, even experienced asylum officials are nevertheless shocked by the unprecedented scale of the challenge that faces them.

'I've never seen this many people, ever,' says an old hand at one of the two main reception centres in Stockholm, as we walk past that day's queues. 'We don't seem to have any more beds in Sweden. We don't have anywhere to send them.'

In the medium term, the situation is not so dire. The government has identified potential space for an extra 66,000 arrivals in sports halls and other public buildings, just under half of which could be converted without too many adjustments. But, in the short term, ready-to-use space is proving hard to find due to a combination of allegedly greedy landlords, arsonists and health-and-safety laws. Vandals have set fire to several sites earmarked for refugees. Private landlords want too much money to let out their properties. And the agency blames legislative bureaucracy for the delay in opening a series of tent cities in southern Sweden.

All this causes a crisis of Swedish identity. Some stoke the fear that Sweden risks being unable to provide for its own citizens if it continues to let in so many outsiders. The Sweden Democrats distribute a flier to refugees landing in Lesvos claiming that thanks to immigration 'our society is falling apart', and warn migrants against trying to reach Sweden. Hours later, Sweden's conservative party, known as the Moderates, calls for increased border controls against refugees, and within days the Social Democrat government grants them their wish.

But others feel that any dereliction of duties to refugees would mark an abandonment of the core tenets of Sweden's social democracy. 'Our society is built on the principle that people are entitled to the same as everyone else,' says the secretary general of the Swedish bar association, Anne Ramberg, as she waits to provide legal advice to new refugee arrivals at Stockholm central station. 'But we are in a situation where we can't even give refugees housing.'

The answer, Ramberg argues, is not for Sweden to lower its standards, but for the rest of the world's richest continent to raise theirs. 'A crisis for us', says Ramberg, 'is very different from the crisis in Jordan or Lebanon', where refugees constitute a far greater proportion of the total population. 'We could take these people if we had solidarity between EU countries. We are a continent of 500 million people – of course we could do it. But there's no solidarity. It's just Germany and Sweden.'

Amid this furore, Hashem falls into a deep gloom. It doesn't help when his brother arrives safely with his family in Germany, and then his sister-in-law reaches Sweden with hers. He's happy for them, of course. But he wonders if he should have brought his family with him too. If his brother managed it, why couldn't he? His mood worsens even further when he finds out that Hayam's other sister has been arrested at a government office in Syria, and has disappeared. Hashem's been in Assad's dungeons. He knows what horrors await her there. Back in Egypt, Hayam is distraught, and Hashem feels tormented by his inability to comfort her. He contemplates trying to get back to Egypt. What good is asylum if he can't be there for his family when they need him most?

Then he hits another setback. Part of the reason Hashem had decided to go by boat in the first place was because he'd given up hope of getting formally resettled by the UN refugee agency. Now, two years after their resettlement was first lodged, the UN finally invite the family for an interview – only to cancel it once they discover that Hashem has already gone to Europe. Even if the interview had gone ahead, the process of being resettled in Europe would still have taken months if not years. But to Hashem, in his current state, it still feels like another cruel blow.

His PTSD symptoms return, and he starts to check the Migrationsverket website almost as a reflex. Every day becomes every hour – and every hour brings a new disappointment. He checks the site before breakfast, and there's nothing. He checks it after breakfast, and there's still nothing. Before lunch: nothing. After lunch: nothing.

One day, Hashem heads to the church hall for his Swedish lesson. Before the lesson, again, there's nothing. During the coffee break, he retrieves his phone from his pocket, types in his code, and again scans his page to find that there's noth—

Hashem blinks. Then he scans the page again. There's . . . something.

No. No, thinks Hashem. He must have logged into the wrong page. There's a problem with the internet. Leaving nothing to chance, he hurries out of the church hall and back to the centre to use the WiFi there. He reaches his room, and logs in once more. And once more, there's . . . something. He takes a deep breath, and reads what it says.

'Application status,' it reads in Arabic. 'Your request for residency, permission to work, permission to study, citizenship or asylum has been received.'

Hashem scrolls down to the next paragraph.

'The Swedish Board of Immigration has taken a decision concerning the granting or refusal of your request.'

And then, again, there's nothing. Nothing that explains whether the decision is positive or negative. Nothing to clarify whether his case is one of the first to be considered under the government's new restrictive measures – or one of the last under the old order. It just says there's been a decision. Hashem has to report once more to the Migrationsverket in Västerås to find out whether he has cause for celebration or despair. So the next morning, he's off again on the 6.45 a.m. bus. It's well before sunrise, and in the darkness Hashem wonders what's in store. It has to be a positive decision, he thinks. It has to be. No Syrian gets their asylum application rejected. But what if he's the odd one out? What if they didn't believe him? As he takes the lift to the seventh floor of the Migrationsverket building, for what he hopes will be the final time, he nevertheless prepares himself for all possibilities.

Well, all apart from one: the anticlimax. The decision isn't actually ready yet. Come back in a week's time, they say. We'll have it ready then. So another week goes by, and on the following Wednesday morning, he finds himself waiting yet again in the darkness for the bus in Skinnskatteberg. He has company, this time – I've flown in to see what happens. We arrive at the bus stop at 6.30 a.m., and once again we shiver together in the chill. The hood of Hashem's coat casts a shadow over his face, but once the bus arrives fifteen minutes later, its lights shining in his eyes, I can see that Hashem is tense. He sits silently for the duration of the journey, hoping, praying that there will be no more surprises. He has an hour to spare by the time he gets to Västerås, but he still hurries to the Migrationsverket building. He wants to be the first in the queue. He gets his wish – there's no one else here. He paces around, sits on the chair, stands up again, and goes for a smoke. He returns, and it's still only 8.30 a.m. Hashem's anxiety rises. Why did they turn him back last week? Has he been rejected? Or are there simply delays to processing his residency? And if the latter, what kind of residency will it be? Permanent? Temporary? If it's only temporary, he might not be able to apply for family reunion. And that would defeat the whole point. His journey from Egypt, across the Mediterranean and then through Europe, would all have been a waste.

People start gathering in the gloomy corridor, so Hashem stands next to the door to the Migrationsverket. He's keen that no one steals his place. Nine o'clock passes – opening time – but still the doors do not open. A crowd builds behind him. Hashem frowns, his heart beating fast. In a few minutes he should know whether he has a life ahead of him in Sweden – or not.

Finally, the door opens. The crowd surges through. Hashem takes a ticket from the machine – number 806. He's one of the first to get inside, so he's one of the first to be called. Within a minute, before he's even had a chance to take a coffee from the drinks dispenser, 806 flashes up in red on the display hanging from the wall. An arrow points to the cubicle that he should enter. He crosses the waiting room and opens the relevant door. Inside, behind a counter, a sombre woman greets him. She pushes an envelope towards him across the counter. Hashem tears it open – and finds a card inside.

He looks down at it. It's Wednesday, 10 November 2015. Three years after he left Assad's jails, two years after he escaped Syria, and seven months after he survived the sea, Hashem finally sees the words he's been waiting for.

'Permanent Uppehållstillstånd,' the card says. 'Permanent Residency.'

Epilogue: What Happened Next?

All the refugees in this book still have asylum applications in the works – so I can't reveal everything about everyone.

Darwin-loving Mohamed Hussein had the swiftest success. Of the group I followed towards the Hungarian border, Mohamed and his friend Nizam were the only two who managed to get through Hungary without being arrested. Now Mohamed is in Germany, studying for a BA in languages and literature at a Bavarian university. Nasser, Fattemah and Hammouda were arrested later in their journey, but they got to a safe place eventually. One of the first things they learned on arrival was that their unborn daughter was still alive. Ilaf was born shortly before Christmas.

After being rescued by Hans Breuer, Galbari al-Hussein and her children took a train to Germany, where they were stopped on the border but later allowed to enter. Ahmad, an engineer I met in the stadium at Kos, is now in Belgium with his nephew, waiting for their asylum claims to be processed.

On Lesvos, the Kempsons continued to patrol the beaches every day for the rest of the year. By the autumn, they weren't alone: hundreds of volunteers descended on the north coast of Lesvos to mount an impressively organised relief effort. It was hugely necessary. Even in the first half of December, the numbers of people arriving per day along the Kempsons' coastline didn't dip below 2000.

Mohamad, a gay Syrian man I met in the chaotic Croatian station, is now in Germany – reunited with his partner. For the first time, they can be open about their relationship. I've lost touch with Ibrahim, the Gambian who survived the Mediterranean's deadliest contemporary shipwreck. But Omar Diawara, one of the other survivors I interviewed, is still stuck in a notorious Sicilian reception centre, waiting for his papers. We talk in a mixture of French and Arabic on Viber, and a lot gets lost in translation. Several of the Senegalese men I met in the Sahara were flown home by the International Organization for Migration after being arrested in Libya. At least one of them is thinking of trying the whole ordeal again.

Further north, on the Libyan coast, Hajj has reportedly shut down his operations. We'll see how long that lasts.

Over in Izmir, smuggling has made Mohamad into a rich man. He's now married, and has his own house in a town far from the coast, and is no longer so closely involved in the day-to-day organisation of his network.

Hashem's family has now finally applied to join him in Sweden. For the second year in a row, Osama didn't get to celebrate his birthday with his dad.

A Message from Hashem al-Souki

The start of the 2011 Syrian uprising against Bashar al-Assad was a beautiful moment. We felt the winds of freedom, democracy, justice and equality for the first time after more than forty years of being ruled by the Assad family, who had governed Syria like a prison. We thought the world had changed, and that this was the end of dictatorship.

But, as time went by, we started to wake from this dream, and returned to reality. We were up against one of the more brutal and experienced intelligence agencies, which knew exactly what to do both inside and outside the country to end the revolution. And they succeeded.

Syria turned into an inferno in which it was impossible to live. Syrian life started to collapse. You had to move from area to area to find safety, and each time you moved the inferno expanded even further, and the risks became even greater – leaving you homeless, incarcerated or humiliated.

At that point, the hard but correct decision was to save ourselves and our children by leaving the country. My children had already lost their home and their education. Had we stayed, they would have been by default raised on weapons and war. The only option was to leave.

Despite experiencing the horrors of war, despite the suffering of displacement, despite the pains and traumas of crossing the sea in old boats, despite the difficulty of adapting to new customs and cultures, the uncertainty about what the future holds, the constant anxiety about my children and my family – despite all this, I have learned many things. First among them is that there are many people who will always give you the hope and determination to plough on through the darkness.

One of them is the journalist Patrick Kingsley. I first met Patrick after my family and I were released from prison, following a failed attempt to reach Europe by boat. Over time, Patrick has become part of my family – he is not just a journalist or a friend, but an important part of my life.

When Patrick asked if he could document my next journey to Europe, I agreed because I wanted the world to understand why people like me are risking our lives. I felt the international community should understand the reasons behind this great migration to Europe. I also wanted to take the chance to speak freely – to use this right that we in Syria have been deprived of for forty years. I want our voice to reach the world.

Through Patrick, I have learned that life has many cultures and ways of thinking – and that goodness exists as well as evil. Through Patrick, I got to know the wonderful photographer Sima Diab, and then Patrick's kind friend Marie-Jeanne, her mother Carol, and his colleagues Milad and Manu. Here in Sweden, I have met many wonderful people, among them the people who taught me my first words in Swedish – Kerstin Wedell, Eva Turen, Eva Sidfeldt, Gosta Gustafsson, Mia Svanberg, Ona Andersen, Ingegerd Staberg and Irene Josefsson – and also the chefs who cooked for us in the refugee centre: Lina, Tina, Camella, Mia and Youny. I also thank the caseworker who investigated my case and made such a difference to my life, Bouzang.

And I send greetings and love to the men and women of all backgrounds who seek to make the world into a better place.

Author's Note

As a journalist, I have the privilege of meeting and learning from many inspiring people whom I otherwise wouldn't usually encounter. Unfortunately, I rarely get to meet most of these people more than once. Hashem al-Souki is an exception. After my story about the shipwreck they narrowly escaped in September 2014, we kept in touch. I would visit his family's flat in the desert every few weeks, and bit by bit we became friends. To my shock, in early 2015 Hashem said he wanted to risk the sea again. I was amazed, given the trauma of his last attempt. Yet Hashem was adamant: in febrile Egypt, his three sons have no future. In Europe, they might win one.

The journalist in me wanted to document this amazing act of heroism, and I will always be humbled that Hashem agreed. So, prior to his departure, he let me, my translator Manu and the brilliant photographer Sima Diab even further into his life, to document his final days in Egypt. Then I gave him a notebook so that he could keep an accurate record of what happened on board, and a camera to supplement his note-taking. Once he arrived in Italy, Sima and I dropped everything and flew to join him (an almost farcical privilege, given the lengths he had had to go to to get there himself). Then I followed him alone as he made his way through Europe to Sweden. I've since visited him twice to see what his new life's like, and in Egypt I regularly visited Hayam and their children.

I'm often asked how I struck the balance between being observer and participant on the journey from Italy to Sweden. As a human being, it was very hard not to get involved. But, as a reporter, I knew I had to let Hashem follow his own course. A good example of this moral quandary came in Copenhagen, where Hashem didn't have a credit card or any Danish krona to pay for the last leg of the journey. At two in the morning, it was so tempting to intervene, but I'm glad I didn't.

I've subsequently wondered whether my sheer presence at the borders helped his cause. In hindsight, I don't think it did. At the German, Danish and Swedish borders it could potentially have made a difference if there had been a cursory border check. Sitting at my table, my smart shirt and leather satchel might have given him cover. But there wasn't a check, so it's an academic point. The French border was the only one where the police boarded the train. If we had been sitting next to each other, it's possible my appearance would have given him some cover, as the policeman wandered down the aisle glancing at every passenger. As it happened, though, we weren't together when the border check in our carriage occurred. Hashem was coming back from the toilet when he encountered the border guards. So the fact he looks a bit French, had a confident stride and didn't seem too scruffy meant his appearance alone was what saved him.

Some people won't be satisfied by both my absence from some parts of the trip – and conversely by my presence on others. But I hope that most readers will recognise that I've done my best to make this as accurate a portrayal of a refugee's journey as I can.

Acknowledgements

Above all, I thank Hashem for letting me into his life. I have learned so much from him – about love, resilience, dedication, parenthood and dignity. I will always be grateful for both the opportunity to write his story and the lessons that he, Hayam and their children have taught me. The same goes for the hundreds of other refugees and volunteers I met in 2015. I can't mention them all. But this book is written in their honour.

The New Odyssey would not have been possible without Jamie Wilson, the *Guardian*'s international editor. It was Jamie's idea to appoint a migration correspondent back in March 2015 – well before anyone realised it would become the story of the year. Without Jamie's foresight, this book could not have happened, since a lot of it was first researched in the line of *Guardian* duty, and adapted from *Guardian* articles. He and our managing editor, Jan Thompson, kindly gave me time off to write – and later very honourably stuck to their promise, even when the refugee crisis did not ebb to the degree that we had expected.

I am also grateful to the Cecil King Memorial Foundation, who gave me a very generous grant to investigate migration in 2014. Without this support, I would not have been able to complete parts of my research. And I couldn't have written up any of it in book form if it wasn't for Faber's Laura Hassan, who edited *The New Odyssey*. I have hugely appreciated Laura's expertise, ideas, patience and masterful edits – and the fact this book has been published so fast is testament to her skill and drive. It is also thanks to the support, advice and professionalism of my agent, Jonathan Conway, who believed in the idea from the start, and whose stable I feel proud to have joined.

On the ground, the success of the research was thanks largely to the fixers, translators and photojournalists I worked with. Sima Diab not only took some of the beautiful photographs that are in this book, but her humanity and insights greatly enhanced my reporting in Egypt, Greece, Hungary and Italy. Manu Abdo's dedication, loyalty, diligence and intelligence were essential to my reporting in Egypt. In Libya, I couldn't have worked without the tireless and wise Yaseen Kanuni. In Niger, it was a privilege to work with Chehou Azizou. The stellar Alessandra Bonomolo put up with me in Sicily, while in Turkey it was the wonderful Abdulsalam Dallal. Abdelfatah Mohamed was an outstanding conduit to Eritrean exiles. In the end, I didn't get to Sudan for this book – but in Khartoum, Reem Abbas helped me with an essential bit of background research. The *Guardian* photojournalists Antonio Olmos and David Levene were fantastic to work with in the Balkans. Throughout it all, Mowaffaq Safadi, a Syrian journalist I worked with in Cairo in 2013, played an important part in helping me to understand the complexity of refugee life. I worked with him only once after I was appointed migration correspondent, but his advice and experiences were a constant influence.

At the *Guardian*, I am very grateful to Jamie's team on the international desk – Lizzy Davies, Martin Hodgson, Mark Rice-Oxley, Simon Jeffery, Alex Olorenshaw, Judith Soal,

Enjoli Liston, Raya Jalabi, Max Benato and David Munk. Feilding Cage and his team did an outstanding job of bringing an early account of Hashem's story to life on the internet. My travel was all down to Jana Harris, Karen Plews and Sarah Hewitt – top-class administrators who got me on around a hundred flights in 2015, often at very short notice, and never once complained at the chaos of it all. I also wouldn't be where I am today without the mentoring or trust of many of our colleagues in other sections. For various reasons, I'll always be grateful to Emily Wilson, Clare Margetson, Jane Martinson, Malik Meer, Martin Chulov, Jon Henley, Max Walker, Ian Black, and Kath Viner – as well as my former colleagues Charlie English, Alan Rusbridger, Stuart Millar, Jenni Russell and Ian Katz. Ian's deep knowledge of Scandinavian culture and history is matched only by the generosity with which he shares it.

Along the refugee trail, I met many wonderful people who helped me in so many ways – not least Tuesday Reitano, Peter Tinti, Joanna Kakissis, Salwa Amor, Justine Swaab, Leonard Doyle, Daniel Trilling, Asteris Masouras, Apostolis Fotiadis and Enar Bostedt. Thank you all for your ideas, contacts, information and advice.

In Cairo, which has been my base for the past three years, I'm grateful for the friendship and assistance during tough times from Carol Berger, Louisa Loveluck, Abdallah Noseir, Milad Magdy, Lotfy Salman, Angus Blair, Jared Malsin, Stephen and Laura Hickey, Maryanne Stroud Gabbani, Mohamed Lotfy, Richard Spencer and Samer al-Atrush. In Istanbul, Izzy Finkel kindly put me up after I missed a flight, and searched for hours to identify a çikotop.

At Faber I thank Donna Payne, for designing the stunning jacket; Lauren Nicoll, who is publicising the book; John Grindrod, who's marketing it; Jill Burrows, the fantastic copyeditor; Emmie Francis and Martha Sprackland, who assisted with the editing; Nick Sidwell of Guardian Bookshop; and Lisa Baker and Lizzie Bishop from the rights department, who did a brilliant job of bringing the book to an international audience. Robert Hahn, the *Guardian*'s head of rights, has also had a key role in this book, since much of it is drawn from *Guardian* reporting. Elsewhere in the publishing world, I'm lucky for the friendship of Rebecca Nicholson and Aurea Carpenter who gave me such a break by publishing my first book.

Daniel Cohen, Elliot Ross, Robert Macfarlane, Sarah Birke, Sima Diab, Raya Jalabi, Carol Berger, my brother Tom and my parents Jenny and Stephen all read parts of the manuscript at short notice. I'm grateful for their feedback and encouragement. More widely, I particularly thank Tom, for inspiring me every day – and my parents, for giving me every chance in life. This book is dedicated to them.

Lastly, thank you, Marie-Jeanne Berger, for your selfless support, advice and inspiration.

References

Prologue

1 'Migratory Routes Map', Frontex; http://frontex.europa.eu/trends-and-routes/migratory-routes- map/ [7 February 2017].

2 *Sea Arrivals to Italy 2010–2014*, UNHCR, 2015; http://unhcr.it/risorse/statistiche/sea-arrivals-to-italy.

3 *UNHCR Refugees/Migrants Emergency Response – Mediterranean*, UNHCR; http://data.unhcr.org/mediterranean/regional.php [9 December 2015].

4 *Western Balkan Route*, Frontex; http://frontex.europa.eu/trends-and-routes/western-balkan-route/ [9 December 2015].

5 This is my own calculation based on data provided by UNHCR and IOM (International Organization for Migration).

6 *2015 UNHCR Country Operations Profile – Lebanon*, UNHCR; http://www.unhcr.org/pages/49e486676.html [9 December 2015].

7 'Eastern Mediterranean Route', Frontex; http://frontex.europa.eu/trends-and-routes/eastern-mediterranean-route/ [7 February 2017].

1 A Birthday Interrupted

1 Ian Black, 'Syrian Regime Document Trove Shows Evidence of "Industrial Scale" Killing of Detainees', *Guardian*, 21 January 2014; http://www.theguardian.com/world/2014/jan/20/evidence-industrial-scale-killing-syria-war-crimes.

2 Martin Chulov, 'Why Isis Fight', *Guardian*, 17 September 2015; http://www.theguardian.com/world/2015/sep/17/why-isis-fight-syria-iraq.

2 The Second Sea

1 This is a collation of data compiled by IOM in June 2015, and my own research in August 2015.

2 This is on the basis that each of the 100,000 passengers will have paid 10,000 CFA to the policemen at the Agadez checkpoint, which comes to a rough total of £1.1 million. Far more money will be made at every additional checkpoint.

3 *UNHCR Refugees/Migrants Emergency Response – Mediterranean*, UNHCR; http://data.unhcr.org/mediterranean/regional.php [9 December 2015].

4 Ibid.

5 *2015 UNHCR Country Operations Profile – Eritrea*, UNHCR; http://www.unhcr.org/pages/49e4838e6.html [9 December 2015].

6 Tom Nuttall, 'Migrants or Refugees?' *Medium*, 6 September 2015; https://medium.com/@tom_nuttall/viktor-orb%C3%A1n-hungary-s-prime-minister-says-the-overwhelming-majority-of-migrants-in-europe-are-69ea2e071f5e#.4ck6z3bbp.

7 Alexander Betts, 'Global Issues Don't Live in Separate Boxes. Why No Mention in Paris of Refugees?', *Guardian*, 13 December 2015; http://www.theguardian.com/commentisfree/2015/dec/13/refugee-status-extended-people-displaced-climate-change.

8 Hein de Haas, 'Turning the Tide? Why Development Will Not Stop Migration', *Development and Change*, 38/5 (2007), 819–41.

3 Trading in Souls

1 These figures are derived from my own research.

2 'Central Mediterranean Route', Frontex; http://frontex.europa.eu/trends-and-routes/central-mediterranean-route/ [9 December 2015].

3 Ibid.

4 Simon Mee and Peter Spiegel, 'Paris Acted within Schengen over Tunisians', *Financial Times*, 25 July 2011; http://www.ft.com/

cms/s/0/98cde586-b6d5-11e0-a8b8-00144feabdc0.html#axzz
3trAo4mic.

5 'Central Mediterranean Route', Frontex; http://frontex.europa.
eu/trends-and-routes/central-mediterranean-route/ [9 December
2015].

6 Ibid.

7 Ibid.

8 *UNHCR Refugees/Migrants Emergency Response – Mediterranean*,
UNHCR; http://data.unhcr.org/mediterranean/regional.php
[9 December 2015].

9 'Libya's Migrant Trade: Europe or Die (Full Length)', *Vice News*,
17 September 2015; https://news.vice.com/video/libyas-migrant-
trade-europe-or-die-full-length.

10 Jeremy Harding, 'The Uninvited', *London Review of Books*,
3 February 2000; http://www.lrb.co.uk/v22/n03/jeremy-
harding/the-uninvited.

11 'EU Anti-migrant Smuggler Operation "needs Libya Access"',
Agence France-Presse, Yahoo News, 27 October 2015;
http://news.yahoo.com/eu-anti-migrant-smuggler-operation-
needs-libya-access-202624208.html.

12 Ibid.

13 This information was provided to me during an interview
with senior Italian coastguards in May 2015; http://www.the-
guardian.com/books/2013/oct/29/alaa-al-aswany-egypt-muslim-
brotherhood.

4 SOS

1 Patrick Kingsley, 'Syrian Refugees Suffer Backlash in Egypt
after Mohamed Morsi's Removal', *Guardian*, 23 July 2013;
http://www.theguardian.com/world/2013/jul/25/syrian-refugees-
suffer-backlash-egypt.

2 'Tenth of Ramadan Victory and Revolution Triumph', *State
Information Service: Your Gateway to Egypt*, 10 August 2011;
http://www.sis.gov.eg/En/Templates/Articles/tmpArticles.aspx?
ArtID=57318#.Vmjr4mR97Zo>.

5 Shipwreck

1 'Mediterranean's Worst Migrant Boat Disasters', Sky News, 20 April 2015; http://news.sky.com/story/1468144/mediterraneans-worst-migrant-boat-disasters.
2 Data provided privately to me by email.

7 Between the Woods and the Water

1 'UNHCR Syria Regional Refugee Response', UNHCR; http://data.unhcr.org/syrianrefugees/asylum.php [10 December 2015].
2 Jack Blanchard, 'Thousands More Syrians Would Flee without British Aid Claims David Cameron on Visit to Refugee Camp', *Daily Mirror*, 14 September 2015; http://www.mirror.co.uk/news/uk-news/thousands-more-syrians-would-flee-6437917.
3 Michael Martinez, 'Syrian Refugees: Which Countries Welcome Them', CNN (Cable News Network), 10 September 2015; http://edition.cnn.com/2015/09/09/world/welcome-syrian-refugees-countries.
4 Data provided to me personally by UNHCR.
5 My own interviews with MSF and Red Cross staff.
6 Alan Travis, 'Judge Blocks Deportation Flight for Rejected Afghan Asylum-seekers', *Guardian*, 22 April 2015; http://www.theguardian.com/world/2015/apr/22/judge-blocks-deportation-flight-for-rejected-afghan-asylum-seekers.

9 A Gate Clangs Shut

1 *UNHCR Refugees/Migrants Emergency Response – Mediterranean*, UNHCR; http://data.unhcr.org/mediterranean/regional.php [9 December 2015].
2 Adrian Edwards, 'UNHCR Viewpoint: "Refugee" or "Migrant" – Which Is Right?'; http://www.unhcr.org/55df0e556.html [27 August 2015].

3 Barry Malone, 'Why Al Jazeera Will Not Say Mediterranean "Migrants"'; http://www.aljazeera.com/blogs/editors-blog/2015/08/al-jazeera-mediterranean-migrants-150820082226309.html [20 August 2015].

4 Hans Breuer, 'In Dem Geto Fun Traiskirchen WanDeRer In the Ghetto of Traiskirchen'; https://www.youtube.com/watch?v=OSkrMdisXl8 [2 September 2015].

5 Hans Breuer, 'KONVOI WIEN BUDAPEST' Vämosszabadi/ Schienenersatzverkehr Für Flüchtlinge 06 09 15 Hans Breuer'; https://www.youtube.com/watch?v=-k9eyMt711E [10 September 2015].

6 Nick Thorpe, 'Migrant Crisis: Will Hungarian Clampdown Work?' *BBC News*, 15 September 2015; http://www.bbc.com/news/world-europe-34253983.

7 'More than 400,000 Migrants Pass through Croatia since Start of Crisis', HINA (Croatian News Agency), 17 November 2015; http://www.hina.hr/#vijest/9072870.

8 This was confirmed to me by the head of the Red Cross's missing persons team in Croatia.

9 Jan Culik, 'Meet Miloš Zeman – the Czech Republic's Answer to Donald Trump', *The Conversation*, 9 December 2015; https://theconversation.com/meet-milos-zeman-the-czech-republics-answer-to-donald-trump-52036.

10 'Europe's Response to the Paris Attacks Is Different This Time', *Economist*, 14 November 2015; http://www.economist.com/news/europe/21678514-je-suis-charlie-was-about-free-speech-time-issue-migrants-europe-sees-paris-attacks.

11 Patrick Kingsley, 'Tens of Thousands Migrate Through Balkans Since Route Declared Shut', *Guardian*, 30 August 2016; https://www.theguardian.com/world/2016/aug/30/tens-of-thousands-migrate-through-balkans-since-route-declared-shut.

12 Daniel Trilling, 'What to do with the people who do make it across?', *London Review of Books*, 8 October 2015; http://www.lrb.co.uk/v37/n19/daniel-trilling/what-to-do-with-the-people-who-do-make-it-across.

13 R. M. Douglas, 'Europe's Refugee Crisis: The Last Time Round It Was Much, Much Worse', *The Conversation*, 18 September 2015; https://theconversation.com/europes-refugee-crisis-the-last-time-round-it-was-much-much-worse-47621.

14 'The State of the World's Refugees 2000: Fifty Years of Humanitarian Action – Chapter 4: Flight from Indochina', *UNHCR News*, edited by Mark Cutts; http://www.unhcr.org/3ebf9bad0.html.

15 Cathryn Costello, 'The Frontline Club and Monocle 24 Present: Crisis in the Mediterranean', Frontline Club, London, 28 May 2015; https://www.youtube.com/watch?v=8lqpVIM0vsI&feature=youtu.be&t=59m53s.

16 Gabrielle Jackson, 'UN's François Crépeau on the Refugee Crisis: "Instead of Resisting Migration, Let's Organise It"', *Guardian*, 22 April 2015; http://www.theguardian.com/world/2015/apr/22/uns-francois-crepeau-on-the-refugee-crisis-instead-of-resisting-migration-lets-organise-it.

10 Status Pending

1 'Statistics', Migrationsverket; http://www.migrationsverket.se/English/About-the-Migration-Agency/Facts-and-statistics-/Statistics.html [20 November 2015].

2 Mikael Ekman and Daniel Poohl, 'Sverigedemokraterna Och Nazismen', *Expo*, 14 January 2011; http://expo.se/2011/sverigedemokraterna-och-nazismen_3614.html.

Index

(Bold numbers refer to maps)